## PRAISE FoR *DARE TO BE* /

"Utterly delightful and fun to read, *Dare to* [
sound advice, great recipes, and tons of usefu[
The mother-daughter team, both lifelong ad[
abundantly of their wisdom and experiences and do so always with a good
dose of humor and worldly wisdom. There's something here for everyone.
As the authors state, this book was written for 'those who are wading in the
pool, splashing around in holistic waters and for those who have moved to
the deep end. There's room in the pool for everyone!' There certainly is in
this warmly written, humorous, and very informative book."

—Rosemary Gladstar, bestselling author of
*Rosemary Gladstar's Medicinal Herbs*

"A story-rich romp through a new territory for those who *Dare to Be A Green
Witch*."

—Susun Weed, herbalist and author of *Healing Wise*

"A fascinating and easy-to-read autobiography and collection of ways to inte-
grate holistic practices into an allopathic lifestyle."

—Heather Chace BSN, RN

"Just when we need it with a world that has become topsy-turvy from a pan-
demic, the Grounded Goodwife's *Dare to Be a Green Witch* provides us with
a manual on how to connect to ourselves and the world around us through
more meaningful practices."

—Suzanne Garvey, director of Seymour Library
in Seymour, Connecticut

"Reading *Dare to Be a Green Witch* was a glimpse into authentic living. Using
the knowledge handed down from generations, these 'witches' have har-
nessed a green lifestyle without even trying to be trendy. This book is full of
heartfelt stories and recipes for living green with plenty of resources cited.

You will see their brews have the science to back up their claims. Pour yourself a cuppa and get ready to be entertained while you learn what green witchcraft really looks like and how easy it is for all of us to get back to our witchy roots!"

—Karen Opper, owner of That Book Store
in Wethersfield, Connecticut

# DARE
## TO BE A
# GREEN
# WITCH

## ABOUT THE AUTHORS

As Grounded Goodwife, mother/daughter duo Velya Jancz-Urban and Ehris Urban encourage audiences to take responsibility for their own health through their hands-on holistic workshops and herstory unsanitized presentations. Ehris grew up in a family passionate about holistic healing and believes, "If you're grounded, you can navigate even the bumpiest roads in peace." Ehris is a master herbalist, holistic nutritionist, Flower Essence Therapy practitioner, Ingham Method reflexologist, and graduate of the New England School of Homeopathy. She became interested in Reiki as a teenager and attained Reiki master certification at age seventeen. She holds a Bachelor of Arts in anthropology/sociology and is a certified ESL teacher. Ehris enjoys beekeeping, tending her organic vegetable and herb gardens, and working in her apothecary. Velya lives her life by the adage, "There is no growth without change." She is a vivacious teacher, public speaker, author, former Brazilian dairy farm owner, and expert on New England's colonial women. Moving into a foreclosed 1770 farmhouse ignited Velya's interest in the colonial era and led to the creation of her entertainingly-informative presentation, The Not-So-Good Life of the Colonial Goodwife. Velya has a few too many rescue dogs and cats, is happiest with a fresh stack of library books, loves thrift shops, and is passionate about alternative medicine.

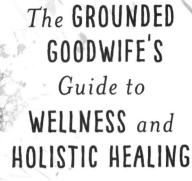

The GROUNDED
GOODWIFE'S
*Guide to*
WELLNESS *and*
HOLISTIC HEALING

# DARE
## TO BE A
# GREEN
# WITCH

"Utterly delightful and fun to read,
*Dare to Be a Green Witch* is laden with sound
advice, great recipes, and tons of useful,
well-researched information."

—ROSEMARY GLADSTAR, BESTSELLING
AUTHOR OF *ROSEMARY GLADSTAR'S
MEDICINAL HERBS*

EHRIS URBAN
VELYA JANCZ-URBAN

Llewellyn Publications
Woodbury, Minnesota

FIRST EDITION
First Printing, 2021

Cover design by Shira Atakpu


Llewellyn Publications is a registered trademark of Llewellyn Worldwide Ltd.

**Library of Congress Cataloging-in-Publication Data**
Names: Urban, Ehris, author. | Jancz-Urban, Velya, author.
Title: Dare to be a green witch : the grounded goodwife's guide to wellness
    and holistic healing / Ehris Urban, Velya Jancz-Urban.
Description: First edition. | Woodbury, Minnesota : Llewellyn Worldwide,
    2021. | Includes bibliographical references and index. | Summary:
    "Mother and daughter duo share recipes and stories for holistic healing
    a wellness"— Provided by publisher.
Identifiers: LCCN 2021021175 (print) | LCCN 2021021176 (ebook) | ISBN
    9780738765457 (paperback) | ISBN 9780738765570 (ebook)
Subjects: LCSH: Holistic medicine. | Healing. | Self-care, Health. |
    Alternative medicine.
Classification: LCC R733 .U73 2021  (print) | LCC R733  (ebook) | DDC
    610—dc23
LC record available at https://lccn.loc.gov/2021021175
LC ebook record available at https://lccn.loc.gov/2021021176

Llewellyn Publications
A Division of Llewellyn Worldwide Ltd.
2143 Wooddale Drive
Woodbury, MN 55125-2989
www.llewellyn.com

Printed in the United States of America

## OTHER BOOKS BY THESE AUTHORS

*How to Survive a Brazilian Betrayal:*
*A Mother-Daughter Memoir*
*(Green Writers Press)*

# DEDICATION

Dr. Rebecca Boorer, MD

Dr. Kathleen Riley, ND

Dr. Elizabeth Herman, ND

Andrea Coakley, LAc

Laura Bryant, RN

We hope to give back what you have given us.

# ACKNOWLEDGMENTS

We can't stress enough the importance of having like-minded people in your life as you embark, or continue, on the green witch path. Neysa Ehrismann Jancz (Velya's mother/Ehris' grandmother) was an early pioneer in the new and uncharted world of holistic living. She had no one's past experience to learn from, and for whatever reason, her husband (Velya's father/Ehris' grandfather) withheld his support—which begs the question: does the reason it was withheld reflect more on him or on her? When someone shows genuine interest in your learning and development, it matters. Eventually, she gave up making whole-grain cranberry nut bread, using molasses, and arguing the merits of health food store vs. grocery store vitamin brands. The Thrifty Chicken Neck Spread grinder and the white ceramic chicken that held our Duo-Kap vitamins went to the thrift shop. By the time she died, there was nothing holistic about her.

The loneliness that sometimes accompanies the green witch lifestyle may be designed to help you discover who you are. But no matter how many people care about you, if you can't be open with them about who you truly are, you're still alone. As Grounded Goodwife, we are buoyed, bolstered, and honored by the thank-you notes, emails, book reviews, phone calls, and social media support we receive from people who attend our workshops and presentations and support our mission of embracing the green witch life.

Long, long before an herbal protocol removed Lyme disease from his body (as evidenced by before/after blood tests), Jim Urban has been fully on board with our nontraditional way of life. His love and support is boundless. He also happily sampled every recipe in this book!

We believe that watching Kathy Vander Eyk's thirty minute video, "Secrets to Landing an Agent," helped us land our publishing contract with Llewellyn Worldwide. We followed her recommendations on how to hook a literary agent and wrote a 297-word query letter (she suggests keeping it under 300 words). We were astounded that we wound up having to choose who would represent us!

Heather Greene, our acquisitions editor at Llewellyn Worldwide and self-proclaimed "book midwife," was with us from conception to labor/delivery. Although we muttered about some of the changes she wanted to see, she had a clear vision of the book we were meant to write.

And, thank you to Llewellyn Worldwide, the world's oldest and largest independent publisher of books for body, mind, and spirit since 1901. We're honored to be included in your mission of bringing holistic health to the forefront.

# CONTENTS

# DISCLAIMER

The authors and publisher are not responsible for the use or misuse of herbs, ingredients, essential oils, recipes, or practices in this book. Like all medicines, plants and holistic practices may be dangerous if used or performed improperly. The authors and publisher do not endorse or guarantee the curative effects of any subjects or recipes in this book. The practices discussed in this book are the lifestyle choices of the authors and may not be for everyone. If you have any physical or mental health issues or are taking any prescriptions/medications, you may want to keep your healthcare professional in the loop about your holistic undertakings and herbal supplements.

The authors do not advocate the internal use of essential oils. Recipes in this book use what are generally considered safe essential oils, but please keep in mind that while completely natural, all essential oils are powerful plant compounds that you, your family, and your pets might have a reaction to. Never use essential oils undiluted or take essential oils internally without the guidance of a professional. Always read about the possible side effects of each essential oil before you use it. Avoid the use of essential oils during the first trimester of pregnancy, on small babies, and on anyone with severe allergies to the plants the oils are derived from. If you see any reactions in yourself, your family, or your pets, stop use of your essential oil products immediately and contact a medical professional.

# INTRODUCTION

## GROUNDED GOODWIFE STORY TIME

*Don't Be Afraid of Being Scared* by Velya

I went into full-blown panic mode the day I got a postcard from our homeowner's insurance company. The intimidating postcard notified me that someone would be dropping by our house sometime in the next two weeks "to conduct a routine exterior inspection" of our Woodbury, Connecticut, home, which would include measuring our house and taking photos.

"OMG!" I texted my daughter, Ehris. "We have to somehow hide the beehives and camouflage the chicken coop!" Even as my thumbs punched out the frantic, dopey text, I knew this was impossible. But every backyard homesteader has heard the horror stories:

- "Liberty Mutual dropped me for keeping *dangerous non-domestic animals*. In my case, that can only mean bees."
- "My neighbor's dog got stung by a bee and *I* got sued."
- "My neighbor is allergic to bee stings and got stung by one of 'my' bees. I guess it wasn't his responsibility to make sure he had his EpiPen handy?"
- "They dropped me because I have an *attractive nuisance*."
- "My insurance company of twenty-six years dropped me because there was the 'potential' of my selling eggs, and that was a risk.

1

They tell me that chickens are farm animals and carry diseases. UGH!"

- "My homeowner's insurance was canceled because 'the number of non-domesticated animals exceeds the maximum allowable.' I have five chickens. I don't have wolves or tigers."

Ehris and I threw branches and pampas grass on top of the buzzing beehives to "hide" them. We kept our free-range chickens locked in the coop for two weeks so they wouldn't be "as noticeable." Although we never saw the "field representative, in possession of a photo identification badge," who had "undergone comprehensive training," the inspection must have taken place, because we received an email from our insurance agent instructing us that we needed to install an outdoor patio railing. There was no mention of the chickens or the bees—and I felt as if we had dodged a bullet.

But then, the Belle by Kim Gravel Flexibelle Petite Pull-On Knit Jeggings I ordered from QVC arrived. I like to call them "the skinny jeans that came with a warning." Securely attached to the front pocket of the jeggings was a hangtag that said: "This garment may contain metallic fibers/threads/yarn. Garment shall not be worn near or during MRI procedures." *So what the heck would happen if I were to wear these jeggings in the MRI I would never agree to have? Would they explode off my body? Melt right into my skin?* Then, I did a little research. People who have MRIs are advised to not wear makeup or nail polish because some cosmetics contain metals that can interact with MRI magnets. People are also told to minimize hair products and forgo antiperspirants and sunscreens, which contain metals, just to be safe. On top of that, first degree burns can result when dyes in tattoos, even from tattooed eyeliner, heat up. And don't forget to remove your bellybutton and toe rings! As I envisioned people in clanking 110 decibel MRI tubes with their eyelashes and fingernails getting sucked off and their tattooed eyelids burned to a crisp, I don't know what shocked me more: that people would agree to undergo a test like this, or that metal is in all of these products! How many people are signing up for

MRIs if companies like QVC routinely include these warnings to avoid litigation?

It was that alarming jeggings tag that made me stop being afraid of my homeowner's insurance company and forced me to really think about stuff. We've had free-range chickens for over twenty-six years. Of course, we love the fresh eggs, but the real reason we have chickens is that they eat ticks but they don't get Lyme disease—and it isn't passed on to their eggs. Our insurance company would be totally cool with us saturating our property with poisonous tick-killing chemicals and posting those little yellow pesticide warning signs. But it's a no-no for Ingrid, Muriel, and Sarah to gobble up ticks so we don't contract Lyme disease and have to take Doxycycline (we wouldn't take Doxycycline because there are proven herbal protocols to help treat Lyme, but you get the point).

We have beehives as a safe place for honeybees to live as they pollinate our non-GMO herb and vegetables gardens. To insurance companies, bees are verboten—but if we had empty bottles of toxic Roundup scattered all over our lawn, the "field representative," with his photo ID badge and clipboard, would have just tiptoed around them as he wrote his report.

How did this happen? How did things get like this?

• • •

Anyone who's watched TV for more than five minutes has been hit by commercials offering a smorgasbord of prescription drugs with extremely disturbing side effects:

- "These changes may include gas with oily discharge, an increased number of bowel movements, an urgent need to have them, and an inability to control them."
- "…may cause benign liver tumors, which can rupture and cause fatal internal bleeding"
- "…coma or death…and trouble swallowing."
- "…life-threatening infection in the skin of the perineum may result…"

…but green witches (like us) are often seen as radicals for drinking raw milk, smoke cleansing, eating fermented foods, and refusing mammograms.

As an herbalist daughter/herstorian mother duo, we offer hands-on holistic workshops and unsanitized herstory presentations at conferences, libraries, historical sites, museums, community centers, colleges, and senior centers. We encourage women to claim their wise-woman knowing and embrace the green witch life.

We're green witches who value and consult the earth, trees, plants, and stones for their healing properties, and we're dedicated to an environmentally-friendly lifestyle. Our focus is on the physical realm and the Earth on which we live. For us, it goes much deeper than "clean living" (an expression we tend to associate more with Whole Foods and Panera). We aren't "anti-witchcraft," but one of our messages is that you don't have to practice spells and talk to faeries to be a green witch.

## GROUNDED GOODWIFE STORY TIME

### *The Higher Your Vibe, the Smaller Your Tribe* by Ehris

People never really "got" me.

I was raised in a family passionate about holistic medicine. My family and I have been following the Blood Type Diet since I was nine years old, and none of us consume corn syrup, wheat, or pasteurized milk. We don't own a microwave or drink out of plastic water bottles. For all of my growing-up years, I remember my mom giving me arnica pellets whenever I fell down. Kids thought I was a weirdo when I ate my Ezekiel bread sandwiches in the cafeteria. When people came over and saw my kombucha, kimchi, and kefir fermenting on the counter, they said things like, "Yuck! Gross! That looks like a science fair project gone wrong!"

At age sixteen, I asked for (and received) a dehydrator and a Vitamix for my birthday. When my parents and I declined my Gardasil vaccine, my health teacher proclaimed, "Your mom is being very irresponsible." I became interested in Reiki in middle school and attained Reiki Master certification at age seventeen.

After freshman year, when I left Shepaug Valley High School to finish school online, my parents were told that I would become a "social outcast" and "never get into college" (I actually graduated college a semester early). After I was diagnosed (by a blood test) with the first documented case of West Nile virus in Litchfield County, Connecticut, an infectious disease specialist nonchalantly stated, "You'll never get the virus out of your system." Our naturopath suggested using castor oil packs to pull the infection out of my liver, where the virus settles. A castor oil pack is a piece of wool or cloth soaked in castor oil, applied to the skin. It's placed on the area to be treated with a piece of plastic on top (we used a plastic shopping bag) to heat it and press against the skin. A heating pad is placed on top for about forty-five minutes. Then, the affected area is wiped clean with a warm, damp towel. This process is repeated for four days on/three days off. After the first treatment, we were amazed at the postcard-sized angry red blotch right over my liver. Six months later, blood tests revealed that I was virus-free.

I hold a Bachelor of Arts in anthropology and sociology and am a graduate of the New England School of Homeopathy. I'm an herbalist, holistic nutritionist, Flower Essence Therapy practitioner, Ingham Method reflexologist, and certified ESL (English as a Second Language) instructor. I used to see clients privately for consultations, but prefer public speaking because I can reach a wider audience.

In my free time, I like to putter around in my apothecary, work in my organic herb and vegetable gardens, and practice yoga and krav maga. Until recently, tending to our beehives was one of my favorite relaxing activities because, as crazy as it sounds, it's easy to become attached to your bees (but after our eighth bear attack, beekeeping is on hold for now).

I've never really had any long-lasting friendships, so I (until recently) didn't think anybody considered me to be warm and personable, and I thought I was totally lacking the ability to be myself with other people. This had been going on since my elementary school days at Burnham Elementary School, where teachers categorized me as "shy." My family understood me, but nobody else did.

As far as my dating life goes, I've spent a lot of time writhing around on the couch having mini-breakdowns, moaning to my mom, "Is there anyone out there who's not a flaky weirdo, or doesn't have a kid, or doesn't spend the whole night bragging about how great they are at playing drums and Fantasy Football and not asking me anything about myself?"

Sometimes I find myself at low points where I'm convinced I'm going to wind up like one of those misunderstood philanthropic "old maids" from the turn of the twentieth century (there were a lot of them in Connecticut, like Caroline Ferriday and Edith Morton Chase). They lived in unique mansions, were educated, owned their own businesses, challenged gender roles, and followed their passions. They were cool—too cool for people of the day to "get" them.

I recently read a very simple anonymous quote that made my whole life make sense: "The higher your vibe, the smaller your tribe." For way too long, I've been trying to fit myself into a world that's not my world. I've been on Meetup hikes where everyone except me was wearing their required "favorite flannel," met investment bankers and orthodontists at speed dating, and spent five minutes on Tinder (until I couldn't take seeing one more shirtless guy holding a Bud Light in front of his bathroom mirror). I've finally learned that that world will never be my thing, I'll never find my people there, and that's okay. I have the ability to be myself with other people—I just haven't ever really been around the *right* people. I'm a green witch who belongs to a tribe of two (my mom is the other member). Instead of feeling sorry for the philanthropic "old maids" from the turn of the twentieth century and dreading becoming one, I now understand them and their refusal to conform. I'd be honored to be in their circle (and, they all had really cool wallpaper!).

I believe that if you're grounded, you can navigate even the bumpiest roads in peace.

• • •

# GROUNDED GOODWIFE STORY TIME

## *There Is No Growth without Change* by Velya

When I was a little kid, my mother added wheat germ to meat loaf, used whole wheat flour, devoured Adelle Davis's books, and listened to Carlton Fredericks on WOR-AM. There was one brand of yogurt in the dairy aisle at the grocery store in Ridgefield, Connecticut. One brand, three flavors: Dannon vanilla, Dannon coffee, and Dannon pineapple. Nobody else I knew ate yogurt, took Duo-Kap vitamins, or ate "Thrifty Chicken Neck Spread" (yep, you read that right)—because in my mother's words, "it was a wonderful calcium source." In our freezer, there was always a plastic bread bag of stockpiled chicken necks that my mother hoarded. Every couple of months, she'd plop the frozen necks into our cast-aluminum pressure cooker. Then, wearing safety goggles (as if she were cooking with explosives and projectiles), she'd monitor the hissing steam vent. When the necks were the consistency of mush, she'd clamp our old-school, hand-cranked meat grinder onto our wooden step stool. While my brother stood on the stool's steps so it didn't dance all over the linoleum floor, I turned the grinder's wooden handle (as if I were crank-starting a Model T Ford), and she'd feed the necks into the mouth of the grinder. If you used your imagination, the final product sort of resembled canned tuna. Then, she'd add chopped celery and onions, Miracle Whip, and hot dog relish. She'd serve Thrifty Chicken Neck Spread sandwiches on whole wheat bread. When we'd complain about the little pieces of bone that got stuck in our teeth, she'd just wave it away and remind us about all the clever WWII prisoners of war she'd read about who ate eggshells as *their* calcium source.

I grew up in blissful ignorance of the medical world. After every office visit, our family doctor would invite us upstairs for tea, served in her mother's collection of translucent bone china teacups. We all called her Becky. I thought everyone invited their doctor to their wedding, and that it was perfectly normal for your doctor to go with you on family vacations. That thinking changed when I was thirty-one years old.

My husband, Jim, and I waited seven years to try and have a baby, then had a hard time conceiving. When I finally did become pregnant, the OB/GYN thought my uterus was a little large for the conception date and suspected I might be carrying twins. Instead, there were no twins—just a dead baby. I have absolutely no idea how we got from the darkened ultrasound room with the glowing monitor to the hospital room many floors below, where I had to have a blood test. All of this happened just days before Christmas, and we had to wait five days before a D&C could be performed. I cried quietly as they wheeled me into the operating room and was still crying when I woke up in the recovery room. I remember thinking, even through the anesthesia, that that was interesting. That was when I found out you don't have to be awake for your heart to be broken.

That's also when I found out that all doctors weren't like Becky. After the procedure, the OB/GYN never went to find concerned and anxious Jim in the waiting room. Nobody bothered to tell him that I was in the recovery room, and that everything was okay.

A week later, I made an appointment with Dr. Kathleen Riley, a naturopath. Aside from thumb surgery for a torn ligament (when my fourteen-year-old son, Mic, flopped down on my hand in a restaurant booth), I never returned to the world of allopathic medicine. We used nurse midwives for the births of our two kids. We do not have primary care physicians, don't take any prescriptions, and we've used that same naturopath for over thirty years. We've always had health insurance but have never used it because it doesn't cover things like acupuncture, yoga, office visits to our naturopath, or supplements. Our family is just like any average American family. We get headaches, sore throats, and colds. We have fevers, diarrhea, we throw up, and contract conjunctivitis. We just don't use allopathic medicine to treat any of these ailments. Of course, this is our lifestyle choice, and may not be for everyone.

Frankly, I never discussed this stuff with anyone outside of family until my life turned upside down in 2010. People always knew we were a gluten-free family and did "whacky" things like follow Peter D'adamo's Blood Type Diet, but that was all they really knew. Then, in 2010, we moved to rural Brazil and were betrayed and swindled by a close family friend. We lost everything and, back in Connecticut, had to reinvent ourselves.

I fumbled around in the dark for a while until I learned to salute my real self.

A recent newspaper article made me appreciate who my real self is. The press release described me as a teacher, author, public speaker, and "the zany, gregarious creator and presenter of the historically entertaining program *The Not-So-Good Life of the Colonial Goodwife*." *Zany? Gregarious? The audience will be expecting me to pop out of a clown car!* Then, I thought back to my early teaching observations from Ridgefield High School. The department chairs and principals always commented on my energy and enthusiasm as I funked up the potentially dry subjects of English and social studies.

My kooky personality and belief that learning should never be boring were ideal in my next job as a gifted students elementary teacher. Why look at prepared slides under a microscope when it's a lot more fun to examine your own (and even an agreeable principal's) earwax? One year, my second graders won first place in the National Statistical Association Poster Contest with the topic "Is your belly button concave or convex?" The kids made a pretty funny bar graph, and I'm sure they never forgot the definitions of the two words.

After we were swindled and betrayed in Brazil, I decided to take the advice of my teacher friends, who urged me to "take my show on the road." I created *How Cool Is That?! Hands-On Science* and began teaching classes like "Dissecting Owl Pellets" and "DIY Pizza Box Solar Ovens" throughout the northeast.

Moving into a foreclosed 1770 farmhouse ignited my interest in the "taboo" lives of colonial women. For instance, in a time when underwear hadn't been invented, what did women do when they had their period? This led to *The Not-So-Good Life of the Colonial Goodwife*, more herstory unsanitized presentations, and eventually, working full-time with my daughter, Ehris, as *Grounded Goodwife*.

When you talk about alternative medicine, people are either really, really interested, or their eyes roll back in their heads and they think you're some kind of woo-woo juju weirdo. For most of my life, I never talked about it, even though it was an important part of me. But after losing everything, I decided to stop caring what other people think—about anything.

I've lived the holistic life since my Thrifty Chicken Neck Spread days, and I know it works. When I started speaking up, I realized there are other women, like me, who take collagen, go to acupuncture on a regular basis, and feed their puppies bone broth. There are also women, like me, who will never have a mammogram. But, unless you're a very strong person, good luck saying that in a roomful of women who will lash out at how "irresponsible" you are.

• • •

Our *Grounded Goodwife* inspiration was born at Rich Farm Ice Cream in Oxford, Connecticut. It dawned on us (over hot fudge sundaes) that we should team up and work together. We got the brainstorm to join forces, combining *Grounded Holistic Wellness* (Ehris's business) and *The Not-So-Good Life of the Colonial Goodwife* (Velya's lively *herstorical* presentation) and merge names. As an herbalist/herstorian duo, we decided that our *Grounded Goodwife* classes would include herbal and historical info, as well as a make-and-take. All good things begin with ice cream!

# GROUNDED GOODWIFE STORY TIME

## *Whangs* by Velya

Even though Ehris detests tomatoes, she grows them in her non-GMO garden. To be more accurate, she likes the *idea* of growing them, especially the ones with jazzy names like Big Yellow Zebra, Cherokee Purple, Mortgage Lifter, Early Girl, Chocolate Stripes, and Blondkopfchen. A few summers ago, she went a little crazy, and we had tomatoes coming out our ears. I'm the only one in our family who eats them, and I wailed, "Ehris! We gotta do something about this! One person can't eat all these tomatoes!" We decided to host a *whang* called "Totally Tomato," where people would come to our farmhouse, pick our tomatoes, and as a group, make herbal Bloody Marys and gazpacho (*whang* is a colonial term for when women got together to do some dreaded task, like making soap, apple butter, or quilting). This event turned out to be one of our greatest brainstorms. As our guests sat around our patio, shared the reward of a simple meal prepared with others, and enjoyed spontaneous and unpredictable dinner table conversation, Ehris and I realized that we hadn't seen a single cell phone in hours, and no one had discussed the heated upcoming presidential election. By the end of the evening, total strangers were making plans to hang out. We learned that the fabric of life is woven by shared experiences and time spent together.

For a year, we hosted a whang a month. One of them, called *Chicks & Quiche*, included our guests taking a trip to our coop for eggs, and cuddling three-day-old chicks. At another one, while we waited for apple pandowdy to come out of the oven, everyone sat around our living room and sang a rousing, off-key version of the 1946 tune, "Shoo Fly Pie and Apple Pan Dowdy."

The whangs reminded us that the fondest memories are made when gathered around the table.

• • •

Now that we've taught hands-on holistic workshops to over eighty thousand people, we've noticed that people are very interested in "witchiness," but they're overwhelmed with how to start and think they're going to harm themselves and their families. They stare longingly at the bulk herb bins in health food stores, but since the bins only list the SKU, price per pound, and the herb's Latin name, it's hard to know how much to buy, and what to do with them.

In our *Grounded Goodwife* hands-on holistic workshops, we constantly hear concerns like:

- "Exactly how many hours should I simmer my bone broth?"
- "Aren't you afraid to eat your free-range chickens' eggs? The ones at Stop & Shop are so much safer!"
- "Isn't raw milk full of disease-causing bacteria?"
- "My kimchi fermented for an extra day. Am I going to poison my family?"

Our hunter-gatherer foremothers didn't set their crockpot temperature dials to medium-low when they whipped up batches of bone broth. Our great-great grandmothers didn't care if the onions in their spring tonic recipes were red or yellow—or even peeled! As more and more people tentatively dip their toes into holistic waters, it's become clear to us that people want to get away from Big Pharma, but they're nervous. Others are already on this path but keep quiet about it since they feel alone.

Fear is one of the most powerful human emotions, but you shouldn't make decisions based on the possibility of what *might* happen. We are living in one of the most fearmongering times in history. There's a lot of power and money available to those who can perpetuate these fears. For insurance companies, Big Pharma, and politicians, fear is worth billions. And fortunately for them, fear is also very easy to manipulate. If you want to control someone, all you have to do is make them feel afraid.

We want to address an issue that we (as people in the holistic world) encounter all the time. We've found that many people don't question how things like Xanax, Ambien, Lipitor, and even Tylenol work. But, they want to know *exactly* how smoke cleansing gets rid of negative energy, how hawthorn regulates blood pressure, how violet dissolves tumors, or how Reiki works. There's a double standard for natural versus allopathic medicine.

People critically judge the natural world. Drinking raw milk or refusing a COVID shot is considered radical, but popping antidepressants with side effects like suicidal thoughts isn't questioned. Using a menstrual cup, taking fermented cod liver oil, healing broken bones with comfrey, and feeding your dogs "raw" are seen as strange. Most people believe that healing cancer without chemotherapy and radiation is impossible. But, allowing someone to slice open your chest and graft your leg veins into your heart is considered normal and conservative.

This book is for those who are in the wading pool, splashing around in holistic waters—and for those who've moved to the deep end. There's room in the pool for everyone! Women have always been the healers. Since time began, women learned from each other, and passed on their wisdom from neighbor to neighbor and mother to daughter. Some called them "wise women," some called them "witches." It *is* possible to thoroughly embrace the green witch life, as we do. It's also perfectly fine to dabble in it, pick and choose the parts that interest you. If you're taking any prescriptions, you may want to keep your healthcare professional in the loop about your holistic undertakings and herbal supplements.

You'll find loads of recipes in this book, and we also explain why each ingredient is in each recipe—like the rhodiola in our Great Granny McWilliams' Restorative Spring Tonic, the spirulina in our Ninja Turtle Spirulina Mask, and the chicken feet in our Rattle-Them-Bones Broth. We'd love this book to serve as your springboard as you experiment with your own remedies and concoctions. We hope our knowledge, research, and anecdotes will give you the confidence to trust your inner knowing, hear your inner voice, and question "the experts."

Welcome to our coven!

# PART ONE
# HEALTH AND WELLNESS

*The best pharmacy is within yourself.*

Your body will tell you the truth no matter how unwelcome, inconvenient, or painful it may be. We hope this book will inspire you to become your own Sherlock Holmes as you investigate what your body is telling you. As you become aware of how to keep yourself healthy naturally, you'll transform your life in powerful, positive ways. You'll learn how to strengthen your immune system, boost your energy levels, and improve the way your body handles stress. You'll not only build up a wellness apothecary, you'll also gain knowledge to put it to use when your body struggles. Making your own medicines is surprisingly easy and inexpensive. You'll be able to take ownership of your own health, and the health of your friends and family.

Herbal medicine refers to using a plant's seeds, berries, roots, leaves, bark, or flowers for medicinal purposes. Imagine knowing the names of these plants, understanding how to use them, when to harvest them, and which parts to use. Envision being able to make these plants into medicines such as salves, oils, teas, syrups, and tinctures. How cool would it be to help others use these herbal medicines for healing purposes? These are the skills of a green witch.

Do you sometimes feel like a kooky oddball? Are you regarded as that wackadoo nut job? We know how that feels! We also know how hard it can be to find your place. If you're ready to follow the path less traveled, we'll guide you through creating healing cold and flu remedies, tonics, broths, ferments, infusions, and decadent treats. Take back your power—the power to heal and renew.

## CHAPTER ONE
# FIRE CIDER AND OTHER GERM-FIGHTING CONCOCTIONS

Why is there so much pressure by Big Pharma, insurance companies, and the United States government to get the flu shot year after year? Why does it seem like every pharmacy posts a sign advertising the shot? Why are free flu shots available at work, school, supermarkets, and big-box stores? Why are there so many pharmaceutical commercials each year around flu season?

There's only one answer: money. Every flu season, the pharmaceutical industry's eyes glow with dollar signs. The making, distributing, and administering of the flu shot is an extremely lucrative business! As vaccine profits climb, there's no denying that Big Pharma is thriving off the flu shot. We recommend you make the best choices for you and your family based upon your own due diligence—but, we've never had a flu shot (and we never will), and we've never had the flu.

We believe that good health starts from the inside out. You can lather yourself with antibacterial soap, wipe your counters down with disinfecting spray, and wear a face mask and gloves, but without a strong immune system, colds and flu are gonna getcha. The recipes in this chapter, along with a "real food" diet including fermented foods, will help keep bacteria and viruses at bay.

# GROUNDED GOODWIFE STORY TIME

## *Aunt Babe* by Velya

As a teacher and mother (and former eight-year-old), I believe that what a child is exposed to at age eight often shapes their interests as adults. Eight-year-olds are readers, writers, scientists, and mathematicians. They want to know, "Why?" and seek out information through reading, experimenting, observing, and asking questions. When I was eight, I was exposed to the information that would trigger my fascination with natural healing and my excitement with things that are a little bit gross (okay, *very* gross).

In 1934, at age twelve, my mom's Aunt Babe developed osteomylitis (a bone infection) in her leg. Today, Aunt Babe would be called gender-nonconformist or gender-expansive. In the 1930s, she was a tomboy. There's confusion as to how Aunt Babe got the injury that would lead to her osteomylitis. She insisted she hit her shin with an axe, but it was also reported that she took a very bad fall while ice skating.

The Aunt Babe story fascinated me when I was a little kid. She developed osteomylitis in a pre-antibiotic, Great Depression world. Babe spent years in the hospital, and her story was featured in newspapers across the United States. At one point, she was discharged from the hospital in a full-length (from her armpits to her toes) white plaster body cast which she wore for a full year. There was an opening in the crotch area, and my grandfather carried Babe around, slid bedpans beneath her, and helped her not only in the bathroom, but with her eventual menstrual needs. When the plaster cast was removed, Babe's leg wasn't healed. She developed horrible sores that abscessed and burst open, and everyone in the family pitched in to help collect the pus that poured from the abscesses. There was so much that they would collect it in cardboard egg cartons (remember, this was a preplastic container world). My mother always said that even though the pus smelled like rotting meat, everyone pretended they couldn't smell a thing to protect Babe's dignity. Eventually, Babe wound up back in the hospital, and amputation was seen as her only option. By that time a teenager, she made my grandfather promise that this would never be allowed.

Finally, a very, very old doctor heard about Babe's case and got involved. He had been a very, very young medic during the Civil War and remembered the wounded soldiers who used to lie on hot, dusty battlefields for days at a time before they could receive medical attention. He'd been fascinated that their exposed wounds were always clean as a whistle and didn't show signs of infection. The reason: maggots (fly larva). Maggots are efficient consumers of dead tissue. They munch on rotting flesh, leaving healthy tissue behind. The doctor noted that soldiers with maggot-infested gashes or bullet wounds didn't have the expected infection or swelling seen in other patients.

Working under a surgical drape (and without her knowledge), doctors inserted live maggots into Babe's wound. They adhesive-taped a metal cage to confine the maggots and allow for ventilation and drainage of necrotic tissue. Three days later, a screaming Babe woke up and saw the satiated maggots clinging to the metal cage. She was convinced she was rotting. Quite the contrary—since maggots can't feed on healthy tissue, their natural instinct is to crawl elsewhere—and that's just what they had done.

Aunt Babe's knee eventually fused and couldn't bend. Although she walked with two canes for the rest of her life, her leg was saved. In an era when there were no provisions for the handicapped, she not only drove a car—she drove an Airstream trailer cross-country, was a proficient wood carver, a genealogist (long before the benefits of Ancestry.com), a foster mother, and dental hygienist.

Aunt Babe's story supports everything I believe about healing. It was the maggots and that doctor's memory of their power on the Civil War battlefields that saved her leg, and probably her life. People are revolted by maggots and leeches, but fecal transplants (transplanting feces from a healthy donor into another person to restore the balance of bacteria in their gut) are seen as cutting edge and routine. For me, western medicine has a place, and that place is in situations of emergency. Conventional healthcare in the western world is still based on allopathy, or the treatment of ailments with drugs. I choose to focus on health rather than disease.

• • •

# FIRE CIDER

We have a love/hate relationship with fire cider. The love part: we consider it to be the ultimate herbal cold and flu remedy, and we call it "a flu shot in a jar." The hate part: it leaves you with dragon breath! Basically, it's a blend of onions, garlic, horseradish, and cayenne (plus other herbs, based on a person's health needs/goals) in a base of raw apple cider vinegar. It's an immune-boosting tonic with antibacterial, antiviral, antimicrobial, antifungal, and antiseptic properties—and can be taken daily as a preventative, or at the onset of colds and flu. We consider it a panacea!

## Benefits of Fire Cider

- It breaks up congestion and helps ward off respiratory ailments.
- It has *diaphoretic* properties (in the herbal world, *diaphoretic* means an herb that stimulates sweating and moves toxins out of the body), which is beneficial in cases of colds, flus, and mild fevers.
- It's beneficial for the cardiovascular system and may help regulate circulation and blood pressure.
- It warms the organs of the digestive system and stimulates the secretion of digestive juices.
- It's anti-inflammatory properties make it a helpful remedy for sore or stiff muscles and joints.

We've created four recipe blends depending on your tastes and needs. We don't peel any of the ingredients and include the skins/peels in our fire cider. Many herbalists believe that skins and peels protect the plant and act as its immune system as it grows. In our workshops, we notice that some people are bothered by adding onion and garlic peels to their jars, so if this idea isn't for you, don't include them. Of course, we encourage you to use organic ingredients.

## BASIC FIRE CIDER

This simple recipe provides general immune support. The ingredients blend to form a potent punch that is immune-boosting, antibacterial, antiviral, congestion clearing, and warming. Makes twenty-four ounces (prior to straining).

### INGREDIENTS

1 medium onion, chopped

4 cloves garlic, chopped

4 tablespoons fresh horseradish, chopped (bottled horseradish is fine, but as we recently discovered, some brands of ready-made horseradish include corn syrup!)

½ teaspoon cayenne powder (or ½ tablespoon fresh cayenne pepper)

Apple cider vinegar (raw, unpasteurized)

### INSTRUCTIONS

1. Chop all ingredients and place in a twenty-four–ounce glass mason-type jar.
2. Fill jar to the top with apple cider vinegar. (Suggestion: the vinegar will eventually erode the lid of the jar. To prevent that from happening, place a piece of wax paper under the lid.)
3. Cover and let sit for at least four weeks (shake jar daily).
4. Strain, bottle, and drink! Does not have to be refrigerated.
5. Some people discard the strained remnants, some people eat them, and some people put them in a blender and add to soups, stews, etc.

## BENEFITS

- **Onion** *(Allium cepa)*: A great source of vitamins C, B1, B6, K, biotin, calcium, folic acid, and dietary fiber. Onions also contain chromium, which isn't a mineral commonly found naturally in food. Chromium helps the body manage blood sugar levels and ensure a slow, gradual release of glucose. So, if you have blood sugar issues, you may want to incorporate more onions into your life! Onions also contain quercetin, a compound that inhibits the development and spread of cancerous cells. Onions are a well-known folk remedy for treatment of coughs.

- **Garlic** *(Allium sativum)*: Garlic, one of the oldest remedies known to humans, is antibacterial, antiviral, antiparasitic, antifungal, and can help lower fevers.[1] A potent internal and external antiseptic, garlic stimulates and supports the body's immune system. Along with the right diet for you (we advocate and follow Peter D'adamo's Blood Type Diet), it can help maintain healthy blood pressure levels.

  Raw garlic contains *allicin*, a compound containing potent medicinal properties, and the one responsible for that distinct "garlic" smell. Allicin is created when two separate ingredients in garlic—alliin (a protein fragment) and alliinase (a heat-sensitive enzyme)—connect with each other. In the intact clove, these substances are isolated in separate compartments. They don't co-mingle until the barriers between them are destroyed by slicing, pressing, or chewing. Heating garlic immediately after chopping it can destroy the heat-sensitive alliinase, which means that allicin won't be created.

  There's a very simple way to fix this: when you chop garlic for cooking, just keep it away from heat for five to ten minutes. During this time, the maximum amount of allicin will be created and you'll get all the medicinal benefits of garlic. Cooking, sautéeing, baking, or frying won't affect the allicin.

--------

1. McIntyre, *The Complete Herbal Tutor*, 104.

# GROUNDED GOODWIFE STORY TIME

## *Garlic's Not an Herb!* by Ehris

When people find out I'm an herbalist, I hear one common question, "If you were trapped on a deserted island, what one herb would you want to have with you?"

That's a tough question for me because I have so many favorites, but my response is always, "Garlic."

"*Garlic?*" People correct me, "Garlic's not an herb!"

To which I respond, "Well, an herb is a plant that has medicinal properties. So, an herb can be anything from well-known kitchen herbs—parsley, basil, rosemary, and thyme—to herbs that most people would consider vegetables—like garlic, onions, and horseradish."

• • •

- **Horseradish** (*Armoracia rusticana*), strongly antibacterial and antibiotic, is useful for fevers, colds, and flu. It's especially helpful for sinus and respiratory issues—and if you've ever smelled or tasted horseradish, you know the feeling as it wakes up your nostrils!

- **Cayenne** (*Capsicum annuum*) improves memory and wards off coughs and colds. People who attend our workshops are always interested in our cayenne flower essence story (see the next page). Flower essences (which have nothing to do with essential oils) are Ehris' favorite mode of healing. They're drops taken sublingually for emotional issues like stress, grief, body image, fear, anxiety, childhood issues, etc. Cayenne flower essence is for lethargy, procrastination, and stagnation.

- **Apple Cider Vinegar** is rich in enzymes and potassium. Since it supports a healthy immune system, many people take plain apple cider vinegar shots every day. Make sure you use the raw, unpasteurized kind with the "mother." Until recently, you could only find raw apple cider vinegar in health food stores. Today, it's available in many grocery stores.

# GROUNDED GOODWIFE STORY TIME

*Cayenne Flower Essence* by Ehris

A few Februarys ago, my mom and I were sitting on the couch in our cold, old house, procrastinating about writing her first hands-on science book for kids. At the time, my mom was a hands-on science teacher, and since I knew all of her lesson plans, I offered to help. I remembered someone had given me a bottle of cayenne flower essence, and kind of as a joke, we each took four drops. By that night, we had written three books! This flower essence doesn't give you a caffeine high—it just keeps you totally focused on the task at hand—like preparing your income tax return, writing a research paper (or this book!), or vacuuming your entire house because guests are arriving in thirty minutes and spiderwebs and dog hair are everywhere. Don't fret about the cayenne aspect—you won't be Puff the Magic Dragon! It's a potentized remedy that comes from the flower, so aside from the brandy it's preserved in, it has no taste.

• • •

## How to Take Fire Cider

We recommend taking one to two ounces (a shot glass is one ounce) daily—especially during cold and flu season. It can be taken straight, diluted in juice or water, or mixed with honey. Ehris insists that adding honey makes it almost bearable. Some people are concerned about the vinegar eroding their tooth enamel—so, we recommend just rinsing your mouth out with water after taking your fire cider.

A clever way to take fire cider is by using it as a salad dressing (mixed with a little olive oil). Some of our followers suggest using it as a meat marinade.

Externally, it can be used as a compress. Soak a washcloth in the tonic, and place it on sore muscles, aching joints, or a congested chest.

## FRUITY FIRE CIDER

Thanks to the elderberries and hibiscus, this blend is purple/red in color. That, combined with the apple, which makes it a little bit sweet, may make it a more pleasant option for kids. Makes twenty-four ounces (before straining).

### INGREDIENTS

1 medium onion, chopped

4 cloves garlic, chopped

¼ cup horseradish, chopped

½ apple, chopped

½ teaspoon cayenne powder (or ½ tablespoon fresh cayenne pepper)

¼ cup elderberries

2 teaspoons elderflower

1 tablespoon hibiscus flowers

Apple cider vinegar (raw, unpasteurized)

### INSTRUCTIONS

1. Chop onion, garlic, horseradish, and apple and place in a twenty-four–ounce glass mason-type jar. Add remaining ingredients.

2. Fill jar to the top with apple cider vinegar. (Suggestion: the vinegar will eventually erode the lid of the jar. To prevent that from happening, place a piece of wax paper under the lid.)

3. Cover and let sit for at least four weeks (shake jar daily).

4. Strain, bottle, and drink! Does not have to be refrigerated.

5. Some people discard the strained remnants, some people eat them, and some people put them in a blender and add to soups, stews, etc.

## BENEFITS

- **Apples** (*Malus domestica*): Despite the saying, "An apple a day keeps the doctor away," apples are often overlooked as a medicinal food. Apples, which have been cultivated since Roman times[2], are cleansing for the system. Studies have shown that apples can reduce blood cholesterol levels.[3]

- **Elderberries** (*Sambucus nigra*) are antiviral, rich in vitamin C, and may inhibit colds, flu, and herpes. As adaptogens, elderberries increase your resilience to stress (learn more about elderberries in our Elderberry Syrup recipe on page 41).

- **Elderflowers** (*Sambucus nigra*) are used to reduce swelling in the mucus membranes, relieving nasal and sinus congestion. They're also calming and soothing—great for tension, anxiety, and insomnia.

- **Hibiscus** (*Hibiscus rosa-sinensis*), high in immune-boosting vitamin C, gives everything a rosy color. Hibiscus supports the heart—physically and emotionally.

  Physically, hibiscus improves circulatory health. According to the *National Geographic Guide to Medicinal Herbs*, "Human studies show that it [hibiscus] reduces blood pressure to the same degree as two commonly prescribed ACE inhibitors, Captopril and Lisinopril. A clinical trial with type two diabetics found that it [hibiscus] lowered blood pressure and increased high-density lipoprotein (HDL), or 'good' cholesterol."[4]

  Emotionally, hibiscus mends grief and brokenheartedness. It releases "stuck" creative forces—especially in the sacral chakra or womb area. It can set you free to enjoy life, and it stimulates passion. Many people only think of romantic passion—which hibiscus can help with—but it'll also support your passion for life, or help you discover what you love to do.

........................................

2. Ody, *The Complete Medicinal Herbal*, 77.

3. Koutsos, et al. "Two Apples a Day Lower Serum Cholesterol and Improve Cardiometabolic Biomarkers in Mildly Hypercholesterolemic Adults," 307–318.

4. Johnson, Foster, and Weil, *National Geographic Guide to Medicinal Herbs*, 339.

## CIRCULATORY TONIC FIRE CIDER

This blend is a tonic for the heart—for both physical *and* emotional heart issues. The herbal additions can help ease grief, sadness, heavy-heartedness, loneliness, and brokenheartedness. Makes twenty-four ounces (before straining).

### INGREDIENTS

1 medium onion, chopped

4 cloves garlic, chopped

¼ cup horseradish, chopped

½ teaspoon cayenne powder (or ½ tablespoon fresh cayenne pepper)

¼ cup hawthorn berries

3 tablespoons linden

1 tablespoon motherwort leaf/flower

Apple cider vinegar (raw, unpasteurized)

### INSTRUCTIONS

1. Chop onion, garlic, and horseradish and place in a twenty-four–ounce glass mason-type jar. Add remaining ingredients.
2. Fill jar to the top with apple cider vinegar. (Suggestion: the vinegar will eventually erode the lid of the jar. To prevent that from happening, place a piece of wax paper under the lid.)
3. Cover and let sit for at least four weeks (shake jar daily).
4. Strain, bottle, and drink! Does not have to be refrigerated.
5. Some people discard the strained remnants, some people eat them, and some people put them in a blender and add to soups, stews, etc.

### BENEFITS

- **Hawthorn** (*Crataegus monogyna*): Hawthorn is an excellent remedy for the heart and circulation, protecting the heart muscle, and regulating heart rhythm. If you take heart medication/prescriptions, you may want to consult your healthcare practitioner before using hawthorn.

- **Linden** (*Tilia* spp.): Linden's cream-colored, honey-scented flowers are one of our favorite remedies for anxiety, tension, headaches, nervousness, and insomnia. In the words of herbalist Robin Rose Bennett, "Linden opens the emotional and spiritual heart even as it improves cardiovascular circulation. If you are willing, linden helps you dance with current grief and clear out old, 'stuck' grief."[5]
- **Motherwort** (*Leonurus cardiaca*): Motherwort's Latin name, *Leonurus cardiaca*, means "the lion-hearted one." Like the other herbs in this blend, motherwort benefits the heart physically and emotionally. This bitter "weed" is known to reduce nervous palpitations and irregular heartbeat, calm anxiety, ease heartbreak, and aid sleep.

# GROUNDED GOODWIFE STORY TIME

### *Hawthorn for the Heart* by Ehris

Many of my clients have experienced physical or emotional heart issues. They'd share heart-wrenching stories about their husband in prison, repeated miscarriages, children dying in school shootings, bitter divorces and custody battles, stillbirths, being ostracized after coming out, and guilt over putting a baby up for adoption. As they opened up, I would immediately think of hawthorn—the premier herbal tonic to support healthy functioning of the heart. The berries, leaves, and flowers strengthen the force of the heart muscle, and help maintain healthy blood pressure and a normal heart rhythm, along with mending a bruised or broken heart. I've recommended it to many clients experiencing heartache, grief, or anxiety.

• • •

## ANTI-INFLAMMATORY FIRE CIDER

Ehris' favorite blend! The turmeric, cinnamon, and ginger seem to make the other ingredients taste a little less intense. This one is helpful for creaky bones/

---

5. Bennett, *The Gift of Healing Herbs*, 235–236.

joints and, along with dietary changes, can help relieve inflammation. Makes twenty-four ounces (before straining).

## INGREDIENTS

1 medium onion, chopped

4 cloves garlic, chopped

¼ cup horseradish, chopped

½ teaspoon cayenne powder (or ½ tablespoon fresh cayenne pepper)

4 tablespoons turmeric powder (or ¼ cup fresh turmeric)

8 black peppercorns, ground

1 tablespoon ginger powder (or 2 tablespoons fresh ginger)

2 teaspoons cinnamon powder

Apple cider vinegar (raw, unpasteurized)

## INSTRUCTIONS

1. Chop onion, garlic, and horseradish and place in a twenty-four–ounce glass mason-type jar. Add remaining ingredients.
2. Fill jar to the top with apple cider vinegar. (Suggestion: the vinegar will eventually erode the lid of the jar. To prevent that from happening, place a piece of wax paper under the lid.)
3. Cover and let sit for at least four weeks (shake jar daily).
4. Strain, bottle, and drink! Does not have to be refrigerated.
5. Some people discard the remnants, some people eat them, and some people put them in a blender and add to soups, stews, etc.

## BENEFITS

- **Turmeric** (*Curcuma longa*) is best-known for its anti-inflammatory properties. It's also a mood lifter, boosts the immune system, and prevents tumor growth. Fun fact: a common misconception is that yellow mustard (which used to be called ballpark mustard) is yellow because of the mustard seeds. The bold yellow color actually comes from turmeric!

- **Black pepper** (*Piper nigrum*) aids in turmeric absorption (this is why golden milk recipes always include pepper!) and is great for coughs and colds. Piperine, the active ingredient in black pepper, has been shown to reduce memory impairment and cognitive malfunction.[6] Pepper was a precious commodity in the ancient world. Legend has it that as a show of honor, black peppercorns were stuffed in the nostrils of Egyptian Pharaoh Ramesses II when he was mummified![7]

- **Ginger** (*Zingiber officinale*), a *diaphoretic* herb (stimulates sweating and moves toxins out of the body), can reduce fevers, and its volatile oils clear out acute bacterial and viral infections.

- **Cinnamon** (*Cinnamomum verum*): Warming and stimulating, cinnamon improves circulation, digestion, concentration, and motivation. With powerful antiseptic, antiviral, and antibacterial properties, this herb wards off winter illness. Cinnamon is also famous for boosting vitality, and reducing muscle stiffness and arthritic pain.

6. Chonpathompikunlert, et al., "Piperine, the Main Alkaloid of Thai Black Pepper, Protects against Neurodegeneration and Cognitive Impairment in Animal Model of Cognitive Deficit like Condition of Alzheimer's Disease," 798–802.

7. Spiegel, "What's the World's Most Used Spice?"

# GROUNDED GOODWIFE STORY TIME

*Let's Be Honest about the Taste* by Velya

People have described the taste of fire cider as warming, tasty, spicy, and sweetly vinaigrette. They are liars. Every shot of fire cider makes my eyes pop out of my head and my hair stand on end! The cloudy, khaki-colored brew tastes much, much worse than it looks. Fire cider gives a wake-up slap to the immune system. Every morning I pour myself a shot glass, make sure the water's running, hold my nose, toss back the shot, get the shivers, gag, and wash it down with *lots* of water. No matter how carefully I try to avoid it touching my taste buds, I fail. Fire cider tastes like a combination of pickle juice, Easter egg dye, Atomic Fireball jawbreaker candies, Italian dressing, and sautéed onions.

My husband, Jim, takes his daily shot at around 4:30 a.m. Some mornings I don't hear any sounds coming out of the bathroom. Other mornings I hear wretching, gagging, and coughing. That's the thing with fire cider—some days it's worse than other days. Of course, we could do what many people do and add a shot to our stainless steel water bottles and sip it throughout the day, but we have a "get it over with" approach to unpleasant things in life.

All of this being said, Jim, Ehris, and I have very busy lives. We're out and about with people and kids coughing all over us, our speaking gig travels land us in many public bathrooms, none of us get enough sleep—and none of us have had a cold (and never the flu) for years. I attribute it to an excellent diet and, *unfortunately*, fire cider.

• • •

# SPRING TONICS

After a blizzard or Nor'easter, we can replenish our fridges and freezers at the supermarket. But for most of human history, winter has been a time of nutrient depletion and starvation.

Today, spring fever is the urge to see the first crocus and put away your Uggs and snowshovels. But prior to 1900, spring fever had a different meaning. By March and April, stored food was gone, and nothing was growing yet. Aside from infancy, early spring was the most dangerous time for children—many children died just before plants started to sprout. Hence, the term "spring fever."

After surviving all winter on a little dried meat, stored grain, and root vegetables, anything fresh and green was literally a lifesaver. Survivors devoured nonpoisonous (and sometimes even semipoisonous) leaves and shoots sprouting beneath the melting snow. Salads, soups, and teas made from these plants were referred to as "spring tonics."

Along with providing nourishment, spring tonics were used to "flush out the pipes," like a modern-day cleanse. Spring tonics were often served with sulfur and molasses to complement the spring cleaning. There was a poor-man's version of sulfur and molasses—a handful of metal nails soaked in a jar of water!

May Proven McWilliams was born in 1889. She handed down her spring tonic recipe to her five daughters, and it eventually made its way down the family tree to us. We tweaked it to add additional medicinal benefits.

Fire cider and spring tonics play two different health roles. The primary purpose of fire cider is to keep your immune system strong to fight off winter's "bugs." Spring tonics, on the other hand, help our bodies come out of hibernation and prepare us to transition to the new seasons.

In the spring, we crave lighter foods like salads and stir fries, in place of meals like meatloaf and mashed potatoes—the hearty comfort foods of winter. It's the time of year when we all start eating what's locally available in the way of wild greens. A traditional spring tonic utilizes herbs gathered from your own yard, just like your great-grandmother would have done. Being indoors all winter, combined with the lack of fresh air and sunshine, can send us into a slump. Many of the earliest plants that pop up in spring are bitter tonic herbs, which can help improve elimination of waste, restore proper function of the organs, and slowly restore the body's health and vitality. These recipes get you ready for spring by gently, yet effectively, cleansing and moving toxins out of the body.

We've created four recipe blends depending on your tastes and needs. As we mentioned in the fire cider section, we don't peel any of the ingredients and include the skins/peels in our spring tonic. Many herbalists believe that skins and peels protect the plant and act as its immune system as it grows. In our workshops, we notice that some people are bothered by adding onion and garlic peels to their jars, so if this idea isn't for you, don't include them.

## BASIC GREAT-GRANNY MCWILLIAMS'S SPRING TONIC

Spring is a time of waking up and bursting forth into the world, and tonics are an easy way to help your body transition from winter to spring. If you're a purist and don't care for any herbal additions, this is Great-Granny McWilliams's original recipe! Makes twenty-four ounces (prior to straining).

### INGREDIENTS

1 small beet, chopped

1 leek, chopped

2 cloves garlic, chopped

½ cup chopped dandelion greens

¼ cup chopped watercress

Juice from 1 lemon (or 3 tablespoons bottled lemon juice)

Apple cider vinegar

### INSTRUCTIONS

1. Place chopped beet, leek, garlic, dandelion, and watercress in a twenty-four–ounce glass mason-type jar. Add lemon juice.

2. Fill jar to the top with apple cider vinegar. (Suggestion—the vinegar will eventually erode the lid of the jar. To prevent that from happening, place a piece of wax paper under the lid.)

3. Cover and let sit for at least four weeks (shake jar daily).

4. Strain, bottle, and drink! Does not have to be refrigerated.

5. Some people discard the strained remnants, some people eat them, and some people put them in a blender and add to soups, stews, etc.

## BENEFITS

- **Beet** (*Beta vulgaris*): You may not have eaten beets since you were a kid and they came sliced in a can. Some people love them, and some people think they taste like dirt! Beets have been used as an aphrodisiac since the time of the ancient Romans. They attributed Aphrodite's (the goddess of love) sex appeal to her insatiable appetite for beets.[8] As most people know, eating fruits and vegetables with rich colors are good for your eyes. Beets contain lutein, which can help slow the progression of age-related macular degeneration, a leading cause of adult vision loss.[9] They add folate, manganese, and copper to this spring tonic, and give it an inviting ruby color.

- **Leek** (*Allium porrum*): Leeks seem to play a "best supporting role," always losing out in popularity to their fellow allium vegetables garlic and onions. With a more delicate and sweeter flavor than onions, leeks add a subtle, nonoverpowering touch to recipes. Leeks are an excellent source of vitamin K. Vitamin K deficiency is fairly rare, but can cause issues like bone loss and excessive bleeding. Other vitamin K rich foods include spring onions, brussels sprouts, cabbage, fermented/cultured dairy, prunes, and broccoli.

- **Garlic** (*Allium sativum*): Garlic has a long history as an antimicrobial herb. In eighteenth-century France, gravediggers drank wine containing crushed garlic to protect themselves from the plague. During World Wars I and II, it was used as an antiseptic for wounds and to prevent infections (like gangrene) in soldiers.[10] We include it in Great-Granny McWilliams' Spring Tonic for its antibacterial, antiviral, antimicrobial, antifungal, antiparasitic, and immunity-building properties.

...........................................

8. Captain Hale, "Beetroots."

9. Buscemi, "The Effect of Lutein on Eye and Extra-Eye Health," 1321.

10. Fenster, *Eating Well, Living Better*, 130.

- **Dandelion** (*Taraxacum officinale*): Some see a weed, some see a wish! In traditional Chinese medicine, emotions and physical health are strongly connected. Put simply, emotions are associated with a particular organ in the body. The emotions associated with the liver are anger, resentment, frustration, irritability, and bitterness. Bitter herbs, like dandelion, cleanse the liver—both physically and emotionally.

  Young dandelion leaves are traditionally eaten in spring to detox the body from the heavy food and more sedentary habits of winter. Dandelion increases the elimination of toxins and waste through the liver and kidneys, cleansing the blood and clearing the skin. This "weed" is especially helpful for anybody who works with, or is exposed to, chemicals—like a mechanic, hair stylist, manicurist, or painter.[11] The diuretic effect of dandelion accounts for its common French name, *pissenlit*, or "piss-in-bed." Obviously, don't harvest your dandelions from areas treated with herbicides (or you'll have an even bigger problem than wetting the bed!).

- **Watercress** (*Nasturtium officinale*) clears toxins and purifies the blood. One cup of watercress contains more than half our recommended daily intake of vitamin A. Lutein, found in watercress (and beets), helps block blue light from reaching the retina, which may result in a reduction in light-induced oxidative damage.[12] The Victorians believed watercress was a cure for toothaches, hiccups, hangovers, and freckles (who knew freckles were something that had to be cured?!).[13]

- **Lemons** are a good source of vitamin C and contain almost the same amount of vitamin C as an orange. There have been a number of studies that indicate lemons may be effective in killing-off cancer cells.[14]

..........................................

11. Bennett, *The Gift of Healing Herbs*, 133.
12. Buscemi, et al., "The Effect of Lutein on Eye and Extra-Eye Health," 1321.
13. Watercress, "Top 10 Benefits of Eating Watercress."
14. Alshatwi, et al., "Apoptosis-Mediated Inhibition of Human Breast Cancer Cell Proliferation By Lemon Citrus Extract," 1621–25; Raimondo, et al., "Citrus Limon-Derived Nanovesicles Inhibit Cancer Cell Proliferation and Suppress CML Xenograft Growth By Inducing TRAIL-Mediated Cell Death," 19514–27; Lee, et al., "Hesperidin Suppressed Proliferations of Both Human Breast Cancer and Androgen-Dependent Prostate Cancer Cells," S15–S19; Crowell and Gould, "Chemoprevention and Therapy of Cancer by d-Limonene," 1–22.

## How to Take Spring Tonics

Near the end of winter, begin taking one to two ounces of a spring tonic daily. It can be taken straight, diluted in juice or water, or mixed with honey. Some people are concerned about the vinegar eroding their tooth enamel, so we recommend just rinsing your mouth out with water after taking the tonic.

A clever way to take Great-Granny McWilliams's Spring Tonic is by using it as a salad dressing (mixed with a little olive oil). Some of our followers use it as a meat marinade.

Externally, it can be used as a compress. Soak a washcloth in the tonic, and place it on sore muscles, aching joints, or a congested chest.

## GREAT-GRANNY MCWILLIAMS'S SEASONAL ALLERGY SPRING TONIC

If you suffer from seasonal allergies, this nettle-rich blend could be your new BFF! Nettle leaf is a natural antihistamine that can be very effective as it naturally blocks the body's ability to produce histamine. This tonic doesn't work like an over-the-counter allergy medicine, so we suggest that you begin taking it at least a month before allergy season begins. Makes twenty-four ounces (prior to straining).

### INGREDIENTS

1 small beet, chopped

1 leek, chopped

2 cloves garlic, chopped

½ cup chopped dandelion greens

¼ cup chopped watercress

¼ cup nettle leaf

2 tablespoons goldenrod leaf/flower

Juice from 1 lemon (or 3 tablespoons bottled lemon juice)

Apple cider vinegar

## INSTRUCTIONS

1. Place chopped beet, leek, garlic, dandelion greens, watercress, nettle leaf, and goldenrod in a twenty-four–ounce glass mason-type jar. Add lemon juice.

2. Fill jar to the top with apple cider vinegar. (Suggestion: the vinegar will eventually erode the lid of the jar. To stop that from happening, place a piece of wax paper under the lid.)

3. Cover and let sit for at least four weeks (shake jar daily).

4. Strain, bottle, and drink! Does not have to be refrigerated.

5. Some people discard the strained remnants, some people eat them, and some people put them in a blender and add to soups, stews, etc.

## BENEFITS

- **Nettle** (*Urtica dioica*): Nettle's antihistamine properties make it an effective remedy for allergies and hay fever.

## GROUNDED GOODWIFE STORY TIME

*Nettle for Allergies* by Ehris

Until a few years ago, I never had any allergy symptoms. Then, one fall, I was hit with allergy woes—runny nose, watery eyes, sneezing. That winter, I started drinking nettle tea every day since I knew it's regarded as a natural vitamin/mineral supplement. When allergy season rolled around in the spring, I was symptom free—thanks to the nettle tea! I still drink it every day. If you decide to try nettle to relieve your allergies, start taking it at least a month before allergy season starts. It doesn't work like prescription medication—you need to give it a chance to kick in.

• • •

- **Goldenrod** (*Solidago* spp.): Don't be put off by the goldenrod in this recipe. Every year in late summer/early fall, allergy sufferers blame goldenrod for causing their hay fever. But the real culprit for the sneezing, runny nose, and itchy eyes is ragweed. Goldenrod and ragweed bloom around the same time. Goldenrod flowers are a bright, noticeable yellow, while ragweed flowers are greenish-white and small. People see the vibrant goldenrod blooming and are convinced it's causing their allergies. Actually, goldenrod helps seasonal allergies! It's an *antiseptic* and *decongestant* that's great for coughs, colds, hay fever, sore throat, flu, sinusitis, bronchitis, and asthma. So, give goldenrod a break!

## GREAT-GRANNY MCWILLIAMS'S RESTORATIVE SPRING TONIC

This blend will nourish you and support a gentle transition to the next season. It's especially helpful if you're trying to regain your strength from an illness or stressful event. Some of our workshop participants have found that it gives them a boost in energy and vitality and addresses their Seasonal Affective Disorder (SAD). Makes twenty-four ounces (prior to straining).

### INGREDIENTS

1 small beet, chopped

1 leek, chopped

2 cloves garlic, chopped

½ cup chopped dandelion greens

¼ cup chopped watercress

½ chopped apple

3 tablespoons lemon balm leaf/flower

5 tablespoons rhodiola root

Juice from 1 lemon (or 3 tablespoons bottled lemon juice)

Apple cider vinegar

## INSTRUCTIONS

1. Place chopped beet, leek, garlic, dandelion greens, watercress, apple, lemon balm and rhodiola in a twenty-four–ounce glass mason-type jar. Add lemon juice.

2. Fill jar to the top with apple cider vinegar. (Suggestion: the vinegar will eventually erode the lid of the jar. To prevent that from happening, place a piece of wax paper under the lid.)

3. Cover and let sit for at least four weeks (shake jar daily).

4. Strain, bottle, and drink! Does not have to be refrigerated.

5. Some people discard the strained remnants, some people eat them, and some people put them in a blender and add to soups, stews, etc.

## BENEFITS

- **Apples** (*Malus domestica*) have long been considered a weather forecaster: If an apple developed a tough skin, it meant that there would be a hard winter. If a young unmarried woman slept with one under her pillow, she would dream of her future husband (Ehris keeps trying this…maybe she needs to stop using Fujis and switch to Granny Smiths…).

- **Lemon balm** (*Melissa officinalis*): Once referred to as the "gladdening herb,"[15] mood-elevating lemon balm reduces tension, anxiety, and headaches. This lemony member of the mint family contains antiviral properties, making it helpful for issues like colds, flus, mumps, and shingles. Studies are showing that lemon balm may be helpful for use in treating HIV.[16] This herb has been valued throughout history for its use in supporting memory and promoting longevity.[17]

- **Rhodiola** (*Rhodiola rosea*), a sedum-like plant that grows in cold and mountainous regions of the northern hemisphere, was used by the

15. Johnson, et al., *National Geographic Guide to Medicinal Herbs*, 34–37.
16. Geuenich, et al., "Aqueous Extracts from Peppermint, Sage and Lemon Balm Leaves Display Potent Anti-HIV-1 Activity by Increasing the Virion Density."
17. McIntyre, *The Complete Herbal Tutor*, 144.

Vikings to improve physical strength and endurance.[18] So, if it could delay a Viking's final journey to Valhalla, think what it could do for you!

Studies have shown rhodiola to be a promising herb for mental health. The Department of Psychiatry at UCLA conducted a study on the effects of rhodiola for patients diagnosed with generalized anxiety disorder. The study found that rhodiola significantly reduced anxiety, with the improvement being similar to the improvement seen with prescription antianxiety medication—but with no significant side effects reported.[19] Rhodiola is also well-known for increasing stamina, fighting fatigue, and enhancing memory and attention span.

## ELDERBERRY SYRUP

For centuries, elderberry has been used in folk medicine to combat colds and flu. However, scientific research proves its effectiveness. At Hadassah-Hebrew University Medical Center in Israel, researchers led by virologist Dr. Madeleine Mumcuoglu, PhD, isolated several proteins and other active principles in black elderberry (*Sambucus nigra*) that disarm the viral spikes by binding to them and preventing them from puncturing cell membranes.[20]

In one placebo-controlled, double-blind study conducted by Dr. Mumcuoglu, 93.3 percent of the people taking an elderberry preparation reported significant improvement in influenza symptoms within two days of starting it, compared with the six days it took for the placebo group to see improvement.[21]

Researchers also have found that people who have taken elderberries have higher levels of antibodies against the influenza virus, showing that the berry may be able to treat flu symptoms, as well as prevent influenza infection.[22]

18. Johnson, et al., *National Geographic Guide to Medicinal Herbs*, 339.

19. Bystritsky, et al., "A Pilot Study of Rhodiola Rosea (Rhodax) for Generalized Anxiety Disorder (GAD)," 175–80.

20. Mumcuoglu, et al., "Elderberry," 235–40.

21. Zakay-Rones, et al., "Randomized Study of the Efficacy and Safety of Oral Elderberry Extract in the Treatment of Influenza A and B Virus Infections," 132–40

22. Zakay-Rones, et al., "Inhibition of Several Strains of Influenza Virus In Vitro and Reduction of Symptoms by an Elderberry Extract (Sambucus Nigra L.) During an Outbreak of Influenza B Panama," 361–69.

Several years ago, elderberries sold for about $15 per pound. Since then, interest in elderberry syrup has risen. During cold and flu season, we've seen the berries cost as much as $75 per pound—a perfect example of supply and demand.

## ELDERBERRY SYRUP RECIPE

Elderberries contain antiviral properties, making them an ideal cold/flu remedy. They're also being studied for their use in treating HIV. Because of its many health benefits, the elder tree has been called "the medicine chest of the country people."[23] It seems impossible that something so tasty can be such good medicine, and so easy to make! Makes about two cups.

### INGREDIENTS

3½ cups water

⅔ cup dried black elderberries

2 tablespoons grated ginger

1 teaspoon cinnamon

1 cup honey (raw and local, if possible)

Optional:

1 teaspoon rose hips

1 teaspoon astragalus root

### INSTRUCTIONS

1. Pour water into medium saucepan. Add elderberries and herbs (including optional herbs)—do not add honey!
2. With the lid on the pot, bring to a boil, then cover and reduce to a simmer for about forty-five minutes. (We've discovered that if you omit the cinnamon and ginger, the simmering berries smell like a combo of cow manure and a vet's office. You know that vet office smell … doggy, but kind of masked by cleaning products.)

23. McIntyre, *The Complete Herbal Tutor*, 156.

3. While it's simmering, pour the honey into a jar that holds at least twenty-four ounces.

4. Remove berry mixture from heat. Put a very large funnel and strainer in the glass jar containing the honey. Strain the berry mixture directly into the jar containing the honey. Smoosh the berries with a wooden spoon or something similar so you get every drop of berry goodness! Discard the strained mixture (or compost it).

5. Shake jar well to combine the berry mixture and the honey (the jar will be very hot, so be careful—you might want to wrap it in a dishtowel and then shake it up).

6. Your homemade elderberry syrup is done! Let it cool, then store in the fridge.

## DOSAGE

- As a preventative measure during cold and flu season, the standard recommended daily dose is one tablespoon for adults and one teaspoon for kids.

- If you're already sick, you can still take elderberry syrup to reduce the symptoms and duration—take the standard recommended dose every two to three hours until symptoms improve.

- Elderberry syrup is an extremely effective remedy, and some herbalists believe that to maintain the best immune-supporting benefits, it shouldn't be taken every single day (for example, take during the week but not on the weekends). Adaptogenic herbs—like elderberry, cinnamon, and astragalus—support your adrenal glands, which manage your hormonal response to stress, and help you cope with anxiety and fatigue. Taking little breaks from adaptogenic herbs can help them maintain optimum effectiveness in your system.

## BENEFITS

Additional herbs in this recipe not only add to the flavor, but deliver a medicinal boost.

- **Ginger** (*Zingiber officinale*): A *diaphoretic* herb (stimulates sweating and moves toxins out of the body), ginger can reduce fevers, and its volatile oils clear out acute bacterial and viral infections. During the Middle Ages, ginger was held in such high esteem that it was said to have come from the Garden of Eden.[24] In fourteenth century England, a pound of ginger was about equal to the price of one sheep.[25]

- **Cinnamon** (*Cinnamomum verum*): Antiviral and antifungal, cinnamon is also an expectorant for coughs and chest infections. In Ancient Rome, cinnamon was at least fifteen times more expensive than silver.[26] In AD 65, in order to show the depth of his grief, Emperor Nero burned a year's supply of cinnamon on the funeral pyre of his second wife, Poppaea Sabina.[27]

- **Rose hips** (*Rosa canina*), the parts left on the plant after a rose is done blooming, are rich in vitamin C.

- **Astragalus** (*Astragalus membranaceus*) is an antiviral *tonic herb* (a tonic herb gives a feeling of vigor or well-being) used to strengthen immunity, vitality, and endurance.

- **Honey:** Every time we see an ingredient list that includes organic honey, we chuckle. Since most beekeepers don't own thousands of acres, there's no way to control or monitor where their bees go and know what kind of pollen they're bringing back to the hive. Bees can travel up to eight miles to find pollen. While the beekeeper might not use pesticides, a neighbor might.

  We recommend that you use raw, local honey. Local bees produce local honey, which means the pollen they collect comes from local plants. Many seasonal allergies are caused by these same plants. We regard local honey as a natural seasonal allergy inoculation.

24. Johnson, Foster, and Weil, *National Geographic Guide to Medicinal Herbs*, 161.

25. Johnson, Foster, and Weil, *National Geographic Guide to Medicinal Herbs*, 162.

26. Johnson, Foster, and Weil, *National Geographic Guide to Medicinal Herbs*, 111.

27. Schapira, Schapira, Shardin, and Schapira, *The Book of Coffee & Tea*, 268.

# ONION COUGH SYRUP

At the beginning of the 1900s, when women were cooking meals from scratch, sewing their own clothes, washing sheets and towels by hand, and buying fresh food from the market almost every day, it took a team of women to run a house. But by the 1950s, shortcuts in the forms of cake mixes, instant dinners, canned soups, premade foods, beauty products, and medicines became very popular. There was widespread abandoning of simple, effective, herbal remedies—one of them being Onion Cough Syrup. In 1653, herbalist Nicholas Culpeper described using onions with sugar (or honey) for coughs in his book *Culpeper's Complete Herbal*.[28]

## ONION COUGH SYRUP RECIPE

Onions, part of the allium family, are traditionally known for their immune-boosting properties, including being naturally antiviral, antibiotic, anti-inflammatory, and expectorant. Traditionally used as a children's cough syrup because of the sweet taste, this remedy must be used fresh, and is ready in six to eight hours. If, like us, you don't like the smell, try holding your nose when taking it. Give this recipe a try even if you're an onion-hater—it's nowhere near as bad as you might imagine! Makes about one cup.

### INGREDIENTS

16 ounce mason jar

1 freshly sliced onion

About ½ cup white sugar

### INSTRUCTIONS

1. In the jar, layer sliced onions with the sugar, adding more onions, then more sugar, etc.

2. Cover jar with lid and let sit for six to eight hours. You'll see the sugar becoming liquidy.

.......................................
28. Culpeper, *Culpeper's Complete Herbal*, 207.

3. Strain the onions (or leave them in so the cough syrup will become more potent). The cough syrup is ready to use! Store in the fridge.

## DOSAGE

This syrup can be used as often as needed, up to every half hour.

- 1 teaspoon for younger than ten years old
- 1 tablespoon for anyone ten years and older

# OTHER GERM-FIGHTING REMEDIES

### Plague-Be-Gone! History

During the Dark Ages, it's believed that many thieves and grave robbers protected themselves from the Black Death (Bubonic Plague) by wearing scarves around their faces dipped in the oils of secret powerful herbs. The story goes that four of these thieves were captured. When they were brought before the king for punishment, he offered them a deal to avoid disemboweling. He demanded to know how the heck they'd stayed healthy, even though they'd been tiptoeing around bodies covered in black boils that oozed blood and pus. If they would reveal their secret, he'd spare their lives. They spilled their guts (so the king wouldn't spill *their* guts). The recipe still lives on!

Use before flying, in malls, schools, hospitals, or when around large crowds. *Highly* effective in supporting the immune system!

**Essential oil disclaimer:** The authors do not advocate the internal use of essential oils. Recipes in this book use what are generally considered safe essential oils, but please keep in mind that while completely natural, all essential oils are powerful plant compounds that you, your family, and your pets might have a reaction to. Never use essential oils undiluted or take essential oils internally without the guidance of a professional. Always read about the possible side effects of each essential oil before you use it. Avoid the use of essential oils during the first trimester of pregnancy, on small babies, and on anyone with severe allergies to the plants the oils are derived from. If you see any reactions in yourself, your family, or your pets, stop use of your essential oil products immediately and contact a medical professional.

## PLAGUE-BE-GONE! ROLL-ON RECIPE

Roll this on pulse points at the first sign of a cold or sore throat. It can also be used as a preventative. During cold/flu season, we never leave the house without putting this behind our ears and on our wrists. We think of it as our bodyguard. Our travels take us to many public bathrooms and rest stops and we feel protected. We always apply it before boarding a plane. If you wake up in the middle of the night with that telltale about-to-get-sick sore throat/tickle in your throat, smear it on and go back to sleep. If you catch it in time, it'll be gone by the time you wake up! We keep bottles of Plague-be-Gone! around the house, in each of our cars, and in our suitcases. It's powerful stuff and seems to last forever! Makes one, 10 ml glass roll-on bottle.

### INGREDIENTS

Essential oils:

- 1 drop clove
- 1 drop lemon
- 1 drop cinnamon
- 1 drop eucalyptus
- 1 drop rosemary
- 1 drop lavender

Carrier oil of choice (our favorites are grapeseed or jojoba)

10 ml glass roll-on bottle

### INSTRUCTIONS

1. With a small funnel, fill the 10 ml glass roll-on bottle almost to the top with your carrier oil.
2. Add essential oils.
3. Put on the roller top, and the cap, and shake well.
4. Label and enjoy!

## PLAGUE-BE-GONE! DISINFECTING ROOM SPRAY RECIPE

Germaphobes sometimes go into full manic-mode on planes. On a flight to Virginia, we watched a mother pull out a prepacked kit full of Lysol spray, disinfecting wipes, and hand sanitizer. Her toddler stood on the plane seat, not touching anything, as the mother started obsessively wiping down the entire area. She sprayed Lysol around them (and everybody nearby!), then sanitized their hands—not once, but twice.

Disinfectant-holics spray their go-to toxic cleaning products on toys, doorknobs, furniture, counters, in bathrooms, and in "sick rooms." If you'd prefer to hit the green road, this recipe is antibacterial, antiviral, and antifungal, doesn't have to be rinsed off, and all ingredients are pronounceable. Makes enough to fill one, one-ounce spray bottle.

### INGREDIENTS

Essential Oils:

- 7 drops clove
- 6 drops lemon
- 4 drops cinnamon
- 3 drops eucalyptus
- 2 drops rosemary

Water

1 ounce glass spray bottle

### INSTRUCTIONS

1. With a small funnel, fill the glass spray bottle almost to the top with water (allow room for the displacement of the spray top).
2. Add all essential oils.
3. Put on the spray cap and shake well.
4. Label and enjoy!

## Hand-It-Over! Chemical-Free Hand Sanitizer

This product isn't meant to replace soap and hot water, but it's a great option for getting you through tough spots when soap and water aren't around. You know, like after you've chucked four leaking bags of garbage into the pit at the dump. Or, after you simultaneously hold your breath and reluctantly open the blue plastic door of a ripe Porta Potty in August. And then, there are the dreaded rest stop bathrooms...

Besides smelling like cheap vodka, many commercial sanitizers contain alcohol that is drying and too strong for kids to use. According to Professor James Scott from the Dalla Lana School of Public Health at the University of Toronto, "One of the problems with putting alcohol on your hands is that just as it disrupts the membranes in germs, it can similarly remove those oils from your skin. So with repeated exposure of skin to alcohol, even if it's diluted, it can slowly over time cause your skin to lose emollients and become at risk of cracking." Having an open, bleeding wound on your skin increases your risk of bacterial infections, potentially causing even more problems.[29] Scott also said, "It [alcohol-based hand sanitizer] is not a panacea, since certain viruses lacking an outer coat (like the one that causes cruise ship diarrhea) or spore forming bacteria (like C.difficile) are not very susceptible."[30]

It may be true that antibacterial products kill 99.9 percent of germs, but that 0.1 percent is the most potentially harmful, since it can resist antibacterial agents. This small surviving percentage breeds, creating lines of antibiotic-resistant "super bugs."[31] Laboratory findings suggest a link between antibiotic-resistance and the use of antibacterial products.[32]

If you're using alcohol-based hand sanitizer to keep the flu away, it might not be as effective as you think it is. A September 2019 study by Japanese researchers revealed, to their surprise, that washing hands under running water—even without soap—is more effective at stopping the spread of flu

29. Dickson, "Don't Panic, You Don't Need Hand Sanitizer to Fight Coronavirus."
30. Hall, "Do Hand Sanitizers Really Work?"
31. Ventola, "The Antibiotic Resistance Crisis: Part 1: Causes And Threats," 277–83.
32. Johnson, "Superbugs: What They Are, Evolution, And What To Do."

germs than using ethanol-based hand sanitizers.[33] In earlier studies, Dr. Ryohei Hirose, the study's lead author and a molecular gastroenterologist at Kyoto Profectural University of Medicine, and the co-authors of the study used virus-containing solutions that had already dried. In those studies, the hand sanitizer was able to reach and inactivate the virus within approximately thirty seconds. In the new study, Hirose and his colleagues took sputum (a mixture of coughed-up saliva and mucus) from people infected with influenza A virus (the most common type of flu virus) and put it on the fingertips of ten volunteers. They next applied an alcohol-based hand sanitizer to the volunteers' fingers—both after the mucus completely dried (a process that took about forty minutes) and while it was still wet. When the mucus was dry, the sanitizer took about thirty seconds to inactivate the virus. When the mucus was wet, however, it took eight times longer—about four minutes. In contrast, when the volunteers washed off the mucus by rubbing their hands together under running water—without soap—the flu virus was eradicated within thirty seconds, regardless of whether the mucus was dry or wet. The findings from this study were meant to address current hand-hygiene practices in hospitals and doctor clinics, which rely heavily on hand sanitizers.[34] However, the results are applicable to all of us. Who's going to wait around four minutes for their alcohol-based hand sanitizer to dry before they touch their steering wheel, pick up silverware, use a drinking glass, or touch a bathroom door handle?

Our alcohol-free, chemical-free Hand-It-Over! Hand Sanitizer is naturally antiviral and antibacterial because of its cocktail of essential oils. And, you won't be spreading toxic ingredients on your biggest organ—your skin—which also happens to be porous.

........................................

33. Hirose, et al., "Situations Leading to Reduced Effectiveness of Current Hand Hygiene against Infectious Mucus from Influenza Virus-Infected Patients," 1–16.

34. Perry, "Study: Washing Your Hands—Even without Soap—Is More Effective than Hand Sanitizers for Flu Prevention."

## HAND-IT-oVER! CHEMICAL-FREE HAND SANITIZER RECIPE

We keep bottles of Hand-it-Over! in our cars year-round. It's not affected by our freezing Connecticut winters, or our steamy summers—and a little goes a long way. Hand-It-Over! doesn't dry the skin and is actually nourishing because of the aloe vera. Don't be put off by the initial sticky feeling—it quickly dissipates. Makes enough to fill one, two-ounce bottle.

### INGREDIENTS

2 teaspoons witch hazel

2 tablespoons, plus 2 teaspoons aloe vera gel

Up to 25 drops essential oil (use any combination of the oils below to reach 25 drops—all are antiviral, antifungal, antibacterial, helpful for stress and anxiety)

- Grapefruit—eases nervous exhaustion, mood elevator, can increase alertness while also calming nerves
- Lavender—improves mood

  According to a study published in European Neurology, people struggling with migraine headaches saw a significant reduction in pain when they inhaled lavender essential oil for 15 minutes.[35]

- Lemon—refreshing, energizing, and uplifting
- Peppermint—ideal for unclogging sinuses, boosts energy level on long road trips
- Orange—brings pleasant thoughts to mind, mood lifter
- Eucalyptus—can reduce muscle pain, swelling, soreness, efficient remedy to ease breathing. May help to clear your airways, allowing more oxygen into your lungs, which relieves brain fog and boosts energy.

2-ounce plastic bottle with flip-cap top

..............................................

35. Sasannejad, et al., "Lavender Essential Oil in the Treatment of Migraine Headache: A Placebo-Controlled Clinical Trial," 288–91.

## INSTRUCTIONS

1. Making this in a small paper cup is ideal because you can squeeze the cup in order to get the ingredients into the plastic flip-top container. In the small paper cup, mix witch hazel and aloe vera gel until combined.

2. Pour into plastic flip-top container.

3. Add essential oils directly to flip-top container. Use any combination of the oils to add up to twenty-five drops.

4. Put on the lid and shake to combine.

5. Label. Use as you would any other type of hand sanitizer.

The best way to arm yourself against colds and flu is by having solutions on hand. Don't wait until you're sniffling, hacking, and wiped out to try to figure out a remedy. Preparing a DIY holistic medicine cabinet in advance of sickness will provide you with the tools to not only calm your symptoms, but also help build your immune system. The extra steps you take now toward optimum health will ensure your body is better prepared to respond.

## CHAPTER TWO
# THE BARE BONES

## GROUNDED GOODWIFE STORY TIME

*Where Did All the Bones Go?* by Velya

When I was a kid, I don't remember anyone getting knee or hip replacements, nor do I remember people hobbling around in bone-on-bone pain. I don't remember walkers. I don't remember so many canes. It's become a "bone of contention" for me that the existence of bone-in/skin-on cuts of beef, chicken, and turkey has waned a great deal since the 1960s. Today, it's almost impossible to even find raw meaty bones for our two dogs, Viola and Myra, who we "feed raw."

I grew up eating bone-in stews and soups that had simmered for hours. When my mother would make Hearty Oxtail Stew, Just Peachy Ribs, or Dutch Oven Beef-Barley Soup, the grass-fed meat eventually fell off the bone, and the bones stayed in the pot until dinner was served. Bones are living tissues. They're rich in vital nutrients like calcium, phosphorus, sodium, magnesium, and other important trace minerals. Bones contain bone marrow, a nutrient-dense superfood released into the meat during cooking, "beefing up" a meal's nutrient density. Animal bones contain high concentrations of collagen, gelatin, glycine, and glutamine. You can't get these nutrients by eating Big Macs, chicken tenders, or muscle meats, such as steak.

• • •

If you do manage to find bone-in meat, corn-fed cattle are now the norm. According to the PBS documentary *King Corn*, "Before World War II, most Americans had never eaten corn-fed beef. Raised on pasture, cattle reared before the 1950s usually took two or three years to be ready for the slaughterhouse. Steers were fed grain only occasionally and in small quantities, and farmers tended to use corn as a supplement—not a staple—of their livestock's diets."[36]

What's all the hubbub over grass-fed meat? Michael Pollan, author of *The Omnivore's Dilemma*, explains, "By the time a modern American beef cow is six months old, it has seen its last blade of grass for the rest of its life....We take them off grass. We put them in pens...and we teach them how to eat something that they are not evolved to eat, which is grain, and mostly corn." Pollan continues, "The problem with this system...is that cows are not evolved to digest corn....ou start giving them antibiotics, because as soon as you give them corn, you've disturbed their digestion, and they're apt to get sick, so you then have to give them drugs. That's how you get in this whole cycle of drugs and meat."[37] On top of that, currently, up to 92 percent of US corn is genetically engineered.[38]

As we trade traditional cooking methods for modern convenience, we're getting fewer and fewer nutrients in our diets. Today, most store-bought stocks, broths, and bouillons contain lab-made meat flavors and monosodium glutamate (MSG)—a controversial food-additive used in canned food, crackers, meat, salad dressings, frozen dinners, and a slew of other products,[39] which bypasses the blood-brain barrier[40] (if the blood-brain barrier is damaged or compromised, it can allow bacteria and other toxins to infect the brain tissue[41]). Just because an ingredient label doesn't state "MSG," the MSG can be hidden within the label. Hydrolyzed soy protein, flavoring, natural fla-

......................................

36. Woolf, *Independent Lens: King Corn*.
37. "Interview Michael Pollan," Frontline: Modern Meat.
38. "About Genetically Engineered Foods," Center for Food Safety.
39. Niaz, et al., "Extensive Use of Monosodium Glutamate: A Threat to Public Health?" 273–78.
40. Schoffro Cook, "Here's Why You Shouldn't Eat Foods with MSG."
41. Götz and Woodruff, "What Is the Blood-Brain Barrier?"

voring, spices, dried whey, disodium inosinate, and guanylate are all tip-offs that a product might contain MSG.[42]

# COLLAGEN AND BONE BROTH

Two of today's most popular health topics are collagen and bone broth. They're often thought of as the same thing, but each has its own benefits. Collagen peptides are generally extracted from bovine hides, while bone broth is made from bones, ligaments, tendons, etc. Our layman explanations and delish recipes demystify the world of bones and hides.

## Collagen Peptides

Collagen, made up of over a thousand amino acids, accounts for one third of the protein in our bodies and 70 percent of the protein in our skin. Our body's collagen production naturally begins to slow down over time.[43] By age twenty-five, collagen levels decrease in the body at a rate of 1.5 percent a year. After the age of thirty, our collagen production slows further, and we begin to lose 2 percent of our collagen stores every year. By the age of forty, we've lost around 15 percent, and collagen becomes depleted much faster than it can be manufactured by the body. And by age sixty, over half of our body's collagen stores are going … going … gone.[44]

## Collagen Peptides Are Beneficial for:

- supporting hair, skin, and nails
- joint health
- encouraging skin elasticity and reducing the signs of aging
- improving digestion
- as a protein source

42. "MSG: A Neurotoxic Flavor Enhancer," Truth in Labeling.

43. Wells, "What Is Collagen Powder (and How to Use It): Wellness Mama."

44. Allison, "Collagen 101: The Merits and the Myths."

## How to Take Collagen

The collagen peptides we take are powdered. They come in a tub with a plastic scoop, and we buy them online. We always stick with the same brand because it dissolves easily, doesn't have a cow-y smell, is hormone/antibiotic-free, and comes from pasture-raised cows (it contains type I and III collagen; we take type II in capsule form). We take one to two scoops per day. In the following recipes, you can't taste the collagen, and it actually makes them a little creamier.

Some people like to mix collagen into oatmeal, yogurt, soup, or baked goods. Personally, we find it changes the consistency of the food, and unless you eat an entire pot of soup or entire pan of brownies, it's hard to know how much collagen you're actually ingesting.

# GROUNDED GOODWIFE STORYTIME

### *Cracky Knees* by Ehris

Even as a little kid, my knees always cracked when I would bend down. On a whim, I decided to see if taking collagen peptides would help. Did they ever! Now, my mom, dad, and I all take them and are amazed by what else we've noticed. My mom has always gotten her hair cut every two weeks (it's choppy and funky). After collagen peptides, she can barely make it two weeks without a haircut—and don't even get us started on how fast our fingernails grow! Even in the winter, we don't need to use any kind of hand or body lotion because of how hydrated our skin is. Our hairdresser, Jenifer Benham (who we turned on to collagen peptides several years ago), is astounded at how quickly the inevitable scissor nicks on her hands heal. I can only imagine what it's doing to my insides!

• • •

# COLLAGEN PEPTIDES RECIPES

## EHRIS'S KRAV SHAKE

I drink this every morning before I go to the gym for my HIIT (High-Intensity Interval Training) Cardio Krav class. If I don't, I'm hungry and lightheaded after ten minutes of roundhouse kicks, uppercuts, and spinning backhammers! Makes one serving.

### INGREDIENTS

¾ cup homemade kefir (see chapter three)

1 scoop collagen peptides

1 frozen banana

½ to ¾ cup frozen berries

¼ cup greens (Depending on availability: spinach, violet leaves, or dandelion greens. I don't put in raw kale because it's a goitrogenic vegetable, and when eaten raw, may inhibit the uptake of iodine by the thyroid gland.)

1 raw egg (from our free-range chickens, but this is optional)

¼ teaspoon astragalus root powder

¼ teaspoon nettle leaf powder

### INSTRUCTIONS

1. Combine all ingredients in a blender. If it's too thick, add a little more kefir.
2. Blend until smooth. Enjoy!

## VELYA'S MORNING COFFEE

Unlike Ehris, who pops off to the gym every morning, I sit on the bed with a cup of coffee and get caught up on social media and emails. In three years, I've never gone a day without collagen or beneficial homemade vanilla extract! While my coffee's brewing, I gag down a tablespoon of fermented cod liver oil for its omega-3 fatty acid benefits, especially beneficial for my eyes and brain. Makes one serving.

## INGREDIENTS

1 scoop collagen peptides

1 teaspoon homemade vanilla extract (see recipe below)

1 cup organic coffee

Heavy cream, to taste

## INSTRUCTIONS

1. Put collagen peptides and vanilla extract in your favorite mug. Add coffee, stir to dissolve collagen, and add cream.

## BENEFITS

- **Vanilla extract** is a well-known dessert flavoring, but it's also antibacterial, antioxidant, and a mental-health booster. It's said to be an effective cold sore remedy. As soon as you feel a tell-tale cold sore tingle, dip a cotton ball in real vanilla extract and apply directly to the sore for a few minutes, and repeat up to four times a day.

### Savor the Flavor! Homemade Vanilla Extract

We began making our own vanilla extract years ago because it's hard to find a store-bought one without corn syrup, artificial fragrances, and fake dyes. Even worse, of the 18,000 metric tons of vanilla flavor produced annually, it's estimated that 85 percent is vanillin made from guaiacol, derived from wood creosote. Most of the rest is from lignin, a byproduct from paper mill waste.[45] Makes one cup.

## INGREDIENTS

6 to 8 vanilla beans

1 cup liquor, around 70 proof (we recommend bourbon, rum, vodka, or brandy)

---

45. Bomgardner, "The Problem with Vanilla."

## INSTRUCTIONS

1. Slice each vanilla bean along the length of the entire pod. Cut each pod in half so it'll fit in the bottle. Place vanilla beans in an eight-ounce mason jar.

2. Pour alcohol over vanilla beans (the beans should be submerged).

3. Now, you get to … wait! Vanilla extract takes about eight weeks to fully mature. Store the jar at room temperature, not in direct sunlight. Shake the jar at least once a week.

4. Once your extract is ready, you can either leave the vanilla beans in the jar (the extract will age and become more flavorful over time) or strain it. We recommend straining it into glass dropper bottles to use for yourself, or to give as gifts.

## EHRIS'S COFFEE ALTERNATIVE

I don't drink coffee, but I like the idea of coffee. This is what I make when I want to wrap my hands around a warm mug and feel like I'm part of the coffee crowd. Makes one serving.

## INGREDIENTS

1 scoop collagen peptides

1 tablespoon cacao powder

¼ teaspoon Real Mushrooms 5 Defenders powder (available online)

⅛ teaspoon Blue Lotus Traditional Masala Chai powder (available online)

1 pinch turmeric root powder

1 pinch pink Himalayan salt

1 pinch cinnamon

8 ounces boiling water

Honey and raw milk, to taste

## INSTRUCTIONS

1. In a twelve-ounce mug, combine collagen peptides, cacao, mushroom powder, chai powder, turmeric root powder, salt, and cinnamon. Pour water into mug and let steep five minutes.

2. Add honey and raw milk to taste, if desired. Stir well and enjoy!

- **Raw cacao** (*Theobroma cacao*) can make you feel all cozy and happy! It contains four "bliss chemicals"—serotonin, tryptophan, tyrosine, and phenylethylamine.

- **Real Mushrooms 5 Defenders powder** contains reishi, shiitake, maitake, turkey tail, and chaga mushrooms. Each mushroom offers its own medicinal benefits, but overall, the ones in this blend enhance immunity. We like this brand because it's made from the medicinally-potent fruiting bodies of mushrooms. Many other mushroom powders are made from just the mycelium, myceliated grain, or myceliated biomass. Additionally, many mushroom powders contain fillers, which are usually some form of powdered grain, "diluting" the medicinal benefit.

- **Blue Lotus Traditional Masala Chai Powder** is a dried black tea blend with organic, powdered non-GMO herbs—ginger root, cardamom, cinnamon, black pepper, nutmeg, and cloves. This particular chai powder doesn't contain corn syrup or sugar, and doesn't have that overpowering cardamom taste like a lot of other chai blends.

### Collagen FYI

Collagen peptides will clump in cold water, but if you mix them in something warm or room temperature, they'll dissolve well.

You have to get collagen from the inside out! Beauty products that contain collagen won't do much when applied topically—collagen molecules are too big to be absorbed by your skin. Save your money on those expensive collagen lotions and foundations! It needs to be taken internally to get the benefits.

## BONE BROTH

When you cook bones in water, good things happen—but as busy "wise women," we can't spend forty-eight hours skimming broth scum or debating the "perfect simmer." Our nutrient-dense bone broth recipe may help plump your skin, cushion your joints, heal your gut, boost your immune system—

and it's ready in two hours without the bland watered-down soup taste of most bone broths.

Initially, we were intimidated by all the steps and processes involved in making homemade bone broth. Online recipes actually say things like:

- "Ask your fishmonger to remove the gills as they can make the broth bitter." (our fishmonger?!)
- "Make use of mirepoix." (what the heck is that?!)
- "The age of the animal is important." (uhh, can we see some ID?)
- "You must reach a chicken Jell-O consistency." (blechh!)
- "Use ankle bones, knuckle bones, feet, femurs, jointy bones, meaty bones, trotters." (cows have ankles?!)

Making bone broth shouldn't be so serious or complicated!

And then came our Goldilocks quest for just the right pot:

1. First, we tried using our blue dutch oven. The tiny batches weren't worth the effort. Plus, we had to leave the burner on for forty-eight hours, so with every brew we became criminals on bone broth house arrest.
2. Next, we used a Crockpot, but constantly had to add more liquid.
3. Then, we bought a giant electric turkey roaster pan. It yielded a huge quantity of broth, but since it was giant, it didn't fit in the sink, and washing the greasy pan became a dreaded task. The entire point of bone broth is to try and drink it on a daily basis, and there shouldn't be any dread in the process!

We have to be honest about the taste: most bone broth recipes just taste like bones and cloudy hot water, with a hint of onion. Finally, the smell, as it's cooking, and cooking, and cooking: picture a kennel—a kennel filled with roasting onions ...

So, after four years of trial and error, we figured out how to make bone broth: simplified!

Our recipe, once it's strained, actually tastes like homemade soup—but with tons of medicinal benefits. You won't waste ingredients by making a gross-tasting broth, or be turned off to the entire process. And, by using a pressure cooker, your broth will be ready in two hours. Smells won't permeate your entire house as they do with the other cooking methods.

There's no need to spend $7 for sixteen ounces of store-bought bone broth!

## RATTLE-THEM-BONES BROTH RECIPE

Ready in only two hours, your house won't smell like a kennel as it cooks, and it doesn't taste like bones and cloudy hot water! This recipe (which took four years to perfect) truly tastes delicious right out of the pot. We add five shakes of pink Himalyan salt to our mugs. Makes about ten cups.

### INGREDIENTS

Carcass of 1 chicken or turkey, plus 2 chicken feet

*Instead of using a carcass, we generally use 1 turkey back and 2 chicken feet, which are inexpensive and readily available at our health food store. We've learned that including fatty meat makes a much more flavorful broth—it tastes like soup!

Or, for beef broth: 3 to 5 pounds beef bones (combination of meaty bones, such as short ribs and marrow bones)—preferably grass-fed organic

2 tablespoons raw apple cider vinegar (like Bragg's)

2 unpeeled onions, cut into chunks (include skins if organic)

4 unpeeled carrots, cut into thirds

1 unpeeled parsnip, cut into thirds

1 bunch celery (including the leaves), cut into thirds

1 unpeeled sweet potato, quartered

4 unpeeled cloves garlic, halved (include peel if organic)

4 whole allspice berries

8 black peppercorns

1 bay leaf

1 teaspoon Himalayan salt

## INSTRUCTIONS

For a pressure cooker:

We use an eight-quart pressure cooker.

1. Put bones in the pressure cooker pot with two tablespoons apple cider vinegar. Add ten cups water and let sit about thirty minutes. This helps extract minerals from the bones.

     * If using beef bones, it's recommended to roast them first. Roasting helps to create a deeper, fuller, and richer flavor from the caramelizing of the meat and marrow. Place bones in a deep roasting pan, and roast in a 425°F oven for thirty to forty minutes.

2. Add remaining ingredients, including any of the following optional ingredients (we use all of them). Not everything in the pot will be covered by water, and that's fine. But if you're using chicken feet, make sure they're at the bottom of the pot so the collagen and cartilage can be extracted.

3. Set pressure cooker on high for two hours.

4. Let the broth cool and strain it into a large pot. Transfer broth to mason jars. Add additional salt to taste now or upon serving. Store in fridge five to seven days, or freezer for up to six months for use in soups or stews.

     – Bone broth enthusiasts insist that you can save the bones in the freezer for a future batch—chicken or turkey bones can be used up to three times, beef bones can be used up to six times—but heads up, your broth won't be as flavorful if you reuse the bones.

## INGREDIENTS

These are optional:

- **Astragalus root** (*Astragalus membranaceus*): We use one tablespoon. Astragalus root strengthens the immune system, boosts vitality, increases endurance, and slows and prevents the growth of tumors. We make sure to include astragalus in our broth, especially during the winter, as a prophylactic against colds and upper respiratory infections.

- **Organic onion/garlic skins:** Antiviral, anti-inflammatory, increases resilience of capillary walls, improves cardiovascular health, helpful for hypertension.

- **Ginger root** (*Zingiber officinale*): We use two tablespoons of fresh ginger root. It's warming, anti-inflammatory, and strengthens immune, digestive, respiratory, and circulatory systems. Ginger root can also improve absorption of essential nutrients.

- **Nettle leaf** (*Urtica dioica*): We add one tablespoon dried, but fresh is fine too. Nettle leaf is a tonic herb—supports the whole body and is very nutrient-dense—contains wide range of vitamins and minerals, good for seasonal allergies

- **Maitake mushrooms** (*Grifola frondosa*): We add one teaspoon dried powder. Maitake mushrooms can provide immune support, are beneficial for diabetes and blood pressure issues, and can help prevent cancer.

- **Shiitake mushrooms** (*Lentinula edodes*): We add three mushrooms, dried or fresh. Shiitake mushrooms can aid in immune support, stop/slow growth of tumors, help prevent cancer, support/improve cardiovascular health, and are rich in antioxidants.

- **Thyme** (*Thymus vulgaris*): We add one teaspoon dried, but fresh is fine too. Thyme is antimicrobial, a mood lifter, good for coughs and sore throats, and a blood pressure regulator.

- **Turmeric root** (*Curcuma longa*): We add one teaspoon of powder; fresh is fine too. Tumeric has anti-inflammatory properties, and may help life the spirits, boost the immune system, and prevent tumor growth.

- **Eggshells** (organic and/or free-range if possible): Eggshells are made of calcium, and some believe that this calcium is the best form for your body to absorb. They also contain iron, magnesium, sulfur, manganese, phosphorus, silicon, gelatin, collagen, and zinc. Since it takes many elements (not just calcium) to build strong bones and joints, we always include eggshells from our free-range chickens in our bone broth!

- **Chicken feet** (we add two per batch): Chicken feet are a good source of hyaluronic acid and chondroitin sulfate. Hyaluronic acid is regarded as "the fountain of youth"[46]; it can prevent the effects of aging. Chondroitin sulfate is helpful for osteoarthritis, and can relieve joint issues.

The healthiest bone broth is one that after cooking and cooling, thickens and gels—just like Jell-O (whether you realize it or not, if you've ever eaten Jell-O, you've eaten gelatin). Ever since we've been adding collagen-rich chicken feet to our broth, it always gels! Before, the gel was hit or miss.

Gelatin acts like a cushion between bones, helping them "glide" without friction. It also provides the building blocks needed to form and maintain strong bones. This helps take pressure off of joints and supports healthy bone mineral density.[47]

## BENEFITS

- **Carrot** (*Daucus carota*): Eye health, blood sugar regulator, boost immunity, aids digestion.
- **Parsnip** (*Pastinaca sativa*): Immune support, aids in enzyme production to manage digestive health, supports brain and eye health.
- **Onion** (*Allium cepa*): Contains chromium (blood sugar regulator), improves immunity to help ward off colds and the flu, supports respiratory system, great remedy for coughs.
- **Celery** (*Apium graveolens*): Anti-inflammatory, improves blood pressure, supports liver health, supports digestion.
- **Sweet potato** (*Ipomoea batatas*): Improves digestion, reduces inflammation, relieves respiratory congestion, boosts immune system.
- **Garlic** (*Allium sativum*): Antifungal, antiviral, antiparasitic, antimicrobial, stimulates and supports body's immune system, supports heart health.
- **Black peppercorn:** Piperine (an antioxidant in peppercorns) is shown to reduce memory impairment and cognitive malfunction, great for coughs and colds.

.................................................

46. "Hyaluronic Acid: the Fountain of Youth," DÉCAAR.
47. Dhar, "What Is Jell-O?"

- **Allspice:** Antibacterial, antifungal, helps the gastrointestinal system function smoothly and protects it from outside attack, aids circulation and heart health.
- **Bay leaf:** Antimicrobial, helpful for digestion, inflammation, heart health.

# RECIPES USING BONE BROTH

## FEEL IT IN YOUR BONES BEEF BURGUNDY WITH BONE BROTH

There are some recipes that are worth the wait. This is comfort food heaven for colder weather, and a great way to "drink" more bone broth! No need to blow your food budget on lean, pricey meat. The low heat and slow cook time turns tougher cuts of beef fork-tender. We recommend that you don't skip the searing step on the beef. Serves six.

### INGREDIENTS

When making this recipes, we save all peels/skins in a big baggie in the freezer for future bone broth batches.

2 tablespoons olive oil

3 pounds stew meat (boneless chuck), cut into 2-inch cubes

2 carrots, peeled and cut into chunks

2 medium onions, peeled and sliced

2 cups white mushrooms, stems removed, quartered

1 teaspoon salt (we use Himalayan salt)

¼ teaspoon pepper

1 cup red wine (Burgundy is best—wine helps develop richer, more complex flavors in your stew—or, omit and just increase the amount of bone broth)

3½ to 4½ cups bone broth

1 tablespoon tomato paste

2 cloves garlic, chopped

5 thyme sprigs

3 bay leaves

¾ cup peas (frozen is fine)

Chopped parsley (optional for garnish)

## INSTRUCTIONS

1. Preheat oven to 325°F.

2. In a large dutch oven, heat the olive oil over medium high heat.

3. Add the beef cubes in small batches to the dutch oven to brown. Brown the beef on all sides, then transfer the pieces to a bowl/ plate. Keep going until all the beef has been browned. Don't move the meat around the pan too much—give it a chance to brown up (if you feel like taking the extra step, use paper towels to dry the pieces of beef before cooking for better browning).

4. Add the carrots, onions, and mushrooms to the dutch oven and brown them, stirring occasionally for three to five minutes.

5. Return the beef and any drippings to the dutch oven. Add the salt and pepper and stir to combine.

6. Add the wine to the dutch oven and add enough bone broth to barely cover the meat. Stir in the tomato paste, garlic, thyme, and bay leaves. Cover the pot with a lid and place in the oven. Cook for three-ish hours or until the beef is tender. Stir in peas five to ten minutes before serving, and garnish with chopped parsley.

We serve this over mashed Yukon gold potatoes (with skins), but it would be great with a loaf of crusty bread. Some people have told us that this recipe is missing flour, but as a gluten-free family, we don't think it needs a thickening agent.

## GOoD-FOR-THE-GuT oNE-POT PASTA

Throw it all in the pot, *including* the uncooked pasta! Some pasta recipes just don't translate well when you use gluten-free pasta, but this one works beautifully with brown rice pasta. The other ingredients cook right along with the pasta and create a rich, warm sauce with bone broth benefits. Unbelievably good and simple, this is one pasta recipe that everyone should have in their repertoire! Add a protein source to create a heartier main dish. Serves four.

## INGREDIENTS

When making this recipe, we save all peels/skins in a big baggie in the freezer for future bone broth batches.

- 12 ounces uncooked brown rice pasta (also works with green pea, wheat, or lentil pasta)
- 1 can (15 ounces) diced tomatoes with liquid (we're not chunky tomato fans, so we use a 15-ounce jar of non-GMO spaghetti sauce)
- 1 small onion, chopped
- 4 cloves garlic, thinly sliced
- 4½ cups bone broth
- ¼ teaspoon red pepper flakes (optional, if you like spice)
- 2 sprigs oregano, chopped
- 2 tablespoons olive oil
- 1 cup spinach or kale (frozen or fresh)
- ⅓ cup peas (frozen or fresh)
- ¼ cup fresh parsley, chopped
- 2 sprigs basil, chopped
- Salt and pepper
- Parmesan cheese for garnish

## INSTRUCTIONS

1. Place pasta, tomatoes/spaghetti sauce, onion, and garlic in large stock pot. Pour in bone broth. Stir. Sprinkle on the red pepper flakes (optional) and oregano. Drizzle top with olive oil.
2. Cover pot and bring to a boil. Reduce to a simmer and keep covered. Cook for ten minutes, stirring every two minutes. Add the spinach/kale, peas, parsley and basil at final two minutes of cooking. Cook until pasta is al dente (or however you prefer it).

3. Season to taste with salt and pepper. Serve in bowls or mugs garnished with Parmesan cheese.

## BYE! BYE! SHEPHERD'S PIE

Say goodbye to joint pain and inflammation and hello to joint healing! The bone broth in this recipe will help you obtain compounds like chondroitin, sulfate, and glucosamine, which may reduce pain and improve joint function. These compounds have been shown to naturally help decrease inflammation, arthritis and joint pain, especially when consumed or used together.[48] Chondroitin is a major component of cartilage and helps keep joints lubricated. Glucosamine has been shown to have anti-inflammatory properties and may help stop progression of degeneration of joint cartilage.

Everyone raves about this Shepherd's Pie. Unlike other versions, it doesn't have a gravy base. Ehris has sampled Shepherd's Pie all over the world, and this one is her favorite! Serves six to eight.

### INGREDIENTS

When making this recipe, we save all peels/skins in a big baggie in the freezer for future bone broth batches.

2 tablespoons olive oil

1 medium onion, chopped

2 big organic carrots, peeled and diced

2 cloves garlic, chopped (allow five minutes for the chopped garlic to "rest" on cutting board so allicin can be created, making the garlic more medicinal)

1 stalk celery, diced

1 ½ pounds ground beef (grass-fed, if possible)

¾ cup bone broth

½ cup green peas, frozen

---

48. "Supplement and Herb Guide for Arthritis Symptoms," Arthritis Foundation.

1 cup shredded cheese (cheddar is the best for this recipe, but we've used mozzarella)

8 medium organic Yukon Gold potatoes, quartered (unpeeled)

4 tablespoons butter for mashed potatoes

Pink Himalayan salt and pepper

⅓ cup yogurt/kefir/heavy cream for mashed potatoes

## INSTRUCTIONS

1. Heat a large frying pan on medium heat (we always cook in cast iron). Add oil, onions, carrots, garlic, and celery. Cook on medium heat, stirring frequently, until the vegetables soften just a bit, but aren't mushy (under five minutes).

2. Turn the heat up to medium-high. Add the ground beef. Stir, breaking up the meat, and continue cooking until the meat is nearly browned (almost no pink left).

3. Remove from heat and spoon off the excess fat.

4. Return to medium heat.

5. Add the bone broth. Stir until combined. Allow the liquid in the pan to slowly "cook off" as you periodically give it a stir.

6. Remove from heat. Gently stir in the frozen peas.

7. Spread meat/vegetable mixture in a 13 × 9-inch pan, and top with ½ cup of the shredded cheese.

8. Boil the potatoes for approximately twenty-five minutes or until fork-tender. Drain. Add butter, two teaspoons pink Himalayan salt, and yogurt/kefir/cream.

9. Mash with potato masher to desired consistency (our family prefers mashed potatoes with lumps).

10. Top meat mixture with the mashed potatoes. Make sure the potatoes come all the way to the edge and form a seal. Sprinkle with remaining cheese (or add more if you're a cheese fan).

11. Bake at 350°F for thirty minutes. Salt and pepper to taste when served.

## GROUNDED GOODWIFE GAZPACHO (AKA "GUT-ZPACHO")

If you get it right, gazpacho can be so good! If, like Velya, you spend all summer with beads of sweat across your upper lip and a constant dribble of perspiration running down your back, then this "summer in a bowl" might be your muggy weather savior.

Many gazpacho recipes suggest that the final step is to "put the vegetable mixture into a blender and whiz until smooth." If that's your kind of gazpacho, this chunky recipe isn't for you—there's nothing mushy about it! This is a soup that's definitely better the next day. Serves fifteen.

### INGREDIENTS

When making this recipe, we save all peels/skins in a big baggie in the freezer for future bone broth batches.

10 ripe tomatoes, chopped

1 onion, chopped

2 cucumbers, chopped

2 red bell peppers, chopped

4 stalks celery, chopped

6 sprigs fresh parsley, chopped

1 leek, chopped

3 cloves garlic, minced

¾ cup red wine vinegar

⅓ cup olive oil

3 tablespoons freshly squeezed lemon juice

3 teaspoons sugar

Salt and pepper to taste

9 or more drops of Tabasco sauce to taste

2 teaspoons Worcestershire sauce

3 cups tomato juice

3 cups bone broth

## INSTRUCTIONS

1. Combine all ingredients in a large pot (we use a giant lobster pot from the thrift shop, which has never been used for lobsters).
2. Refrigerate for at least an hour to let the flavors meld. It tastes even better the second day!

## KARTOFFELSUPPE RECIPE

During what we call our "blur time" (life after our Brazilian betrayal when we still weren't grounded), we were both ESL (English as a Second Language) teachers for German families who had immigrated to the US for corporate jobs. Recipe-swapping was a great way for all of us to learn about each other's cultures. Kathrin Lauw, the mother of the family Velya worked with, was shocked that the United States doesn't have parsnip baby food, while Velya had never heard of a popular German dairy product called quark. Kathrin's recipe, Kartoffelsuppe (Potato Soup) has become one of our favorite winter dishes! Makes four servings.

## INGREDIENTS

When making this recipe, we save all peels/skins in a big baggie in the freezer for future bone broth batches.

2 tablespoons olive oil

2 cloves garlic, chopped

1 onion, chopped

3 stalks celery, chopped

6–8 carrots, peeled, cut into cubes

2 leeks, chopped (discard the tops)

8–10 potatoes, cut into cubes

6 cups bone broth

1 bay leaf

1 small green cabbage, cut into cubes

1 beaten egg

⅓ cup chopped fresh parsley

Optional: meatballs (see recipe)

## INSTRUCTIONS

1. Heat olive oil in large pot (we use our dutch oven). Add garlic and onion. Cook until garlic becomes fragrant and onion becomes soft (about three to five minutes).
2. Add celery, carrots, and leeks. Mix and cook for a few minutes.
3. Add potatoes, bone broth, and bay leaf.
4. Cover with a lid and bring to a boil.
5. Simmer until vegetables are softened (about thirty minutes).
   - Optional step if you choose to add meatballs: Meanwhile, using ground beef, turkey, or pork (your choice), make your favorite meatball recipe. If you don't have a meatball recipe, there's one at the end of this recipe.
6. Remove the bay leaf. Without draining any of the liquid, use a potato masher to *slightly* mash the vegetables (leave it good and chunky).
7. Add cabbage to mashed vegetables.
8. While stirring over medium heat, add beaten egg. Stir gently for approximately two minutes until egg is cooked.
9. Add chopped parsley.
10. Serve in soup bowls with optional meatballs on top.

## EASY GLUTEN-FREE MEATBALLS

Having a batch of these meatballs in the freezer can be a lifesaver on those nights when you don't have any dinner inspiration. Also, there's no messy frying pan involved! Makes twenty-four meatballs.

### INGREDIENTS

2 eggs

¼ cup bone broth

1 small onion, finely chopped

⅔ cup grated Parmesan cheese

2 garlic cloves, minced

½ teaspoon dried oregano

½ teaspoon dried thyme

½ teaspoon dried rosemary

½ teaspoon dried parsley or basil

1 ½ teaspoon pink Himalayan salt

¼ teaspoon pepper

2 pounds ground meat (beef, turkey, pork, chicken, or any combination)

### INSTRUCTIONS

1. Preheat oven to 375°F.
2. In a large bowl, combine all ingredients. Mix well (we think the only way to do it is to get in there with your hands).
3. Shape into 1½-inch balls (bigger than a cherry tomato, smaller than a lime). Place meatballs on a broiler pan (or whatever works for you).
4. Bake, uncovered, for fifteen to eighteen minutes.
5. To freeze, allow meatballs to cool and freeze in containers.

## PEACE OUT, TAKEOUT! CROCKPOT BEEF AND SNOW PEAS

This healthier twist on a Chinese take-out favorite is so easy to make at home, right in your Crockpot! No MSG, no cornstarch, and the beef becomes tender as it simmers in a flavorful bone broth-based sauce. Serve over white/ brown rice, or quinoa. Makes four servings.

### INGREDIENTS

1 ½ pounds boneless beef chuck roast (or use what we call "stew meat"), sliced into thin strips

1 cup bone broth

¼ cup Bragg's Liquid Aminos

3 tablespoons maple syrup (or, in a pinch, use brown sugar)

1 tablespoon sesame, grapeseed, or olive oil

3 cloves garlic, chopped

2 tablespoons arrowroot starch

2 cups snow peas, whole (with ends trimmed)

### INSTRUCTIONS

1. Place beef in Crockpot.
2. In small bowl, combine bone broth, Bragg's Liquid Aminos, maple syrup, oil, and garlic. Pour over beef and cook on low for six to eight hours.
3. In a mug, combine arrowroot starch with two tablespoons sauce from the Crockpot. Stir until smooth. Add to slow cooker and stir to combine.
4. Cover and cook for ten minutes longer to let the arrowroot starch thicken the sauce (arrowroot thickens below the boiling point).
5. Add the snow peas just before serving so they stay crispy and green.
6. Serve over cooked rice or quinoa. Garnish with red pepper flakes and sesame seeds if that's your thing.

- **Bragg's Liquid Aminos**: We use this as a replacement for soy sauce. Unlike soy sauce, this is a gluten-free liquid seasoning made from non-GMO soybeans, and contains both essential and nonessential amino acids. Amino acids—the building blocks of protein—are necessary for healthy muscles, bones, and skin.

- **Arrowroot starch** is a fine white powder made from starches in the tubers of the tropical arrowroot plant, *Maranata arundinacea*. We use it in place of cornstarch. If (like us) you avoid corn and gluten, arrowroot is an easily-dissolvable, flavorless thickener to add to savory or sweet recipes.

# WHAT'S HEALTHIER— CHICKEN, TURKEY, OR BEEF BONE BROTH?

Ultimately, the broth you prefer will come down to personal flavor preference. Beef bone broth tends to have a richer, heartier, flavor, and chicken or turkey bone broth is lighter. Charmaine Jones, registered dietician and nutritionist (MS, RDN, LDN), explains, "There is no concrete evidence that shows whether chicken is healthier than beef bone broth."[49] The "better" option will come down to taste preference. Bone broth must be enjoyable for you to want to drink it in the first place.

One of the reasons we prefer turkey bone broth is that organic turkey bones are much easier to obtain than the grass-fed oxtail, shortribs, or knucklebones (cut in half by the butcher) needed for beef bone broth.

In addition, we've been following Dr. Peter D'adamo's *Eat Right for Your Type* Blood Type Diet for twenty years. Dr. D'adamo's premise is that each of the four blood types developed in different parts of the world at different times, and have evolved through human evolution. Your blood type is closely tied to your ability to digest certain foods. Dr. D'adamo writes, the "Blood

---

49. Whitney, "The 5 Best Bone Broths You Can Buy Off the Shelf."

Type Diet lets you zero in on the health and nutrition information that corresponds to your exact biological profile."[50]

Following a diet that suits your blood type can improve digestion, help you reach and maintain an ideal weight, increase energy levels, and improve health.

The Blood Type Diet divides food into three categories: Highly Beneficial, Neutral, and Avoid. Highly Beneficial is a food that acts like a medicine. Neutral is a food that acts like a food, providing nutrients and calories. Avoid is a food that acts like a poison, increasing your chance of disease.

Our entire family is Blood Type B. The Rh (+/-) factor doesn't really matter with this way of eating. Either turkey or beef is Neutral for us, but we prefer the lighter taste of the turkey bone broth (and its milder flavor makes it easier to incorporate into recipes). See the chart below to learn what Dr. Peter D'adamo recommends for your blood type in regard to chicken, turkey, and beef.

|  | Chicken | Turkey | Beef |
|---|---|---|---|
| Blood Type O | Neutral | Neutral | Highly Beneficial |
| Blood Type A | Neutral | Neutral | Avoid |
| Blood Type B | Avoid | Neutral | Neutral |
| Blood Type AB | Avoid | Highly Beneficial | Avoid |

## Something to Chew On …

According to Dr. Phil Bass, an assistant professor in the Department of Animal and Veterinary Science at the University of Idaho, "Being on the cusp of the Millennial generation, I must admit going to the grocery store with my mom while growing up allowed me to see that the majority of beef cuts in the meat case were boneless. This was contrary to the bone-in steaks in our freezer at home from the farm-raised cattle we harvested. T-bones, porterhouses, cowboy rib eyes—all classic steakhouse fare found in some of those 'old school,' dimly lit carnivore havens of yore. But the popularity of bone-in

..................................................
50. D'Adamo and Whitney, *Eat Right for Your Type*, 30.

beef cuts has waned a great deal over the decades. ... Rarely will one find a bone-in chuck roast anymore."[51]

The first modern total hip replacement was performed in the early 1960s. It remained a fairly rare procedure until the late 1980s, when the number of cases grew from an estimated 9,000 in 1984 to 310,800 in 2010.[52]

In 1974, "the total condylar knee gave patients with advanced knee arthritis a chance to live without pain."[53] In 2018, the most common total joint replacement procedures in the United States were total knee replacements (about 700,000 a year).[54]

There are more than one million total joint arthroplasty procedures performed in the United States annually, and this number is expected to increase to nearly four million by 2030.[55] According to a January 23, 2019 report by BlueCross BlueShield, "Across the country, the average cost for an inpatient knee replacement is $30,249. ... For a hip replacement, the average cost in the inpatient setting is $30,685."[56]

## Bone Broth: Is It Beneficial or Just a Fad?

Dr. William H. Percy, an associate professor and biomedical scientist at the University of South Dakota, says the health claims surrounding bone broth are "loosely based" on nutrition science, adding, "Anecdotes along the lines of 'I ate bone broth and my gut problem cleared up' do not count as evidence-based medicine."[57]

Our accounts of bone broth healing would not count as "evidence-based medicine," but we find it interesting that over two thousand years ago, its therapeutic benefits were recognized.

....................................................

51. Bass, "Bone-In Beef Cuts: A Bone Of Contention."
52. Dotinga, "Hip Replacements Skyrocket In U.S."
53. "Inventing The Modern Total Knee Replacement," Hospital for Special Surgery.
54. Scutti, "More Men, Younger Americans Having Joint Replacement Surgery."
55. Etkin and Springer, "The American Joint Replacement Registry-The First Five Years," 67–69.
56. "Planned Knee and Hip Replacement Surgeries Are on the Rise in the U.S.," BlueCross and BlueShield.
57. Heid, "Science Can't Explain Why Everyone Is Drinking Bone Broth."

Chicken soup has long been recognized as an important part of the physician's arsenal.[58]

Back in AD 60, the therapeutic benefits of chicken soup were recorded by Pedacius Dioscorides, an army surgeon under the emperor Nero, in his pharmacopeia *De Materia Medica*.[59]

And in the twelfth century, the theologian and physician Moses Maimonides wrote, "Chicken soup … is recommended as an excellent food as well as medication."[60]

Wellness physician Dr. Josh Axe agrees: "Bone broth benefits literally every part of your body, from your gut to your brain, muscles and ligaments."[61]

### Collagen Peptides vs. Bone Broth—Which One Is Better?

Collagen peptides (collagen that's undergone a process called *hydrolysis*, which breaks down collagen's amino acids into smaller molecules, making it easier for your body to absorb) come from animal hides. Bone broth is made from animal bones.

If your goal is to target specific areas in your body, like skin, hair, joints, gut, bones, and muscles, then collagen peptides may be the better option. If you're more interested in boosting your immune system and overall health, then bone broth could be a better choice.

Honestly, our bone broth "factory" slows down in the summer. Drinking hot bone broth on a muggy morning in August isn't very appealing. Instead of sipping it during the summer months, we tend to use it as the liquid when we make quinoa, rice, or sautéed vegetables.

You don't have to decide between collagen or bone broth. To get the best of both worlds, we suggest incorporating both into your life!

..............................................

58. Rosner, *The Medical Legacy of Moses Maimonides*, 242; Hopkins, "Chicken Soup Cure May Not Be a Myth, " 16; Ohry and Tsafrir, "Is Chicken Soup an Essential Drug?"

59. Cohen, "Asthma, Allergy and Immunotherapy; A Historical Review: Part II," 47–58.

60. Rosner, *The Medical Legacy of Moses Maimonides*, 243.

61. Axe, "Bone Broth Benefits For Digestion, Arthritis, and Cellulite."

## CHAPTER THREE
# FEVERISHLY FERMENTING

Fermented vegetables have been prepared and consumed throughout history by people all over the world. The earliest record of fermentation dates back as far as 6000 BC in the Fertile Crescent (modern-day southern Iraq, Syria, Lebanon, Jordan, Israel, and northern Egypt).[62] Fermented cabbage was a staple food for those who built the Great Wall of China 2,700 years ago.[63] Today, sauerkraut is still Germany's national dish.

For thousands and thousands of years, fermenting was just a preservation method. Unfortunately, the development of preservation methods like pasteurization and freezing has made fermenting and culturing unpopular in most "developed" countries.

## WHAT'S THE DIFFERENCE BETWEEN FERMENTED AND CULTURED FOODS?

Most people use the terms interchangeably and refer to all live fermented foods as cultured foods. Some nitpickers feel that a food can only be considered "cultured" if you use a culture to start it, like with yogurt, kombucha, and some types of cheese (to add to the confusion, these are also fermented foods). Fermented foods are usually raw, but some of them can be cooked after fermentation (think of traditional sourdough bread).

Until recently, traditionally fermented/cultured foods included ketchup, sauerkraut, pickles, soy sauce, cod liver oil, Tabasco sauce, Worcestershire

62. Paramithiotis, *Lactic Acid Fermentation of Fruits and Vegetables*, 107.
63. Wells, "Sauerkraut: It All Began in China."

sauce, yogurt, some cheeses, and sour cream. Today, if you buy these at a supermarket, they're just pickled or processed versions of traditionally fermented/cultured foods.

So, the average American is eating very little—if any—fermented food!

## REASONS TO EAT FERMENTED/CULTURED FOODS

Isn't it interesting that seventy-five years ago, people ate fermented foods on a daily basis, and nobody had even heard of probiotics—but now they're the new "craze?" Today, we're faced with an increasing number of bacteria that have become resistant to antibiotics. Scientists are now conducting experiments on fermented foods and finding that they do have therapeutic qualities (duh!).

Fermented foods may help restore the proper balance of bacteria in the gut. Seventy-five years ago, these health problems weren't the widespread issues they are today: gastrointestinal disorders, cardiovascular diseases, allergies and central nervous system-related diseases, autism, obesity, cancer, inflammatory bowel disease (including Crohn's disease and ulcerative colitis), rheumatoid arthritis, celiac disease, severe food allergies, and asthma. All of these conditions have been linked to a lack of good gut bacteria.[64]

Interestingly, gut bacteria play key roles in behavior. A 2010 animal study published in the journal *Neurogastroenterology and Motility* found that mice lacking in gut bacteria behave differently from normal mice, engaging in what would be referred to as "high-risk behavior."[65] We had fun joking around about possible mouse high-risk behavior! Do they leap over mousetraps? Tease cats?

Your gut serves as your second brain.[66] It produces more serotonin (which is known to have a positive influence on your mood) than your brain does.

..............................................

64. "Can Gut Bacteria Improve Your Health?" Harvard Health Publishing; Wang, et al., "Good or Bad: Gut Bacteria in Human Health and Diseases," 1075–80; Zhang, et al., "Impacts of Gut Bacteria on Human Health and Diseases," 7493–519; "Gut Microbiome Can Suppress Food Allergies: Just Add "Good" Bacteria"; Rivas, Crother and Arditi, "The Microbiome in Asthma," 764–71.

65. Neufeld, et al., "Reduced Anxiety-like Behavior and Central Neurochemical Change in Germ-Free Mice," 255–65.

66. "'Second Brain' Neurons Keep Colon Moving," *ScienceDaily*.

Fermented foods help us absorb nutrients and improve digestion. You can ingest huge amounts of nutrients, but unless you actually absorb them, they're not doing you any good (kind of like putting lotions or creams onto skin that hasn't been exfoliated). Fermented foods are rich in enzymes, which our bodies need to digest, absorb, and make full use of our food. Fermenting is like partially digesting food before you eat it. You probably know people who insist they can't drink milk, but can tolerate yogurt. The lactose (which is usually the part people can't tolerate) in milk is broken down as the milk is cultured, and turns into yogurt. The same applies to pasteurized vs. raw milk.

## GROUNDED GOODWIFE STORY TIME

### *Raw Milk* by Ehris

Last winter, we hosted a holiday house tour, and served our guests George Washington's Christmas Eggnog. I'm crazy about eggnog, and I was hoping there would be a lot leftover so I could drink it all when everyone went home. That night, I ladeled a huge glassful out of the punch bowl and blissfully sipped it as we watched *Shark Tank*. The next morning, I felt like a total bloated blob. You know the Michelin man? He had nothing on me! All day, I was thinking, *What happened to me? I didn't eat anything weird … I didn't drink anything weird … !* Then, I gasped, "The eggnog! The milk! The cream!" My family only drinks raw milk, but for the eggnog recipe we used pasteurized milk, since some people get a little weird about drinking raw milk. I'm totally fine with raw milk, but milk pasteurization damages the delicate enzyme lactase, which is required to digest the lactose. Sorry, George, but I won't be making your recipe again!

• • •

Fermenting helps preserve food. For example, milk in the fridge will quickly spoil, but if it's made into kefir, it'll last much longer. And, if you've got a huge garden harvest you don't know how to use up, ferment it!

Finally, fermenting food is inexpensive. The ingredients in these recipes—like the cabbage in kimchi, the SCOBY in kombucha, and the milk in kefir—don't cost very much. There's nothing fancy required to make fermented/cultured foods!

## CAN'T I JUST TAKE PROBIOTICS?

In our classes and workshops, many people reassure us, "My gut health is just fine! I don't need to eat fermented foods. I take probiotics!" The issue with probiotic capsules is that over time, the live bacteria cells they contain die off—especially in warm or humid conditions. The chances of the bottle staying refrigerated from its manufacturing site until it gets into your hands is very slim. We think it's more effective and much less expensive to create your own fermented/cultured foods.

## KIMCHI

Kimchi is a traditional Korean spicy fermented cabbage dish. As a teenager, Ehris spent six weeks in South Korea on a 4-H exchange program. She was served kimchi as a side dish with every meal, including breakfast! Korean households make kimchi in large quantities, and Ehris remembers watching her friend Ji-Hye's grandmother make kimchi with her neighbors, using over one hundred cabbages. In Korean homes, there can never be too much kimchi!

Kimchi isn't chopped veggies simply marinated in vinegar, and it's not a poor man's coleslaw. Kimchi's funky sourness can be pungent enough to clear a room. Some kimchi is salty with a fishy undertone or shrimp-y aftertaste, some is bland and rubbery. All kimchi should have a tangy fizz, because it's "alive."

Kimchi was mentioned in the ancient Korean book *Samkuksaki*, published in AD 1145, as well as in many other documents such as *Naehun*, *Hunmong-jahoe*, *Sinjeung-yuhap*, and *Kanibuckonbang*.[67] According to these texts, kimchi was the result of a simple vegetable-in-brine fermentation prepared in a stone jar and stored underground, which worked very well in its preservation.

...............................................

67. Patra, et al., "Kimchi and Other Widely Consumed Traditional Fermented Foods of Korea: A Review."

The name "kimchi" descends from the older Korean word *chimchae*, which means "brining of vegetables." Kimchi possesses anti-inflammatory, antibacterial, antioxidant, anticancer, probiotic, and antiaging properties.[68] The same bacteria that's used in making yogurt, lactobacillus, is used in kimchi's fermentation process.

Some people incorrectly believe that sauerkraut is interchangeable with kimchi. Sauerkraut is a German cabbage preparation that undergoes fermentation, but unlike kimchi, which includes many ingredients, sauerkraut usually consists only of salt and cabbage. Kimchi's cabbage is cut into big chunks, but sauerkraut's cabbage is cut into fine pieces, and only the upper parts of the cabbage are used. Sauerkraut takes about six weeks to ferment, while our kimchi recipe is ready overnight.

## EASY KIMCHI RECIPE

It took us a long time to perfect this recipe! So many kimchi recipes make the process way too complicated with way too many steps, and the ferment takes too long. We served this at the 250th birthday party for our Grounded Goodwife farmhouse. None of our guests had ever eaten kimchi before, but they all went back for seconds! This recipe can be made vegan by omitting the fish sauce (personally, we don't add it because we don't care for the fishy taste). Makes about eight cups.

### INGREDIENTS

For the cabbage:

5 pounds napa cabbage (about 2½ cabbages), cut into 1-inch, bite-sized pieces

– save 1–2 outer leaves, you'll use these later

½ cup coarse sea salt (other types of salt pull out too much moisture, making the cabbage too soft and wilted)

---

68. Patra, et al., "Kimchi and Other Widely Consumed Traditional Fermented Foods of Korea: A Review."

1 cup water (preferably non-chlorinated—chlorinated water can inhibit fermentation)

Seasonings:

½ medium onion

5–6 garlic cloves, peeled

¼ cup water (preferably non-chlorinated—chlorinated water can inhibit fermentation)

¼ cup Korean red pepper powder (we use gochugaru, which is available online and at some grocery stores)

1 bundle green onions/scallions (we cut them into ¼-inch pieces with scissors)

Optional, if you like it fishy: 2 tablespoons fish sauce or salted shrimp paste

## INSTRUCTIONS

1. Place cabbage in a very large bowl.

2. Mix sea salt and water, and stir until sea salt has dissolved as much as possible (FYI, you probably won't get it to totally dissolve, and that's okay). Pour over cabbage and mix together with your hands. Let sit unrefrigerated for one and a half to two hours.

3. In the meantime, in a blender or food processor, puree onion and garlic with ¼ cup water. Pour into a medium bowl. Add red pepper powder, green onions/scallions, and optional fish sauce/shrimp paste and mix well.

4. Once the cabbage has significantly wilted, rinse cabbage, which will remove most of the salt. Place back into the very large bowl. Toss cabbage with the seasoning mixture until well-coated; as with meatloaf, using your hands works best.

5. Place seasoned kimchi into a wide-mouth half gallon jar. Using your fist, punch down the cabbage to compress it all in the jar. Keep stuffing the jar until it's completely full. Cover with the cabbage leaves you saved, and press down. The leaves will help keep the cabbage submerged.

6. Tightly close the lid on the mason jar and leave out at room temperature overnight. Taste the kimchi after twenty-four hours. If you think it tastes fine, put the jar in the fridge. If you like it more pungent, leave out for another day or two, then put it in the fridge. It's ready to eat!

Since it's fermented, kimchi can last for about three to six months in the fridge (ours never lasts that long since we eat it every night with dinner!). We eat it as a side dish, on top of salad, on hamburgers, on BLTs, and on hotdogs. Once your gut health has been established, you can keep it thriving by eating a tablespoon of kimchi per day. Keep the kimchi submerged below the brine and it will get better and more flavorful with time.

Play around with different kinds of cabbage! Purists will insist, "No, kimchi won't be the same if you use plain old 'American' cabbage," but we've tried this recipe with green, napa, and savoy cabbage. We love using a combo of all three, but experiment to discover which taste you prefer!

## KOMBUCHA

Kombucha is a fermented tea drink that's made with black tea, sugar, and a SCOBY (more on that later). "Booch" flows at coffee shops and health food stores. Boozy "booch" (longer ferment) is often on tap at bars—with enough alcohol to rival an IPA beer. We started making kombucha at least fifteen years ago, before hipsters had even heard of it. Since then, it's become extremely trendy, but many people still don't know why it's good for them.

This fermented "tea of immortality" has come a long way from its reported beginnings in China more than 2,000 years ago. It's evolved into a $475 million industry in the United States.[69]

Kombucha originated in Northeast China around 220 BC. It's believed that the name comes from Dr. Kombu, a Korean physician who brought the fermented tea (cha) to Japan as a curative for Emperor Inkyo.[70] Get it? Kombu + cha!

..............................................

69. Mackeen, "Are There Benefits to Drinking Kombucha?"

70. Troitino, "Kombucha 101: Demystifying The Past, Present and Future of the Fermented Tea Drink."

Kombucha tastes kind of like sparkling apple cider with a tang of vinegar. Kombucha's bacteria—the *good* kind of bacteria—supports everything from immune function and mental health to nutrient absorption.[71] Participants in our DIY Kombucha workshops report that the benefits they've noticed most from drinking kombucha are increased energy, improved digestive health, and a stronger immune system.

If you can make tea, you can make kombucha. To brew your own kombucha, you need black tea, white sugar, water, vinegar, and a SCOBY (which stands for symbiotic colony of bacteria and yeast). Although a SCOBY looks and feels like a raw, skinless chicken breast, and people refer to it as a "mushroom," it's neither of these things. It's similar to "the mother" in raw, unpasteurized apple cider vinegar, or the starter in sourdough bread—it's a living thing. Every time you make a batch of kombucha, another SCOBY will be created. Eventually, you'll be inundated with them (but don't worry about it right now, we'll get to that later).

In order to make your first batch of kombucha, you'll have to find a SCOBY source. They're available online, like on Etsy, but we don't recommend getting them that way. SCOBYs that are shipped in the mail are put in a plastic baggie or container. The problem is that your SCOBY is alive— it needs to breathe! The better way is to find a kombucha maker (trust us, they're out there). They'll probably be happy to hook you up with a SCOBY!

## KOMBUCHA RECIPE

After experimenting for years, we've found that this is the easiest way to brew a batch of kombucha. A sixteen-ounce bottle of store-bought kombucha averages about $4. Brewing your own costs about 6¢ for sixteen ounces. This batch-brew method recipe makes one gallon.

........................................

71. Link, "This 'Immortal Health Elixir' Protects Your Gut & Fights Food Poisoning Pathogens (and More!)."

## INGREDIENTS

14 cups water

1 cup white sugar (required for the fermentation process—don't bypass or substitute! During fermentation, the sugar is broken down and transformed into acids, vitamins, minerals, and enzymes)[72]

8 tea bags of black tea or 2 tablespoons loose black tea (any kind of black tea—we usually use organic assam, but we've also used Lipton—both work equally well!)

2 cups "starter tea"—homemade or store-bought unpasteurized plain kombucha—or 1¾ cup water + ¼ cup white vinegar (*not* apple cider vinegar)

1 SCOBY per jar

## INSTRUCTIONS

1. Boil eight cups water.
2. Meanwhile, put the eight teabags (or two tablespoons loose-leaf tea) in a large metal pot (big enough to hold fourteen cups of water).
3. Pour the boiling water over the teabags or loose-leaf tea.
4. Steep for five to ten minutes and remove teabags or loose-leaf tea.
5. Add one cup sugar and stir. Add remaining six cups cold water to tea solution. Let cool to room temperature.
6. Pour the tea/sugar solution into a gallon-size glass jar.
7. Add two cups of "starter tea" to your gallon-size glass jar.
8. Add the SCOBY (it may sink or float—either way is fine!).
9. Cover the jar with a paper towel/breathable cloth (your SCOBY is a living thing) and a rubber band.
10. Let sit, undisturbed, at room temperature for three to four weeks, until you see a baby SCOBY form at the top of the jar. This might sound confusing... but you'll know when you see it.
11. Fish out both SCOBYs and place them in a glass jar that's big enough to accommodate their size. It's easiest for future batches not to fold

..................................................
72. Sussman, *Cold Press Juice Bible: 300 Delicious, Nutritious, All-Natural Recipes for Your Masticating Juicer*, 12–14.

or squish them. Cover them with kombucha so they don't dry out. This will become your SCOBY hotel—more on that later.

12. Put the lid (the real jar lid) on your kombucha and put it in the fridge. It's ready to drink! Or, you can flavor it...

## FLAVORING

Flavor ideas:

- **Fruit**: peaches, apples, cherries, berries, pears, pineapple, coconut
    For a gallon of kombucha, add one to two cups fresh or frozen fruit.
- **Herbs**: ginger, cinnamon, vanilla beans, holy basil
    For a gallon of kombucha, add two to three tablespoons fresh or dried herbs.

Our favorite kombucha flavors are hibiscus/raspberry and ginger/holy basil. Of course, it's a matter of personal taste, but there are a few kombucha flavors that don't sound very appealing to us, like banana, mint, or goji berry.

### Batch Brew vs. Continuous Brew

Kombucha can be made either by batch brew (made in a mason-type jar) or continuous brew (made in a glass container with a spigot). We prefer the continuous brew system. It's less maintenance, since it can be cleaned periodically rather than with each new batch. It's also the healthiest environment for the SCOBY. Instead of disturbing the ecological environment through moving to new containers and regular cleaning, continuous brew allows the yeast and bacteria to develop relatively undisturbed with a consistent supply of new food.

## BREWING

Instead of washing the container at the end of the ferment...

- Take out the baby SCOBY and leave the mother SCOBY in the container.
- Drain off the kombucha, but leave at least two cups of the kombucha in the container to act as starter tea for the next batch.

- Prepare new sugared tea using the normal ratios. Allow the sugared tea to cool thoroughly, then slowly pour the solution into the top of the brew system.
- Cover with paper towel/cloth and let sit for three to four weeks!

## INSTRUCTIONS

Add your flavorings of choice to your plain kombucha and close the jar. Let it *second ferment* on the counter for two to four days. Remove flavorings and refrigerate. It's ready to drink!

Kombucha will last for months in the fridge, but gradually loses effervescence. We suggest drinking about eight ounces of kombucha a day.

We strongly recommend that you don't use herbal tea to brew kombucha. In order to thrive, the SCOBY needs nutrients provided by black tea such as nitrogen and tannins.[73] Some people brew with green tea, but we've found that the SCOBY seems to stay more "robust" with black tea. Herbal teas contain much lower levels (or none) of the nutrients needed by the SCOBY. Making kombucha with herbal tea will eventually make your SCOBY mutate (yikes!) or degrade, so we recommend that you just stick to brewing with black tea.

Sometimes, people are concerned about the sugar and caffeine in kombucha. The sugar in kombucha is food for the SCOBY, which digests and converts it into beneficial enzymes and nutrients. When it's done fermenting, eight ounces of kombucha will contain about two to six grams of sugar (eight ounces of orange juice contains around twenty-four grams of sugar). The longer kombucha ferments, the less sugar it will contain.[74] Regarding caffeine, as your kombucha ferments, the caffeine level decreases. But if you're concerned about caffeine, you can brew your kombucha with decaf black tea.

We've noticed in our Grounded Goodwife workshops that people are often embarrassed to ask if kombucha is alcoholic. The answer is yes and no. It contains a *very* small amount of alcohol—usually about 0.5 percent, depending on length of fermentation. Just to compare, beer contains 4 to 6

.................................................
73. Crum, "Best Tea for Kombucha - How to Choose a Tea Blend Recipe."
74. Crum, "Top 10 Questions about Sugar & Kombucha."

percent. Some kombucha makers ferment it longer to increase the alcohol content.

The "danger" question is one we hear for almost everything we teach, but especially when it comes to the topic of fermented foods. We feel that as long as you're using a clean jar, your hands are clean when you're handling the SCOBY, and your SCOBY isn't moldy, no, it's not dangerous. If something happens to your SCOBY (it happens to the best of us), it'll be obvious, and you'll just have to find a new SCOBY source. As always, use common sense.

## What to Do with Your Excess SCOBYs

Be prepared to be inundated with SCOBYs! This is like that Amish Friendship Bread situation where it feels like a chain letter in bread form. The bread starter kind of takes over your life and eventually extends out to a friend of a friend of a friend because it's alive, and you feel terrible about killing it. Every time you make a batch of kombucha, a new SCOBY will be created.

You can create a "SCOBY hotel"—kind of like SCOBY storage. To start the hotel, put your extra SCOBY in a clean jar with about ⅔ cup kombucha (make sure there's enough kombucha to cover the SCOBY). Cover the jar with something breathable—like a paper towel or clean dishtowel held on by a rubber band—and store at room temperature (not in the fridge). You can keep adding SCOBYs to the hotel, and add more kombucha as needed so they don't dry out. The theory is that you can just peel these SCOBYs apart to share with other "boochers," but after a few months, they'll grow into one massive clump, which is fine because you can cut them with a knife to separate them. Here are some ways to use your inevitable excess SCOBYs:

- Compost them (you'll have to ignore their screams as they beg for mercy).
- Add little SCOBY pieces to a vase of water to perk up fresh flowers. Who needs those powdered "flower food" packets that come with bouquets?
- Put SCOBY pieces under a Band-Aid to help heal a cut/burn.
- Blend SCOBY slices into smoothies. Mmm mmm, that's good eatin'!
- Try a SCOBY face mask! Just slop one on your face, eyeholes optional. You may feel like the hapless heroine in a sci-fi movie, but the increased

circulation in your face may regenerate skin cells. The pH level of the SCOBY creates a mild acid peel that sloughs away dead skin. Keep a towel handy to catch the drips, and lie down while you're doing this.

- Our dogs *love* to eat SCOBYs!
- Make SCOBY Fruit Leather!

## SCOBY FRUIT LEATHER

This recipe is easiest if you have a dehydrator, but an oven works too. When dehydrated at a low temperature, the SCOBY keeps its healthy acids and good bacteria.

### INGREDIENTS

2 cups pureed SCOBY (use a blender)

2 cups chopped fruit (berries, pineapple, peaches, pears, apples, etc.)

¼ cup sugar

1–2 teaspoons herbs (cinnamon, ginger, cloves, nutmeg, etc.)

### INSTRUCTIONS

1. Combine the fruit and sugar in a medium saucepan. Cook over medium heat, stirring frequently, for about ten minutes.

2. In a blender, add the fruit mixture, SCOBY puree, and herbs. Blend until all ingredients are combined.

3. Spread the mixture onto wax paper, parchment paper, or dehydrator sheets in a layer about ¼-inch thick.

4. Dehydrate in a dehydrator or oven for twelve to thirty-six hours.
   - Dehydrator: use the lowest setting (95–110°F)
   - Oven: put it on the lowest temperature and prop the door open

5. Once the mixture is dried and isn't sticky, remove from the wax paper/parchment paper/dehydrator sheets. If it's hard to remove, put the leather in the freezer for about ten minutes—then it should peel off easily.

6. Cut the leather into strips—they can be rolled up or bite-size, your choice! Store in an airtight container at room temperature. They'll last for a long time (we've had ones that have lasted over a year, but they dry out a little bit over time).

## KEFIR

Kefir—a fermented and cultured milk drink that tastes like thin, yeasty, effervescent yogurt—originated with nomadic shepherds on the slopes of Russia's North Caucasus Mountains. Many people choose to drink kefir because it contains far more strains of beneficial bacteria than yogurt. Kefir contains vitamin B12, calcium, magnesium, folate, enzymes, and several important probiotics strains.[75] Some studies suggest that consumers of kefir have abundant probiotic gut bacteria, which correlates with optimum health.[76]

The health benefits of homemade kefir far outrank any store-bought variety. Store-bought kefir is pasteurized and homogenized during manufacturing, so much of its beneficial bacteria is lost. Also, if you're buying kefir products at a store, they're probably made with powder instead of grains. Powdered kefir starter contains about seven to nine strains of bacteria. Milk kefir grains contain a much longer list of beneficial bacteria and yeast strains, making kefir grains the more probiotic-rich culture for making kefir.[77] Kefir—which many people of the Caucasus claim to be their secret to longevity and health—is one of the easiest things you can make at home. It's so much easier than making yogurt!

## GROUNDED GOODWIFE STORY TIME

### *Life of a Kefir Maker* by Ehris

If someone followed me around for the day, they'd see that I start my morning with a kefir smoothie. They'd also see that I end my day by taking a sixteen-ounce mason jar from the top of our fridge and

75. Link, "Kefir Benefits, Nutrition Facts, Types and How to Make."

76. Prado, et al., "Milk Kefir: Composition, Microbial Cultures, Biological Activities, and Related Products," 1177.

77. Mitts, "How to Make Kefir (the Only Guide You Need)."

spooning what looks like white miniature cauliflower clumps float-
ing around in ranch dressing from that jar to an empty sixteen-ounce
mason jar and adding a cup of raw milk. This is the life of a kefir
maker!

• • •

## History of Kefir

Kefir dates back two thousand years to the shepherds of Russia's Caucasus
mountains. They discovered that fresh milk carried in leather pouches would
occasionally ferment into an effervescent beverage, which we now know as
kefir. The word "kefir" comes from the Turkish word "keyif," which means
"good feeling."[78]

The original method for making kefir was very simple. Fresh cow, goat,
or sheep's milk was poured into watertight bags made from animal skins.
Then, gelatinous kefir "grains" were added, and the bag was suspended in
the sun during the day (just as with the SCOBYs needed for kombucha,
nobody seems to be quite sure where the first kefir grains came from). When
the sun went down, the bag was hung near the door, and each person passing
through the doorway would poke the bag to keep the milk and kefir grains
mixed while fermenting.

Kefir was a great on-the-go food for shepherds! Who needs trail mix or a
granola bar? When leaving home, they'd take an animal-skin bag containing
milk and kefir grains, and as they traveled, the contents of the bag would
constantly be sloshing around. The shepherds would add fresh milk from the
animals they were herding to replace the kefir they drank.[79]

In order to make kefir, you have to start with kefir "grains." Legend
has it that kefir grains (not really a true grain) were a gift from the prophet
Mohammed (AD 571–632), who instructed his followers on how to use the
grains. There was a belief that kefir grains would lose their potency if the
secret of their use became common knowledge. They were closely guarded

78. Pothuraju, et al., "Fermented Milk in Protection against Inflammatory Mechanisms in
Obesity," 389–401.
79. Seifi, "Magical Kefir."

as part of the wealth of each family within a tribe and were secretly passed down through the generations. Foreigners were sometimes given a taste of kefir (it's said that Marco Polo wrote about his kefir taste-test in the book of his eastern travels), but the method of making it remained guarded.[80]

Hospitals in the former USSR used kefir as part of the diet for patients with gastrointestinal and metabolic disorders, high blood pressure, heart disease and allergies, and in neonatal wards for the newborn and mother.[81]

### Where To Get Kefir Grains?

While we don't advocate getting a SCOBY online, milk kefir grains seem to survive being mailed (just make sure you're ready to use them as soon as they arrive). A plus with kefir grains is that they don't require as much TLC as a SCOBY, and just seem more hardy. If you know someone who makes kefir, they'll probably have extra grains to share with you.

### KEFIR RECIPE

Ehris makes kefir every day—it's so simple! All you need to get started are kefir grains, milk (preferably raw), and a sixteen-ounce (or larger) glass jar. Such an easy way to get more "cultured!" Makes one cup of kefir.

### INGREDIENTS

1 cup milk (we use raw cow's milk)

1 teaspoon kefir grains

### DIRECTIONS

1. Place kefir grains in a glass mason jar (we use a sixteen-ounce jar). Add milk and stir.
2. Cover the jar with something breathable (because kefir is a living organism)—like cheesecloth or a paper towel—and place a rubber band around it.

80. "Kefir's History." La Coprologie sur le Web.

81. Shavit, "Renewed Interest in Kefir, the Ancient Elixir of Longevity," 14–18.

3. Let the mixture rest at room temperature for twenty-four hours. We put it on top of the fridge because it's safely out of the way, and the warmth seems to help with culturing.

4. Your kefir is done! Remove the grains (which will look like miniature cauliflower florets) from the jar (but *don't* throw them away— you'll need them to make more kefir). Place a lid on the kefir, and put it in the fridge. It will last at least a week.

   – In order to have constant kefir production (aka a "kefir factory"), immediately put the grains (which you saved) in a clean sixteen-ounce glass mason jar. Add one cup of raw milk to start the process all over again.

## TIPS

The general rule is to use one teaspoon of kefir grains per cup of milk. So, if you want to make two cups of kefir, use two teaspoons kefir grains, etc.

Just as with your SCOBY hotel, be prepared for these grains to grow pretty quickly over time! You can share the grains with other people. When we're inundated with grains, we give them to our dogs, Myra and Viola— they *love* them!

While we use raw cow's milk, it's okay to use pasteurized cow's/goat's milk too. Some people use almond, soy, or coconut milk, but that's not something we advocate.

### Putting the Grains on Pause (for up to Three Weeks)

Don't fret! You *can* take a break from making kefir. You *will* go on vacation again!

1. Make sure your grains have been culturing for at least a month before taking a "vacation" (this is for the health of your grains).

2. Add your kefir grains to two to four cups fresh milk (more milk for longer breaks is best, to keep the grains well-fed).

3. Put a tight lid on the container and place in the refrigerator. The kefir grains should be safe and healthy for up to three weeks.

### Re-starting Kefir Production

1. Separate the grains from the storage milk. Place them in fresh milk, and culture as usual.

2. It might take a few batches for the grains to wake up and get back to work.

3. You can drink or discard the storage liquid—your choice.

### What to Do with Your Kefir

As soon as your kefir is done culturing/fermenting, it's ready to drink. If you're used to buying kefir from a store, you'll probably be expecting your homemade kefir to look nice and smooth. It won't be. It will be weirdly chunky. Personally, we think plain kefir tastes like a combo of cottage cheese and milk that's going bad, so we don't drink it this way. We make kefir smoothies—with enough berries and bananas, it camouflages the tang and obliterates the chunks (we also add spinach, nettle, spirulina, shatavari, eleuthero, alfalfa, astragalus, and Amazing Grass Green Superfood powder). We've used kefir (instead of milk) in mashed potatoes, gluten-free macaroni and cheese, alfredo sauces, stroganoffs, and gluten-free cake batters.

If you make kefir long enough, you're going to become sick of kefir smoothies. Like Ehris did, you'll hold your head and cry in exasperation, "What else can I do with this stuff?!" One day, we got the brilliant idea to pour some kefir through cheesecloth, tie it onto a wooden spoon like a hobo's bindle, and let it drain for eight hours. Our lives were changed, and yours will be too (you're welcome).

### CREAMY GREEK-STYLE KEFIR "YOGURT"

We were never into making yogurt. Reason #1: it involves a thermometer, and Ehris hates using thermometers (it's why we don't make candy or chocolate). Reason #2: we only drink raw milk, and it always seemed counterproductive to heat up raw milk (thereby killing its beneficial stuff) in order to make its culture into yogurt. So, if you use raw milk, this kefir "yogurt" is not only a reprieve from drinking kefir smoothies, it's probiotic-rich, as well as raw! Makes about one cup.

## INGREDIENTS

4 cups kefir

⅛ to ¼ teaspoon pink Himalayan salt, to taste

Sweetener ideas: honey, maple syrup, stevia

Topping ideas: berries, apples, granola, coconut, vanilla extract, nuts, cacao
nibs, etc.

## INSTRUCTIONS

1. Line a colander with cheesecloth, a very thin dishtowel, or an old
   T-shirt. Place the colander in a pot or bowl. Pour the kefir in the
   cloth-covered colander. Then, gather the corners of the cloth and
   tie at the top with a rubber band or string. Tie cloth to a wooden
   spoon and hang it over a pot, or suspend elastic from your kitchen
   faucet and let it drain into a pot. Let strain for about eight hours,
   until it reaches a thick Greek-yogurt consistency.

2. Transfer strained kefir to a mixing bowl.

3. Add sweetener to the kefir "yogurt," if desired. Store in a container in the fridge, and use within a week. Mix in toppings when
   you're ready to eat it.

4. The strained liquid you'll be left with in your pot or bowl is whey.
   You can pour it down your sink or dump it in your compost pile,
   or check out our uses in "Ways to Use Whey."

### GARLIC-HERB KEFIR CHEESE

Kefir makes a delicious sour soft-style raw cheese (it's raw if you use raw
milk). You can use it in place of ricotta for dishes like lasagna. Or, use it on
bagels, crackers, celery, or baked potatoes! Jim describes the taste as very
much like blue cheese or feta. Makes about one cup.

## INGREDIENTS

4 cups kefir

¼ to ½ teaspoon pink Himalayan salt, to taste

2 cloves minced garlic

1 tablespoon basil

1 tablespoon fresh parsley

1 teaspoon fresh thyme

1 teaspoon fresh oregano

## INSTRUCTIONS

1. Line a colander with cheesecloth, very thin dishtowel, or an old T-shirt. Place the colander in a pot or bowl. Pour the kefir in the cloth-covered colander. Then, gather the corners of the cloth and tie at the top with a rubber band or string. Tie cloth to a wooden spoon and hang it over a pot, or suspend elastic from your kitchen faucet and let it drain into a pot. Let strain for about eight hours, until it reaches a thick Greek-yogurt consistency.

2. Transfer strained kefir to a mixing bowl.

3. Mix in the salt, garlic, and herbs, and refrigerate in a container.

4. Use the cheese within a week (it will continue to culture).

5. The strained liquid you'll be left with in your pot or bowl is whey. You can pour it down your sink or dump it in your compost pile, or check out our uses in "Ways to Use Whey."

## APRICOT-MAPLE KEFIR "CREAM CHEESE"

You can use this recipe instead of flavored cream cheese. So good on Ezekiel toast, or Ezekiel sprouted English muffins, or a gluten-free bagel! Makes about one cup.

## INGREDIENTS

4 cups kefir

2 tablespoons maple syrup

½ teaspoon astragalus root powder (optional, for immune health)

¼ teaspoon ground cinnamon

⅓ cup chopped dried apricots

⅛ to ¼ teaspoon pink Himalayan salt, to taste

## INSTRUCTIONS

1. Line a colander with cheesecloth, very thin dishtowel, or an old T-shirt. Place the colander in a pot or bowl. Pour the kefir in the cloth-covered colander. Then, gather the corners of the cloth and tie at the top with a rubber band or string. Tie cloth to a wooden spoon and hang it over a pot, or suspend elastic from your kitchen faucet and let it drain into a pot. Let strain for about eight hours, until it reaches a thick Greek-yogurt consistency.

2. Transfer strained kefir to a mixing bowl. Add maple syrup, astragalus, cinnamon, and dried apricots, and mix with beaters.

3. Keep refrigerated in a container, and use within a week.

4. The strained liquid you'll be left with in your pot or bowl is whey. You can pour it down your sink or dump it in your compost pile, or check out our uses in "Ways to Use Whey."

## KEFIR TZATZIKI

Who doesn't love a gyro? For us, the tzatziki sauce is the best part. Our kefir tzatziki recipe isn't only tasty on grilled meat or vegetables at summer BBQs, it's healthy for the digestive system. Try it as a dip, or as a creamy, probiotic salad dressing in place of ranch dressing. Makes about one cup..

## INGREDIENTS

4 cups kefir

1 chopped pickling cucumber (we like our tzatziki chunky, but finely chop if that's not your bag)

2 cloves garlic, minced

2 tablespoons olive oil

1 tablespoon lemon juice

4 tablespoons fresh dill

½ teaspoon pink Himalayan salt

**INSTRUCTIONS**

1. Line a colander with cheesecloth, very thin dishtowel, or an old T-shirt. Place the colander in a pot or bowl. Pour the kefir in the cloth-covered colander. Then, gather the corners of the cloth and tie at the top with a rubber band or string. Tie cloth to a wooden spoon and hang it over a pot, or suspend elastic from your kitchen faucet and let it drain into a pot. Let strain for about eight hours, until it reaches a thick Greek-yogurt consistency.

2. Transfer strained kefir to a mixing bowl. Add cucumber, garlic, olive oil, lemon juice, dill, and salt. Mix well. Keep refrigerated in a container, and use within a week. Enjoy!

3. The strained liquid you'll be left with in your pot or bowl is whey. You can pour it down your sink or dump it in your compost pile, or check out our uses in "Ways to Use Whey."

## WAYS TO USE WHEY

A person can drink just so many kefir smoothies! Recently, we've been experimenting with straining our kefir to create cheese, yogurt, and cream cheese. If you're tried any of our recipes on the previous pages, you know that the results are pretty darn tasty, but we've run into one glitch: what do we do with all of the whey?

Wait, whey? What's whey?

*Little Miss Muffett, sat on her tuffet, eating her curds and whey.* You probably remember this classic nursery rhyme, but have you ever wondered, *What are curds and whey?* (and, in case you've also wondered what a tuffet is, it's a foot-stool or low seat).

Whey is that mysterious liquid at the top of a yogurt container, which you probably pour down the drain, or mix into the yogurt without even thinking about it. It's watery, slightly sour, tangy, and cloudy, with a really faint milk taste.

Simply put, milk (and, therefore, kefir), is made up of liquids and solids. When you strain kefir through cheesecloth or a coffee filter, you're separating some of the liquid from the solids. The liquid that's separated is whey, a natural component of milk. We're not ones to be wasteful, so when our kefir creations provided us with cups of whey, we did some experimenting to see what we could do with it. Turns out, you can do a lot!

If you take a walk down the sports nutrition aisle of a grocery store, you'll come across an overabundance of whey protein products.

Hippocrates used liquid whey as a medicine to provide strength and vigor, and Greek physicians called it "healing water."[82] Today, however, whey is considered a waste product of the cheese and yogurt industries. The booming Greek yogurt business has been criticized by environmental agencies for the gallons and gallons of "whey waste" that they must get rid of after processing their strained yogurt products. According to a 2013 Cornell University report, for every seven thousand gallons of milk used in making Greek yogurt, as much as 4,900 gallons of whey gets produced.[83] The problem is what to do with all that liquid whey. It can't just be dumped in rivers. According to George Bevington, an engineer who deals with wastewater treatment in Johnstown, New York, the whey would set off a boom of sugar-eating bacteria, "and that means there'd be no oxygen left in the river, and that means there'd be no fishies left in the river!"[84]

Drowning in whey, industries have been "whey-ing" their options about what to do with all of this tangy liquid. They've found a market in the sports nutrition industry, which is transforming their leftover whey into powder, marketing it as a muscle-building, energy-boosting supplement. Sounds like a good solution—but, the beneficial nutrients are destroyed as this whey is high-heat pasteurized and given several toxic acid baths. So, even though you might be tempted by flavors like chocolate hazelnut and French vanilla crème, commercial whey protein powders probably aren't as healthy as they claim to be.[85]

........................................

82. Milner, "Why Whey?"
83. Smith, "There's a Downside to All That Greek Yogurt You're Eating."
84. Charles, "Why Greek Yogurt Makers Want Whey to Go Away."
85. Grossmann, "Homemade Whey vs. Protein Powder: Rediscovering Nutrient Dense Foods."

We don't typically see liquid whey for sale in stores—which is a shame, because when it's made properly (in small batches from cultured dairy), whey contains unique healing properties. Whey is a complete protein—meaning it contains all essential amino acids (the building blocks of protein), which are used to support vital biological functions in the body. Amino acids are involved in almost every body function—everything from growth, development, healing, repair, and digestion to providing energy for your body.

Whey can be used in a variety of different "wheys" (clever, huh?). Experiment with our recipes, and come up with some of your own!

## LITTLE MISS MUFFETT'S STRAWBERRY LEMONADE

A fizzy, fermented lemonade that's easy to make and is ready in only two days. There's no "whey" you'd know this probiotic-rich drink contains whey! You'll be so captivated by the pink grapefruit color, you won't even care if a spider sits down beside you! Makes about twelve cups.

### INGREDIENTS

¾ cup sugar (don't be scared off by the amount of sugar—it's needed for the fermentation process—the final product yields a very low sugar content)

2 cups warm water

1 cup chopped strawberries (if frozen, thawed to room temperature—the leftover berry liquid can be included in this recipe)

8 cups room-temperature water

Juice from 10 lemons, or 1 cup bottled lemon juice

1 cup whey

### INSTRUCTIONS

1. In a gallon-size glass jar, stir together sugar and warm water until sugar is dissolved.

2. Add the lemon juice, strawberries, and room-temperature water.

3. Make sure the liquid is at room temperature, then add the whey.

4. Cover with a lid and let sit on the counter for two days.

5. Refrigerate. Drink and enjoy!

## WHEY-BACK-WHEN GINGER ALE

In our great-grandmothers' day, homemade ginger ale was the tonic of choice for an upset stomach, menstrual cramps, nausea, or the flu. To make old-fashioned ginger ale, all you need are a few basic ingredients and a large glass jar. Golden ginger ale fell out of favor during Prohibition (1920–1933). Bootleg liquor/moonshine was very potent, and a strong soft drink was needed to mask the flavor. Dry ginger ale, which was less sweet, exploded in popularity in the 1920s, and was a hit at speakeasies, at parties, and with flappers. Dry ginger ale became a permanent fixture in America's grocery stores. This golden ginger ale recipe isn't supposed to taste like grocery store ginger ale. It's only mildly fizzy, but it packs a strong ginger punch, and no corn syrup! Makes about eleven cups.

### INGREDIENTS

3 cups warm water

¾ cup chopped ginger root (we don't peel it)

¾ cup sugar (don't be scared off by the amount of sugar—it's needed for the fermentation process—the final product yields a very low sugar content)

7 cups room temperature water

1 cup whey

### INSTRUCTIONS

1. Boil three cups water. Stir in ginger root, and simmer for thirty minutes. Remove from heat.

2. Add sugar and stir until dissolved. Add remaining seven cups room-temperature water. Cool mixture to room temperature.

3. Stir in whey.

4. Pour into a gallon-size glass jar. Keep at room temperature for two to three days.

5. Strain to remove ginger root.

6. To enhance the fizz, let it sit in capped bottles for another day at room temperature.

7. Refrigerate, and enjoy within a week.

## WHEY TO GO! CHoCOLATE PEANuT BUTTER PRoTEIN SHAKE

If you use your imagination a bit, this protein shake is good enough to pass for a healthy peanut butter cup milkshake! There are loads of protein shake recipes out there, but this one is a great way to curb the chocolate craving without reaching for the cookies or peanut butter cups. Whey is a complete protein—meaning it contains all essential amino acids (the building blocks of protein). Makes one serving.

### INGREDIENTS

¼ cup raw cow milk, or unsweetened almond milk (or milk of choice)

¼ cup whey

½ tablespoon cacao or cocoa powder

1 tablespoon natural peanut butter or almond butter (chunky, smooth— you're the boss!)

1 teaspoon honey or other sweetener (optional)

½ frozen banana, cut in half

Optional: ½ cup ice cubes

### INSTRUCTIONS

1. Add all ingredients to a blender and secure the lid.

2. Blend on a medium speed for fifty to sixty seconds, or until well-mixed.

**Other Whey Ideas**

1. Try substituting whey in a baking recipe that calls for water, milk, or buttermilk.

2. Add whey to smoothies (unless you're smoothied out).

3. Use it on your hair! When we're inundated with whey, we use it as a shampoo (neither of us uses regular shampoo). To use: wet your hair, then pour about one cup of whey over your head (this might not be a good time to sing in the shower—the whey tastes a little tangy). Massage it into your scalp, then rinse well. It nourishes, strengthens, and softens the hair. Even if you use regular store-bought shampoo, rinsing your hair with whey can make it smoother and shinier.

4. Feed it to the dogs! People who feed their dogs dry food often mix in a little whey.

5. Add a little to your chickens' water as a protein source, especially if they don't free-range.

Stored in a container in the fridge, whey will keep for several months. You can also freeze it for later—we recommend freezing it in ice cube trays, and storing the frozen cubes in a baggie.

## GROUNDED GOODWIFE STORY TIME

### *Mommy Wars* by Velya

I was recently at a friend's house as she was getting ready to feed her newborn. As I inwardly cringed, it took everything in my power to bite my tongue and not engage in Mommy Wars as she nonchalantly measured baby *formula* with *low-fat* pasteurized cow milk into a pink *plastic* baby bottle—and *microwaved* it!

I stole a glance at the formula container and winced at the first three ingredients: corn maltodextrin, whey protein concentrate, and vegetable oils. The BPA and phthalates released from the microwaved plastic bottle into the formula is a whole 'nother issue.[86]

86. "Is Plastic a Threat to Your Health?" Harvard Health.

We stopped using microwaves over twenty-five years ago after a see-it-for-myself accidental experiment. I was making yogurt and impatient for the milk to reach 180°F on the stove. So, instead, I microwaved it. I'd been making yogurt for years, but this was the first time it didn't "set"—at all. I'm convinced that the microwave's radiation killed the culture. The microwave went to the dump the next day and was never replaced.

• • •

## GUT HEALTH AND BABiES

Establishing normal gut flora in the first one thousand days—the period from conception to two years of age—is critical to a baby's immune system.[87] Gut health has a major impact on the development of the digestive tract and immune system. The process of establishing the gut microbiota has the potential to be a main determinant of lifelong health.[88]

The results of a 2015 clinical study involving seventy-five infants are astonishing! Researchers gave half of the newborns a probiotic (specifically, *Lactobacillus rhamnosus*) for the first six months after birth, while the control group didn't receive the probiotic. Thirteen years later, all of the children were assessed for ADHD and Asperger's syndrome. Seventeen of the children in the control group were diagnosed with ADHD or Asperger's, while none of the children who received probiotic supplementation were diagnosed. The researchers concluded that probiotic supplementation "may reduce the risk of neuropsychiatric disorder development later in childhood."[89]

While more research studies with more participants are needed to provide more evidence, multiple studies show that an abnormal gut microbiota is related to autism spectrum disorder (ASD).[90]

........................................

87. Robertson, et al.,"The Human Microbiome And Child Growth—First 1000 Days And Beyond," 131–47.

88. Tanaka and Nakayama, "Development of the Gut Microbiota in Infancy and Its Impact on Health in Later Life," 515–22.

89. Pärtty, et al., "A Possible Link Between Early Probiotic Intervention and the Risk of Neuro-psychiatric Disorders Later in Childhood: A Randomized Trial," 823–28.

90. Fattorusso, et al., "Autism Spectrum Disorders and the Gut Microbiota," 521.

A 2017 study in *Frontiers in Cellular Neuroscience*, by researchers in China, the Philippines, and the United States[91] made a persuasive case for the important role of gut bacteria in ASD. The study described how children exposed to antibiotics during their first three years of life show less diverse bacterial species and strains in their gut bacterial populations, and how this may relate to ASD risk. Additionally, the researchers described how antibiotics taken during pregnancy might also be a potential risk factor for ASD.

The study found that breastfeeding, because of its role in establishing a newborn's gut bacteria, is associated with a decreased risk for ASD, and concluded that "breastfeeding for more than six months is associated with a lower risk of developing ASD."[92] However, breastfed babies aren't guaranteed to have healthy intestinal flora. For mothers who breastfeed, it's equally important that their own gut flora is thriving long before they begin nursing.

This study looked at interventions like probiotics, prebiotics, and dietary interventions as possible therapeutic tools for the treatment of ASD. Dr. David Perlmutter, a board-certified neurologist and Fellow of the American College of Nutrition, called the study, "an important publication as it calls attention to the importance of viewing ASD holistically, as opposed to simply focusing on the brain."[93]

For parents who choose to vaccinate their kids, be aware that most vaccines are given in early childhood when both the microbiome and the immune system are developing. Careful attention should be given to understanding how the early microbiome affects vaccination, and how vaccination may influence the development of the early microbiome.[94]

According to the European Society for Neurogastroenterology and Motility "current CDC (Centers for Disease Control and Prevention) vaccine protocol beginning within twelve hours of birth does not factor gut microbiota as crucial to immune response."[95]

..............................................

91. Fattorusso, et al., "Autism Spectrum Disorders and the Gut Microbiota," 521.

92. Li, et al., "The Gut Microbiota and Autism Spectrum Disorders."

93. Perlmutter, "Autism Spectrum Disorder and Gut Bacteria: Hope Moving Forward."

94. Jamieson, "Influence of the Microbiome on Response to Vaccination," 2329–31.

95. Bell, "Gut Microbiota and Infant Vaccine Protocol."

Dr. Natasha Campbell-McBride, a medical doctor with two postgraduate degrees (master of medical sciences in neurology and master of medical sciences in human nutrition) is well-known for developing the concept of GAPS (Gut And Psychology Syndrome), which she describes in her book, *Gut And Psychology Syndrome: Natural Treatment for Autism, Dyspraxia, A.D.D., Dyslexia, A.D.H.D., Depression, Schizophrenia.* Campbell-McBride argues that the one thing that all the diagnoses of childhood asthma, eczema, diabetes, allergies, digestive disorders, ADHD, and austism have in common is a compromised immune system.[96] Campbell-McBride explains, "A compromised immune system is not going to react to environment insults in the normal way."[97] In some of these children [with compromised immune systems], vaccination, putting an enormous strain on the already compromised immune system, becomes that 'last straw which breaks the camel's back,' and brings on the beginnings of autism, asthma, eczema, diabetes, etc."[98]

Fermented/cultured foods are an acquired taste. You don't have to love kombucha, kimchi, *and* kefir. As long as you add some sort of fermented or cultured food to your diet, there's no reason to make all three.

A modern Western diet heavy on processed foods can upset the balance of your gut. Fermented/cultured foods help inoculate the gut with a variety of helpful bacteria. One of Mother Nature's easiest health hacks is to try mixing and matching gut-healthy foods like kefir, lacto-fermented pickles, good yogurt, sauerkraut (not the stuff in a can, it must be refrigerated and say "unpasteurized") and its bubbly cousins kimchi and kombucha. Just a couple of tablespoons of these foods, a few times a week, will add millions of probiotic bacteria to your gut.

More than two thousand years ago, Hippocrates said that "all disease begins in the gut." Who are we to argue with the ancient Greek physician known as the "father of medicine?" However, we prefer to put a more positive spin on his words and say that "all *health* begins in the gut." We agree with Michael Pol-

....................................................

96. Colletti, "Gut and Psychology Syndrome: GAPS: Part III."

97. Campbell-McBride, *Gut and Psychology Syndrome*, 68.

98. Campbell-McBride, *Gut and Psychology Syndrome*, 68.

lan, author of *Cooked: A Natural History of Transformation*, that fermenting your own foods is "a declaration of independence from an economy that would much prefer we remain passive consumers of its standardized commodities, rather than creators of idiosyncratic products expressive of ourselves."[99]

.................................................
99. Pollan, *Cooked: A Natural History of Transformation*, 414–15.

## CHAPTER FOUR
# HERBAL INFUSIONS

Women have always been healers. We were pharmacists, growing and harvesting healing herbs, and sharing the wisdom of their uses. We were nurses, counselors, and midwives. We learned from each other, and passed our knowledge from neighbor to neighbor and mother to daughter. Those in power called us "witches." The people called us "wise women."

## GROUNDED GOODWIFE STORY TIME
### *Herbal Beginnings* by Ehris

Unsuspectingly, I began my herbal studies in the safety of my gardens. Originally, I just wanted to grow vegetables. With only organic and heirloom seeds, I grew cherry tomatoes, kale, cucumbers, radishes, leeks, lettuce, squash, and sunflowers. My dad built me raised wooden planting beds, which we filled with four truckloads of horse manure shoveled from our neighbor's farm. In the Vitamix blender, I concocted homemade insect repellents from garlic, chili powder, and dish soap. The garden was my therapy, and I spent many peaceful hours building twig arbors and harvesting the bounty.

Then something magical started to happen. As I spent time alone weeding, watering, and working, the plants themselves began to mentor me. When I researched how to harvest the catnip I'd planted for our cat, Harry, I stumbled upon the use of catnip for menstrual cramps, insomnia, and nightmares. This led to a strong thirst to learn the healing energies of all the plants I was growing. I came home from the Woodbury library with piles of medicinal herb books, and signed up for classes.

As nerdy as it may sound, reading about the Latin names of herbs and their actions was cathartic. I loved the idea that every malady has a cousin that heals it. It wasn't just the actual herbs that cured me. It was also medicinal to work with them. I planted borage, mostly because of the unusual look of the flower; but when I brewed tea from its leaves and blossoms, it lifted my heavyheartedness. In one of my old botanical books, I read that jousters used borage because they believed it brought them courage, which was what it did for me. It gave me the courage to release my anger at Jose (a close family friend who'd betrayed and swindled us) and my grief over the dead end of our Brazilian dream. I delved deeper into my herb garden, and the perfumed walk became a mystical part of my world. Even the coldest winter eventually transforms into a field of green, flowers, and new life. The wise words in old herbal remedy books written by my healer foremothers brought me comfort. I felt empowered to stop being a broken heart.

When I first began my herbal studies, I never really thought any medicinal plants could grow in Connecticut because our winters are too cold and harsh. When I learned more, I realized how ridiculous that was! So many medicinal herbs grow wild in Connecticut and are considered "weeds"—like mullein, violet, nettle, St. John's wort, red clover, and mugwort. In our herb garden, we grow over thirty differ-ent non-GMO plants—classic ones like mint, lemon balm, rosemary, thyme, sage, and fennel—and lesser-known herbs like boneset, bor-age, rue, anise hyssop, and milk thistle.

Working with my plants gave me the courage to know that since I had healed myself, I could help others. I took the advice of one of my dog-eared herb books, which included a quote by Maya Angelou, "As soon as healing takes place, go out and heal somebody else." During my early days in the herb garden, I never dreamed that I'd go on to become an herbalist and public speaker (I guess the borage really worked!).

• • •

One of the easiest ways to make herbal medicine is by making herbal tea. In our herbalism basics class called "There's still thyme...," people always ask, "Is there caffeine in the loose-leaf tea we're going to make?" In reality, herbal tea isn't "tea" at all. Technically, only beverages derived from the *Camellia sinensis* plant—like black, green, oolong, white, and pu-erh—should be called tea. English Breakfast, Earl Grey, Darjeeling, and orange pekoe are all black teas that have been mixed and blended. Beverages made from plants other than *Camellia sinensis* should be referred to as "herbal infusions." So, if you're drinking "tea" made only from herbs, you're actually drinking an *herbal infusion*.

Many of the herbal teabags sold in stores are really just "dust," and don't have much medicinal value. People often think of herbal infusions just as something cozy to drink when you curl up with a good book or during a Netflix binge—not something that really does anything to improve your health. Herbal infusions *can* taste good, but they're blended specifically for health purposes. We like to think of them as "tea with a mission."

## HARVESTING HERBS

No matter where we teach our workshops, one of the top questions people ask is, "How do you harvest your herbs? Do you use bypass pruners, needle-nose hand shears, cultivation scissors, or straight-cutting loppers?"

Honestly, if we'd consulted books or online articles about how to harvest herbs, we would have been overwhelmed, disenchanted, and probably wouldn't have an herb garden today. In the years since we planted our first herb garden, we've come across so many rigid harvesting decrees. If you're new to the world of herbs, these unnecessary rules could be a complete turn-off: *Water your basil the night before you intend to harvest. Only pick herbs when they're dry. Only harvest oregano on a warm morning. If you are pinching with your fingers, clean your hands before starting. Begin harvesting the herb when the plant has enough foliage to maintain growth. Clean your scissors or cutting instrument before cutting each herb, since some herbs are susceptible to disease, which can spread to other plants.*

When to harvest an herb really depends on the part of the plant you plan to use. For leaves, like mint, skullcap, lemon balm, lemon verbena, catnip, anise hyssop, and comfrey, it's best to harvest them before a plant is in full bloom. If the leaves seem alive, full of color, healthy, and in their prime, it's time to harvest! It's best to harvest blossoms like borage, lavender, and chamomile when the flowers are just about to bloom, or are fully opened. For roots, like burdock, dandelion, astragalus, or valerian, harvest them when the plants are dormant—late fall to early spring. This is when the energy of the plant has gone from growth above the ground back to its roots.

We believe in doing things the simplest way possible. To harvest leaves, when an herb is at its peak, we go out to the herb garden with clippers from our junk drawer and cut the stalks at the base of the plant. To harvest flowers, we just use our fingers and collect the blossoms in a basket. We have mixed feelings about harvesting roots. Root medicine is powerful and effective, but it's hard to dig them up without damaging the entire plant. The only real exception we make are dandelions, because the roots are small and easy to dig up, and they're so plentiful at our house.

## Drying Herbs

And then, there's the second-most-popular herb question: "How do you dry your herbs? Do you use a dehydrator? Oven? Microwave?"

While it would be every herbalist's dream to be able to use fresh herbs year-round, that just isn't the case in most parts of the world. Drying herbs preserves their medicinal benefits for future use. Because dried herbs that are used as medicine should smell, taste, and look as close as possible to how they did before harvesting, it's not a good idea to dry them in the sun, microwave them, or leave them hanging for months on end.

To dry our herbs, we divide the herbs into bundles about the circumference of a pickling cucumber (if the bundles are too thick, they won't dry out). We put rubber bands around the bottom of the stalks and hang them upside down from square-cut nails in our kitchen's hand-hewn beams. A lot of our followers hang the bundles in their hot, dry attics. It takes about a month for the herbs to totally dry (you'll know when they're ready because they'll feel kind of crispy). If you let them hang for too long, they'll get kind of dusty.

## Garbling

Next, get ready to *garble* (a fancy way of saying "the process of separating the leaves, flowers, and stems, and discarding the unwanted parts"). Garbling your herbal harvest is the final step to ensuring you're just keeping the parts you're going to use as herbal medicine. When we garble, we keep the leaves and flowers, and compost the stems.

## Storing Herbs

Store dried herbs in airtight containers. We like to use glass jars, since we're not advocates of plastic. It's taken a few years, but we've built up a nice assortment from thrift shops. Label and date the jars, and place them in a cool, dry place out of direct sunlight.

If you store the leaves whole and crush them when you're ready to use them, the herbs will retain more flavor.

## GROUNDED GOODWIFE STORY TIME

### *Everything Looks Green* by Ehris

I wasn't prepared for my first bountiful herb garden harvest and didn't have enough glass jars for storing the dried herbs. I wound up temporarily storing some herbs in baggies and putting them on the floor of my apothecary. The next day, I came downstairs and saw that one of the baggies was kind of ripped open, and herbs were all over the floor. I swept them up and put the baggie back on the floor. The same thing happened the next day … and the next day. Finally, I realized that the herb was catnip—which I'd grown as a special treat for our cats,

Harry and Anthony. For those few days, we heard the cats running around upstairs, sounding like elephants, and we couldn't figure out why. Catnip is relaxing for humans, but the nepetalactone in catnip is a stimulant when sniffed by a cat. It produces a high similar to marijuana or LSD. So, the moral of the story is to *label your herbs*! You'll be convinced you'll remember what the herbs are—but as your apothecary shelves fill up with green "medicine," the contents of the glass jars will all start to look the same.

• • •

## HOW TO MAKE LOoSE-LEAF TEA/HERBAL iNFUSiONS

It always astounds us that many people don't realize they can use fresh herbs growing in their garden to make herbal infusions. It's also perfectly fine to use dried herbs. Fresh herbs generally have more volatile oils, giving them more flavor, but (at least in Connecticut) you can't harvest them year-round.

Many people shy away from making loose-leaf tea because they think it's too complicated or overwhelming. It's as simple as going out to your garden with a pair of scissors, or chopping up herbs you bought at the store.

For fresh herbs, use one tablespoon herbs per cup of water.

For dried herbs, use one to two teaspoons herbs per cup of water.

## GROUNDED GOODWIFE STORY TIME

### *The Secret to Herbal Infusions* by Ehris

Until recently, I used a tea ball/infuser to brew all of my blends. I can't believe it took me so many years to figure out the ultimate way to make herbal infusions. A friend of ours, who owns a chain of coffee shops in New York City, brought a French press coffee maker to our house for a weekend women's writer retreat because she knew we only had a pod coffee maker (my mom was actually embarrassed to tell her this, since our friend is a coffee connoisseur!). After the retreat ended, my mom went back to her pod coffee, and the French press was just sitting around in our pantry. One day, my mom went into the pantry to get some raisins, and came out enthusiastically waving the French press around in her hand. In her usual perky way, my mom said excitedly, "Ehris! Do you think you could make herbal tea with the French press?" My life was changed (I'm not even kidding). I make all of my herbal tea blends this way now. It's great because it strains the herbs so well that you don't end up drinking any leaves, and the tea stays hot.

• • •

## Steeping Herbal Infusions

Boxes of premade herbal teabags usually suggest steeping their blends for four to seven minutes, and then removing the teabag. But if you're looking for optimal health benefits, that's simply not long enough.

We steep all herbs (covered, to keep the herbal properties in your mug and not evaporating into the air) for at least ten minutes. It'll take some experimentation on your part, but herbs like chamomile and lavender get a little bitter after steeping for ten to fifteen minutes. For some herbs, like nettle, alfalfa, lemon balm, and linden, we usually steep them overnight to make a really medicinal tea. We strain them, and then warm them up (but never in a microwave!).

## Herbalism 101

Herbs are divided into at least forty different categories based on their medicinal action. For example:

- *Bitters*—like dandelion, burdock, and gentian—stimulate the gallbladder to release bile and the stomach to release hydrochloric acid, preparing the body for digestion. If you eat way too much at Thanksgiving and you're sitting on the couch feeling like a total blob, unable to move because you had too many pieces of pumpkin pie, you might want to try some bitters! Once that bitter taste hits your tongue, you'll be surprised how fast it works (within thirty to sixty seconds!) and that blobby feeling will go away. You can take bitters a bunch of different ways— chewing on fresh leaves, drinking tea, or taking tinctures. In order for this to work, the bitter taste has to actually touch your tongue, so bitters as capsules don't have this same effect.

- *Vulneraries*—like aloe, calendula, comfrey, and witch hazel—are soothing and healing for wounds, cuts, and burns. As we all know, aloe is a popular remedy for sunburn.

## GROUNDED GOODWIFE STORY TIME

### *Vulneraries in Action* by Ehris

When we moved into our Woodbury farmhouse, we didn't have an outdoor grill. An old neighbor offered us one they were getting rid of, but it was very temperamental when it came to lighting. Every time my dad wanted to buy a brand-new one, my mom insisted, "Nah, that's okay. This one's good enough."

One day, I saw my mom fiddling around with the knobs on the grill. Suddenly, a literal fireball blasted straight up out of the grill, engulfing my mom's hand. She screamed, "I can't look! I can't look!" I got her in the house and examined her charred hand. My mom doesn't remember too much of this whole story because I immediately started giving her shots of grain-alcohol-based sedative herb tinctures for the pain: valerian, passionflower, and hops. I soaked her hand in three vulnerary herbs: aloe gel, calendula, and comfrey (along with a few drops of Five Flower Formula). Since I'd pretty much drugged her and she was out of it (sedative herbs really work!), she got into bed. I slathered her hand with more aloe gel and wrapped comfrey leaves around it as an herbal Ace bandage. When I unwrapped her hand the next morning, all the charring was gone! Except for one tiny blister near her thumb, there was no damage. My mom insists, "The funniest part of the story was the morning after the fireball. Jim, of course, insisted that we buy a new grill. When I told the store owner, who looked just like Bruce Springsteen, about the terrible explosion and what had happened to my hand, it was very anticlimactic because there was nothing to see! I remember him looking at my hand and not being very amazed or impressed by the story. I'm a vulnerary believer!"

• • •

- *Nervines*—like lemon balm, lavender, chamomile, rosemary, spearmint, and hops—nourish the nervous system and help relieve stress and anxiety. Typically, if an herb has a strong smell (whether you think it smells good or bad), it's a nervine. We always try to include at least one nervine in our herbal infusion recipes, since *everyone* could use help with stress and/or anxiety.
- *Astringents*—like yarrow, elderflower, and sage—contract and tighten. They dry up bleeding, phlegm, and weeping poison ivy.

## GROUNDED GOODWIFE STORY TIME

### *Wilma* by Velya

I was forty-five minutes away from home when I heard the voice-mail from Mic: "Mommy, I just got home! Wilma bit off her own toe! There was blood all over the living room rug but it's okay now, I cleaned it up with Clorox. And, I found her toe."

To translate, Wilma was our 155-pound, six-year-old rescue Great Dane. That's it for the translation. I had no idea what the toe business meant. What was I most upset about: the thought of our poor maimed dog or the visual image of our decolorized living room rug? A CSI crime scene came to mind with an outlined chalk drawing of Wilma's stiff body surrounded by patches of bleached-out brown Berber synthetic carpeting. Blood! Clorox! The kid was in college, and the one time in his life that he cleans up a mess, he's got to do it with *bleach*?!

When I got home, Wilma enthusiastically greeted me at the door with a paper towel masking-taped around her front right paw. It promptly fell off. Blood dripped onto, and all over, the wooden kitchen floor. When she finally calmed down, I was able to see that although it looked gruesome, she hadn't bitten off her toe. For some reason, she had torn her toenail out by the roots and the bloody, meaty stump was exposed. With every step, blood dribbled out. Mic bounded down the stairs, eager to show me the bloody living room and the *toe*. The toe turned out to be her entire black toenail—and although the living room had the eye-watering smell of a heavily chlorinated hotel pool, the rug—thankfully—was still brown. Wilma followed us and left a fresh bloody trail on the rug. After experimenting, unsuccessfully, with paper towels and adhesive tape, I realized any bandage I constructed was just going to be eaten off.

Just then, Ehris got home from her job at New Morning (our local health food store), saw the blood, hurried out to her herb garden, and picked some yarrow leaves. She crushed them between her fingers, held them on Wilma's bloody toe, and within a minute, the yarrow's styptic properties stopped the bleeding. If I hadn't seen it, I never would have believed it could work so well.

About a week later, I got *another* type of voicemail—the kind where you feel vindicated and get to have the last laugh. I checked my cell phone after grocery shopping and heard the following message from Mic: "Yo, you know how I'm taking that Body Sculpting class for my gym requirement? Well, on the first day the guy said he wanted us to get a pedometer and wear it all semester and I was like 'F that.' Yesterday, he said that he'll be collecting our pedometers next week! I bought one and Googled it and it said the average person takes 5,000 steps a day. I did the math on a calculator to figure out how many times I have to shake this stupid thing to make it look accurate. 450,000 times! I have to shake it 450,000 times!"

I smiled all the way home.

Epilogue: If you ever need to rack up fake miles on a pedometer, it can be accomplished by sticking a wire coat hanger in a battery drill and attaching the pedometer to the other end. The miles accumulate slowly. I'm not sure what happened first—450,000 steps, or Wilma's new grown-in toenail.

• • •

# HERBAL INFUSION RECIPES

## WOMEN'S TONIC LOOSE-LEAF BLEND

This refreshing and uplifting nervine blend can help reduce stress and anxiety, increase energy and vitality, and support the adrenals. We serve this at many of the workshops we host at our farmhouse. Makes a little over three-quarters cup dried (enough for about eighteen cups of tea).

### INGREDIENTS

2 tablespoons dried lemon verbena

4 teaspoons dried spearmint

3 teaspoons dried nettle

2 teaspoons dried raspberry leaf

2 teaspooons dried licorice root

1 teaspoon dried red clover

### DIRECTIONS

1. Combine all herbs in a glass jar. Label the jar!
2. To make a cup of tea, use one teaspoon dried herbs per one cup water.
3. Steep (covered) for fifteen to thirty minutes.
4. Strain and drink!

## BENEFITS

- **Lemon verbena** (*Aloysia citrodora*) lifts the spirits and relaxes, and helps you get through tough times when life gives you too much to handle.

- **Spearmint** (*Mentha spicata*) renews, energizes, and refreshes without depleting or using up energy reserves.

- **Nettle** (*Urtica dioica*) is rich in a full spectrum of vitamins and minerals, especially calcium and iron. This stinging "weed" is Ehris' favorite tonic herb (a *tonic herb* helps fortify and build energy, and is nourishing for the body).

- **Raspberry leaf** (*Rubus idaeus*) has been used to strengthen the uterus during pregnancy since the sixth century. Today, many herbalists still recommend raspberry leaf during pregnancy to shorten labor and ease delivery. High in nutrients, especially iron and calcium, raspberry leaf has also been used to help regulate the menstrual cycle and ease menstrual cramps.[100]

- **Licorice root** (*Glycyrrhiza glabra*) is an *adaptogen*, which means it improves resistance to mental and physical stress—when stressful situations arise, you'll be more balanced and less affected. Licorice root is soothing for sore throats, has antiviral and anti-inflammatory properties, and supports the endocrine system. With its naturally sweet taste, this tonic herb is a great addition to tea blends. It seems that every time we serve this tea during one of our events and people read the ingredient label, there's always someone who's convinced we've chopped up Twizzlers (you know, the licorice candy) and thrown them in the teapot!

- **Red clover** (*Trifolium pratense*), considered a lawn weed by many, is one of nature's best vitamin and mineral supplements—containing beta-carotene, vitamin C, B vitamins, magnesium, manganese, zinc, and copper. It's calming and a mild sedative (don't worry, it won't make you groggy throughout the day—we've found that it just takes the edge off if you're feeling tense, stressed, or anxious). You may remember chewing on fresh red clover as a kid. You know how it's a little bit sweet? This

..................................................
100. Johnson, Foster, and Weil, *National Geographic Guide to Medicinal Herbs*, 301–3.

shows that red clover can add more sweetness to your life—especially if you're feeling bogged down, heavy-hearted, or if your daily routine is seeming kind of dull.

## BERRY HEALTHY LOOSE-LEAF BLEND

An immune-enhancing mix of fruity antiviral herbs, this blend is especially tasty with the addition of a little sweetener (we recommend honey or stevia!). Makes about ⅔ cup dried (enough for about eight cups of tea).

### INGREDIENTS

4 tablespoons dried lemon balm

3 tablespoons dried elderberry

3 tablespoons dried hibiscus

2 teaspoons dried mullein leaf

1 teaspoon dried rose hips

1 teaspoon cinnamon powder

### INSTRUCTIONS

1. Combine all herbs in a glass jar. Label the jar!
2. To make a cup of tea, use one teaspoon dried herbs per one cup water.
3. Steep (covered) for fifteen to thirty minutes.
4. Strain, add sweetener if desired, and drink!

### BENEFITS

- **Lemon balm** (*Melissa officinalis*): Antiviral lemon balm is a great herbal ally for cold and flu season! With its lemony flavor, this mood-elevating *nervine* is a nice addition to any herbal infusion. A member of the mint family, lemon balm reduces stress, tension, anxiety, and agitation, and also improves memory. It's also considered an *analgesic* (to use lemon balm to relieve pain, we've found it works best drunk as a tea *and* used as a poultice). But, since we're all about getting to the root cause of issues, make sure you examine possible reasons *why* you have the pain in the first place. Could it be caused by an emotional issue? Something you're eating that you shouldn't be? Don't expect lemon balm to cure all of your "junk." You have to put in some work, too!

- **Elderberries** (*Sambucus nigra*): Rich in vitamin C, elderberries are antiviral, inhibiting colds, flu, and herpes. As *adaptogens*, elderberries increase your resilience to stress (learn more about elderberries in our Elderberry Syrup recipe).

- **Hibiscus** (*Hibiscus rosa-sinensis*): This flower has a tart, almost cranberry-like flavor. Hibiscus supports the heart—physically and emotionally. In parts of Africa, hibiscus fruits are a favorite side dish, often served with ground peanuts.[101]

- **Mullein** (*Verbascum thapsus*): Whenever we talk about mullein in one of our workshops and show its photo, the audience in unison always bursts, "Oh! Is *that* what that is? That grows alongside my garage/road/rock garden!" Mullein is our favorite herb for supporting the respiratory system. Its fuzzy leaves, which feel similar to lamb's ear (the plant, or the animal), are an effective remedy for deep-seated coughs, bronchial infections, chest colds, allergies. Mullein moistens, softens, and clears congested "gunk," easing chest pain and inflammation.

  Mullein's yellow flowers, combined with garlic and olive oil and steeped in a glass jar for two to three weeks, are a traditional ear infection remedy. A few drops of the strained mixture, put directly into the ear every few hours, can fight the infection while relieving the pain just as effectively as an antibiotic (without any of the negative side effects of antibiotics).

  Herbalist Robin Rose Bennett recommends mullein to soften hard-heartedness, dissolve learned toughness, and open the mind to new possibilities.[102]

101. Johnson, Foster, and Weil, *National Geographic Guide to Medicinal Herbs*, 127.
102. Bennett, *The Gift of Healing Herbs*, 250–57.

- **Rose hips** (*Rosa canina*) are high in vitamins A, B, C, and K. One of the most well-studied rose hip benefits is their ability to treat osteoarthritis.[103]
- **Cinnamon** (*Cinnamomum verum*): A warming and relaxing herb, cinnamon is also antibacterial, antiviral, antifungal, and antioxidant. Along with dietary changes, it can help regulate blood sugar, and it improves mental energy, concentration, and motivation. *Avoid large doses during pregnancy.*

## JOURNEY TEA LOOSE-LEAF BLEND

Warning: avoid this tea if you're taking birth control or HRT! The herbs in this recipe may help regulate your hormones, which can override prescriptions. This is Velya's favorite tea blend. She says, "It tastes important," and loves its unique bitter/sweet taste, either hot or cold.

Supporting the liver's cleansing process assists the hormonal state of the body, and the herbs in this infusion are designed to do just that. They stimulate the liver and normalize hormonal function. It's a perfect blend for issues involving menstruation, premenopause, and menopause (as long as you're not taking birth control or HRT). Makes a little over ¾ cup (enough for about ten cups of tea).

### INGREDIENTS

5 teaspoons dandelion root

4 teaspoons Vitex (aka chaste tree berries)

4 teaspoons sassafras bark

3 teaspoons shatavari root

2 teaspoons licorice root

1 teaspoon dried ginger root

---

103. Cohen, "Rosehip - An Evidence Based Herbal Medicine for Inflammation and Arthritis," 495–8; Christensen, et al., "Does the Hip Powder of *Rosa canina* (Rosehip)Reduce Pain in Osteoarthritis Patients?: A Meta-Anaylsis of Randomized Controlled Trials," S220.

## DIRECTIONS

1. Combine all herbs in a glass jar. Label the jar!
2. Use two teaspoons dried herbs per one cup water.
3. Steep (covered) twenty to thirty minutes.
4. Strain and drink!

## BENEFITS

- **Dandelion root** (*Taraxacum officinale*) is a bitter *hepatic* herb—it cleanses the liver. This "weed" is also a *diuretic*. Pharmaceutical diuretics can dangerously deplete your potassium levels, but dandelion increases the elimination of toxins and wastes through the liver and kidneys as it replenishes the body's potassium.

- **Vitex** (*Vitex agnus-castus*), aka chaste tree, has been used for thousands of years to treat menstrual and hormonal issues. Today, many herbalists (and some European gynecologists) still recommend chaste tree berries for menstrual irregularity, breast tenderness, fertility issues, and hot flashes.[104] A three-month study, published in the *British Medical Journal*, tested the effectiveness of chaste tree in 178 women with PMS. The results showed that chaste tree users had a significant improvement in their PMS symptoms, which included irritability, moodiness, anger, headache, and breast fullness.[105]

- **Sassafras** (*Sassafras albidum*) has been long-valued as a liver-supporter and blood purifier—especially to purify the blood of winter stagnation. We both take sassafras bark internally, but unfortunately, it's not mentioned in many herbal books anymore. Rosemary Gladstar writes in *Herbal Recipes for Vibrant Health*, "In the 1970s, *safrole*, a highly toxic chemical constituent found in sassafras, was isolated, extracted with chemical solvents, and tested on laboratory rats. It was found, not surprisingly, that in large amounts, it produced carcinogenic cells in the rats. No human case of cancer from sassafras has ever been reported. ... Interestingly, the population of the southeastern United

104. Johnson, Foster, and Weil, *National Geographic Guide to Medicinal Herbs*, 286–89.
105. Shaw, et al., "Vitex Agnus Castus for Premenstrual Syndrome."

States, where sassafras tea is a traditional folk remedy, has the lowest rate of throat cancer in the county."[106] We continue to use it, and find it extremely valuable and effective. Of course, the decision is up to you.

- **Shatavari root** (*Asparagus racemosus*): Arguably the most important herb in Ayurvedic medicine for women, shatavari has been used for centuries—mainly for treating issues relating to women's health. Shatavari has been valued among Ayurvedic practitioners as a nourishing, cooling, soothing herb helpful in treating conditions where the body and mind are depleted or out of balance. It's especially used for fertility issues, irregular menstrual cycles, PMS, and during menopause.[107]

- **Licorice root** (*Glycyrrhiza glabra*) is excellent for toning and strengthening the endocrine system—including the adrenal glands (licorice root is a specific remedy for adrenal exhaustion).[108] To combat stress and live a more balanced life, it's essential to optimize adrenal gland function. Especially if you're feeling stressed and overworked, supporting the adrenals can help sustain healthy energy and stress levels.

- **Ginger** (*Zingiber officinale*): Warming and decongesting, ginger is an effective (and tasty!) remedy for menstrual cramps, PMS, nausea, motion sickness, seasickness, poor circulation, respiratory congestion, colds, and flu.

## GROUNDED GOODWIFE STORY TIME

### *Trees Without Fruit?!* by Velya

Menopause is the time when a woman passes from her childbearing years into a transformational process. To many people, menopausal women are regarded as prunes, their shriveling ovaries making them dried-up versions of their former selves. John Oldham, the seventeenth century English poet, believed that menopausal women were "nothing but lost and nasty souls." He argued that "were they trees without fruit," they would be "hewn down and cast into the fire."[109]

....................................................

106. Gladstar, *Rosemary Gladstar's Herbal Recipes for Vibrant Health*, 363.

107. Johnson, Foster, and Weil, *National Geographic Guide to Medicinal Herbs*, 305–7.

108. Gladstar, *Rosemary Gladstar's Medicinal Herbs*, 163.

109. Foxcroft, *Hot Flushes, Cold Science*, 127.

In the 1692 Salem witch trials, the accused were overwhelmingly women because they were "known" to be weaker and more susceptible to sinful impulses than men. Postmenopausal women were particularly vulnerable as they no longer served the purpose of procreation, and these women deviated from accepted norms and expected roles.

In his 1972 (not 1572!) best-selling book, *Everything You Always Wanted to Know About Sex, But Were Afraid to Ask*, Dr. David Reuben declared, "To many women, the menopause marks the end of their useful life. They see it as the onset of old age, the beginning of the end. They may be right. Having outlived their ovaries, they may have outlived their usefulness as human beings. The remaining years may be just marking time until they follow their glands into oblivion."[110]

I think people, especially men, are afraid of postmenopausal women—and that delights me. I think it's because we're assertive, strong, and unafraid. The statistics are all over the internet. By the year 2030, there will be 1.2 billion menopausal and postmenopausal women, with an added forty-seven million new entrants each year.[111] Can you imagine what we women could accomplish with all that collective zest? Banning GMOs, taking on Big Pharma and insurance companies, tackling climate change, fighting vaccine mandates, eliminating fracking, fixing our educational system and health cost messes, instituting paid maternity leave, addressing reproductive freedoms, establishing equal pay—and, it's high time to get a woman on a hundred dollar bill. And there are millions of sisters "hot" on my heels to make changes!

• • •

110. Rovner, "Healthtalk: The Myths Of Menopause."

111. Haan, "Women's Health," 16528–32.

## CHILL OUT! LOOSE-LEAF BLEND

This minty nerve-tonic blend, which feeds and nourishes the brain, gently increases mental alertness and vitality while reducing stress, anxiety, and tension. This blend actually tastes better served cold!

Makes a little over half a cup dried (enough for about ten cups of tea).

### INGREDIENTS

2 tablespoons dried spearmint

2 tablespoons dried green milky oat tops

2 tablespoons dried lemongrass

2 teaspoons dried ginkgo

2 teaspoons dried gotu kola

### INSTRUCTIONS

1. Combine all herbs in a glass jar. Label the jar!
2. To make a cup of tea, use two teaspoons dried herbs per one cup water.
3. Steep (covered) for fifteen to twenty minutes.
4. Strain, add sweetener if desired, and drink!

### BENEFITS

- **Spearmint** (*Mentha spicata*): Uplifting and refreshing, spearmint has *amphoteric* properties (amphoteric herbs know what your body needs). Interestingly, it can be either calming *or* energizing depending on what your body needs. If you're feeling stressed, tense, or exhausted, a cup of spearmint tea can be a relaxing nerve-tonic. Conversely, some people who take long car drives sniff spearmint essential oil along the way to keep them focused and alert.
- **Green milky oat tops** (*Avena sativa*): Fully-ripe oats are served as oatmeal. Green milky oat tops are oats in their green stage, which release a

tiny bit of "oat milk" when squeezed. Green milky oat tops are one of the best nutritive tonics for the nervous system, and can relieve nervous exhaustion, irritation, and anxiety. Research has been conducted that shows milky oat tops, in combination with lemon balm, can counteract hyperactivity in kids and adults.[112]

- **Lemongrass** (*Cymbopogon citratus*): increases the body's ability to repair damaged connective tissue like cartilage, ligaments, and tendons. As a *diuretic*, this citrus-flavored herb helps the body remove toxins by cleansing the kidneys and liver, increasing urination. We recommend lemongrass tea if you're feeling exhausted, burned out, or stressed. It heightens awareness and promotes a positive outlook. Lemongrass is also known as "fever grass," and is used for malaria and cholera.

- **Ginkgo** (*Ginkgo biloba*) helps relieve anxiety and depression. It's also been used to improve memory, diminishing eyesight, and hearing loss.

- **Gotu kola** (*Centella asiatica*), a nerve tonic, calms insomnia, anxiety, stress, and mental turbulence. In China, gotu kola is sometimes called "the fountain of life."[113] According to legend, a gotu kola–eating herbalist named Li Ching-Yuen lived for over two hundred years.

  Gotu kola is considered a brain food. You know the saying, "An elephant never forgets"? It may be because elephants love gotu kola! In Sri Lanka, it's common knowledge that elephants (who are known to have long lives and great memories) love to eat this herb. The locals follow their example, eating a few leaves a day.[114]

## FORTY WINKS LOOSE-LEAF BLEND

This is a blend of effective, yet gentle, sleep-inducing herbs. It's also helpful in reducing stress and anxiety! Makes about ½ cup dried (enough for about sixteen cups of tea).

..................................................

112. Gladstar, *Rosemary Gladstar's Medicinal Herbs*, 181.

113. "Mountain Rose Herbs: Gotu Kola." Mountain Rose Herbs.

114. "Gotu Kola." Penn State Hershey Health Information Library.

## INGREDIENTS

¼ teaspoons dried chamomile

4 teaspoons dried skullcap

3 teaspoons dried licorice root

1 teaspoon dried catnip

1 teaspoon dried passionflower

½ teaspoon dried rosemary

## INSTRUCTIONS

1. Combine all herbs in a glass jar. Label the jar!
2. Use two teaspoons dried herbs per one cup water.
3. Steep (covered) ten to fifteen minutes.
4. Strain and drink!

## BENEFITS

- **Chamomile** (*Matricaria chamomilla*): Many people hold their tension, worry, or stress in their stomach or solar plexus. After a while, all that junk accumulates, and can lead to insomnia (usually caused by repetitive thoughts). Chamomile helps release this tension, and promotes calm and serenity.
- **Licorice root** (*Glycyrrhiza glabra*): As an adaptogen, licorice root improves resistance to mental and physical stress—when stressful situations arise, you'll be more balanced and less affected. Licorice root is soothing for sore throats, has antiviral and anti-inflammatory properties, and supports the endocrine system. With its naturally sweet taste, this tonic herb is a great addition to tea blends.
- **Skullcap** (*Scutellaria lateriflora*) has traditionally been used to help quiet the mind, treat insomnia, and ease anxiety and irritability.

# GROUNDED GOODWIFE STORY TIME

*Feel a Headache Coming On?* by Ehris

To me, skullcap is one of the most relaxing herbs. When I drink a cup of hot skullcap tea, I can actually feel my neck and shoulder tension releasing. I very rarely get headaches, but if I feel one coming on, I drink a cup of skullcap tea, and my headache is gone in less than thirty minutes.

• • •

- **Catnip** (*Nepeta cataria*)—calming for humans—has the total opposite effect on cats! For humans, catnip soothes the nerves, relaxes tension, and relieves stress.
- **Passionflower** (*Passiflora incarnata*): Passionflower's leaves and extravagantly beautiful blossoms are extremely calming and soothing to the nervous system. Ehris very rarely experiences anxiety or insomnia, but if she does, she drinks a cup of passionflower tea as a gentle sedative.
- **Rosemary** (*Salvia rosmarinus*): Many people use rosemary only as a seasoning on their roasted potatoes or roasted chicken. Little do they know that rosemary can be made into an herbal tea! It tastes kind of minty, and is helpful for anxiety, depression, exhaustion, and insomnia.

If you can boil water, you can make a medicinal infusion. Herbal infusions can be used on a one-time basis for an acute situation. They can also be used on a regular basis as part of a healthy diet. Many of the plants you can use are free wild "weeds" growing right outside your door, or they can be easily cultivated in your own garden, or purchased in bulk. The simple act of cupping your hands around an infusion you created will directly involve you in your self-healing process.

## CHAPTER FIVE

# HEALTHFUL DECADENCE: LIQUEURS AND CHOCOLATES

Kale chips and hummus... rice cakes topped with vegan "cheese" spread... mushroom jerky...

Do these "treats" sound indulgent and decadent? Umm... they don't sound very thrilling to us either! Yet so many people think that living the green witch life is synonymous with deprivation and denial. We definitely do *not* recommend living a life completely devoid of tasty goodies. Even the strictest keto, paleo, gluten-free, fat-free, raw food, vegetarian, or vegan followers have to admit that nothing compares to a fudgy brownie, crackly on top, moist inside, with a glass of cold raw milk. Let go of guilt! It's not realistic to go through life never enjoying "forbidden" foods and drinks.

Our herbal liqueurs are an enticing way to experiment with unfamiliar beneficial herbs, and our chocolate truffles are filled with medicinal herbs, healthy fats, and just enough natural sweetness to satisfy even the fiercest sweet tooth.

Stress can't exist in the presence of these recipes!

## HERBAL LIQUEURS AND CORDIALS

A liqueur or cordial is an alcoholic beverage that's been flavored with fruit, herbs, nuts, spices, flowers, or cream, and bottled with added sugar. They're usually not aged for long, but may have resting periods to allow flavors to marry. Italian monks, during the thirteenth century, developed liqueurs/cordials as a way to infuse herbs for medicinal use.[115]

Many liqueurs can trace their roots back to the apothecaries of the fifteenth and sixteenth centuries. These were used as medicines, prescribed to invigorate the body, settle the stomach, and cure diseases. Some were considered aphrodisiacs, which made them very much sought after among the nobility. Some even had gold flakes or pearls added, as these precious ingredients were considered a great help in preventing disease.

By the eighteenth century, liqueurs were popular amongst the aristocracy—more so for their intoxicating effects than for medicinal purposes.[116] We prefer the original approach to liqueurs, emphasizing their medicinal herbal benefits.

When we offered our very first Grounded Goodwife class at our 1770 farmhouse, we had no idea if anyone would come, but we thought if the workshop topic involved alcohol, we would have a better chance of getting a crowd. We decided to invent an herbal Apple Brandy Cordial recipe and scheduled the workshop for September. Considering we don't even drink, it's pretty astounding how great the recipe turned out. We knew we were on to something with our Grounded Goodwife idea when we had a waiting list for the class. When they sipped the cordial samples, everyone oohed and aahed, "This tastes just like apple pie in a glass!"

Herbal liqueurs, the historical descendants of herbal medicine, are a nonintimidating way to start incorporating unusual herbs into your repertoire. As you make our Apple Brandy Cordial, Kith-and-Kin Bloody Mary, Shatavari Cocoa Cordial, and Pumpkin Rum *Yo-ho-ho!* Cider, perhaps you'll see yourself as a robed monk, working in silence behind monastery walls to create delicious alcoholic concoctions.

..............................................
115. Hajeski, *National Geographic Complete Guide to Herbs and Spices*, 217.

116. Ming Lee, "Steeped in History: A Cordial, Liqueur or Schnapps Is a Tonic Whatever You Call It."

## APPLE BRANDY CORDIAL: HOW DO YA LIKE *THEM* APPLES?

This premier Grounded Goodwife recipe tastes like apple pie in a glass! With a pretty ribbon tied around the neck of the bottle, this cordial makes a great gift. In the 1800s, approximately fourteen thousand apple varieties were grown in North America. Today, fewer than one hundred varieties are grown commercially, and only a handful are available in grocery stores.[117] Makes about three cups.

### INGREDIENTS

6 medium apples, preferably organic, chopped (unpeeled, but we remove the seeds)

1 ½ cups sugar

½ teaspoon cinnamon

½ teaspoon vanilla extract

2 teaspoons dried organic astragalus root

¼ cup dried organic alfalfa

3 cups brandy (no need to buy the expensive brand)

### INSTRUCTIONS

1. Combine all ingredients in a gallon glass screw-top jar or mason jar.
2. Let the jar stand for twenty-four hours. Turn it upside down and let stand another twenty-four hours. Repeat until sugar dissolves.
3. Store in a dark place for a minimum of four weeks, shaking the jar occasionally.
4. Strain and pour into bottles (we use narrow-neck bottles). This liqueur makes a very appreciated housewarming, hostess, or thank-you gift.

......................................................
117. Hensley, "A Curious Tale: The Apple in North America."

Suggestion: Make your own "Tipsy Applesauce" with the strained apples for a potent boozy treat! People love it served on top of apple crisp or ice cream. It lasts in the fridge for a long, long time.

- **Astragalus** (*Astragalus membranaceus*), native to Mongolia and China, is a popular tonic herb used to increase vitality, strengthen immunity, and enhance endurance. An *adaptogen*, it helps the body adapt and respond to stress. It's used in the treatment of cancer, chronic hepatitis, HIV, and autoimmune disease. We take it during the winter as a prophylactic against colds and upper respiratory infections. *Use cautiously with immunosuppressive drugs.*

- **Alfalfa** (*Medicago sativa*): "Alfalfa? Isn't that what they feed cows, horses, and rabbits?" A tonic herb, alfalfa contains one of the highest chlorophyll contents of any land plant. Alfalfa may be used to relieve arthritis, ease menopause symptoms (when combined with sage), and alleviate allergies. It's been known to send its roots forty-nine feet underground to reach nutrients it can't get on the surface. *Don't use alfalfa in combination with blood thinners.*

- **Cinnamon** (*Cinnamomum verum*) is antibacterial, antiviral, antifungal, and antioxidant. It can help regulate blood sugar, and improves mental energy, concentration, and motivation. *Avoid large doses in pregnancy.*

- **Apples** (*Malus domestica*): Hildegard von Bingen (the famous twelfth-century German Benedictine abbess, writer, composer, philosopher, Christian mystic, visionary, and healer) prescribed raw apples as a tonic for healthy people, and cooked apples as the first treatment for any sickness.[118]

### KITH-AND-KIN BLOODY MARYS

Don't be put-off by the pinkish color—this is what Bloody Mary mix without additives or dyes looks like! According to the US Department of Agriculture,

---

118. Wallace, "Commonly Used Medicinal Plants."

there are twenty-five thousand tomato varieties.[119] We suggest conducting your own research (wink, wink) to see which of the twenty-five thousand varieties makes the best Bloody Mary! Makes four cups.

## INGREDIENTS

4 large tomatoes, preferably organic, chopped (unpeeled, leave the seeds in)

Juice from 1 lime

4 teaspoons Worcestershire sauce

1¼ teaspoons horseradish (fresh, or the stuff in the jar is fine—but, as we recently discovered, some brands of ready-made horseradish include corn syrup!)

1 sprig oregano

2 sprigs thyme

2 sprigs parsley

1¼ teaspoons salt

1¼ teaspoons black pepper

4 ounces vodka

Ice

## INSTRUCTIONS

1. In a blender, puree the tomatoes, lime juice, Worcestershire sauce, horseradish, herbs, salt, and pepper until smooth.
2. Fill each glass with ice, one ounce vodka, and approximately ⅔ cup fresh Bloody Mary mixture.
3. Garnish with celery and/or lemon, and add Worcestershire sauce if desired.

### SHATAVARI COCOA CORDIAL

Of all of our Grounded Goodwife recipes, this is by far the most popular. This creamy cordial—with hints of lightly-toasted caramel and warming vanilla—

..................................................
119. Childress, "Tomato Varieties! Humble to Humongous & More!"

includes shatavari, the most important rejuvenating tonic herb for women in Ayurvedic medicine. Men, as well as women, are crazy about this cordial! Makes five, twelve-ounce bottles.

## INGREDIENTS

27 ounces coconut milk

28 ounces sweetened condensed milk

4 tablespoons instant coffee

2 tablespoons almond extract

1 tablespoon vanilla extract

4 tablespoons organic chocolate syrup

2 teaspoons organic shatavari root powder

1 teaspoon organic ashwagandha root powder

1½ cups spiced rum

## INSTRUCTIONS

1. Blend all in a blender.

2. We recommend pouring it into mason-type jars, and shaking the jars well before pouring into glasses. If you pour the blender contents into narrow-neck bottles, the coconut milk will eventually solidify at the top, making it hard to pour.

3. All of these ingredients are shelf-stable, so it doesn't have to be refrigerated.

## SUGGESTIONS

- You can totally omit the rum from this recipe. As Ehris, who loves creamy drinks, insists, "It's like twelve million times better without alcohol!"

- Try experimenting with different types of milks—goat, raw, almond, etc. (Obviously, if you use dairy, you'll have to refrigerate your cordial.)

## BENEFITS

- **Shatavari** (*Asparagus racemosus*) translates to "she who possesses a hundred husbands." It's the most important rejuvenating tonic for women in Ayurvedic medicine. Used widely throughout other parts of the world, especially India, it's not well-known in the United States. Shatavari (wild asparagus) is an *adaptogen*, meaning it helps the body respond to stress. It reduces anxiety, is effective for children with ADD/ADHD, enhances fertility, regulates hormonal imbalances, is useful during menopause, and is antibacterial and antitumor.[120]

- **Ashwagandha** (*Withania somnifera*) native to India, is one of the most important herbs in Ayurvedic medicine. Also an *adaptogen*, it boosts strength and vitality, and is an exceptional nerve and reproductive tonic. As an immune-enhancing herb, ashwagandha is often used for chronic immune issues like fibromyalgia, HIV, lupus, and MS. The plant kind of smells like burned rubber. *Avoid using more than three grams daily during pregnancy.*

## PUMPKIN RUM *YO-HO-HO!* CIDER

This warm twist on spiked apple cider is perfect for those first chilly fall days when you can wear a sweatshirt and shorts. Those are the days when Velya, who's dripped with sweat all summer, comes back to life. This recipe is perfect for a Halloween party for kids and adults. You can ladle the alcohol-free "cider" into mugs, and adults can add their own rum (or not). Makes about three and three-quarters cups.

## INGREDIENTS

1 cup pureed pumpkin (not pumpkin pie mix)

2½ cups apple cider

1¼ teaspoon cinnamon

¼ teaspoon ginger

¼ teaspoon nutmeg

....................................................
120. McIntyre, *The Complete Herbal Tutor*, 111.

⅛ teaspoon allspice

3 ground cloves

1 teaspoon organic eleuthero root powder

1 teaspoon organic hawthorn berry powder

⅓ cup spiced rum

## INSTRUCTIONS

1. In a medium pot, mix together the pumpkin puree, apple cider, spices, and herbs (don't add the rum yet!).
2. Bring the mixture to a boil, then reduce to low and simmer for twenty minutes.
3. Remove from heat, pour into mugs, add rum, stir, and serve warm.
4. Top with whipped cream for an extra treat!

## BENEFITS

- **Eleuthero** (*Eleutherococcus senticosus*) has been used in China for over two thousand years. In Russia, research has been conducted on the effects of eleuthero on athletes and workers.[121] It's been shown to help people cope with, and recover from, adverse conditions and physical performance. Eleuthero increases blood flow through the arteries to the brain, and is used for ADHD, as well as failing memory in the elderly. It enhances immunity against infections, including coughs and colds. *Avoid using with digoxin.*

- **Hawthorn** (*Crataegus monogyna*) is considered a supreme cardiac tonic. It strengthens and tones the heart and blood vessels, and can help regulate blood pressure. It's also a wonderful herb to heal the emotional heart from deep grief, sadness, or broken heartedness. *If you're taking heart medication/beta blockers, check with your physician before taking hawthorn.*

- **Allspice** (*Pimenta dioica*) Maybe we're the only ones that didn't know this, but allspice is made from the dried berries of a plant known as the

---

121. McIntyre, *The Complete Herbal Tutor*, 127.

*Pimenta diocia*, which is a member of the myrtle family. We thought it was a blend of cinnamon, cloves, and nutmeg.

- **Pumpkin** (*Cucurbita pepo*) contains beta-carotene (which acts as an internal sunscreen and protects against UV damage) and amino acids (which strengthen the connective tissue and reinforce elasticity). Pumpkin contains one of the highest contents of naturally-occurring vitamin A and beta-carotene over any other fruit (yes, it's a fruit, not a vegetable).

## CHoCOLATE TRUFFLES

One of the most celebrated episodes of *I Love Lucy* features Lucy and Ethel frantically working on a chocolate factory assembly line with Lucy's cheeks bulging as she tries to "hide" chocolates. Many people today still love Lucy—and chocolate—as much as they did when the episode first aired in 1952! Lovestruck Americans spend $448 million every year on Valentine's Day candy—which amounts to fifty-eight million pounds of chocolate and thirty-six million heart-shaped boxes.[122] But what does chocolate have to do with the most romantic day of the year?

It turns out that chocolate really *does* have a history as a love food. It was a highly-prized luxury among Olmec, Maya, and Aztec upper-class elites, who claimed that cacao (the raw form of cocoa) was a supremely powerful aphrodisiac. They indulged in a spicy, frothy drink combining fermented, roasted cacao seeds with cornmeal, vanilla, honey, and chili peppers.[123]

By 1670, advertising pamphlets in London proclaimed that a mere lick of chocolate would "make old women young and fresh, and create new motions of the flesh."[124]

Until this point, people had only been *drinking* chocolate, but Richard Cadbury, whose British family manufactured chocolate, was searching for a way to use pure cocoa butter. He created "eating chocolates" in 1861, which

...............................

122. Klatell, "How Much Caffeine Is In That Piece Of Chocolate?"

123. Johnson, Foster, and Weil, *National Geographic Guide to Medicinal Herbs*, 107.

124. Green, "How the Decadence and Depravity of 18th-Century London Was Fueled by Hot Chocolate."

he packaged in unique heart-shaped boxes adorned with cupids and rose-buds. Even when the chocolates had been eaten, people could use the ornate boxes to save mementos such as love letters.[125]

Chocolate pioneer Milton Hershey started as a caramel maker, but in 1894 began covering his caramels with sweet chocolate. In 1907, Hershey launched production of teardrop-shaped "kisses." According to Philomena Krosmico, director of manufacturing for West Hershey and Reese's plants, "There's a belt the chocolate goes down, it pulls up, makes a little kiss sound, and that's where legend says the name came from."[126] The kisses were afford-able, mass-produced, and advertised as "a most nourishing food."[127]

We like to think that our medicinal chocolate truffles are more nourishing than Milton Hershey's "Kisses" because of our herbal additions. A chocolate truffle is a type of chocolate confectionary traditionally made with a choc-olate ganache center, coated in chocolate, cocoa powder, or chopped nuts, usually in the shape of a ball. The name "truffle" comes from the traditional shape of the mushroom/fungus truffle.

Cacao, the raw, unprocessed form of cocoa, is nutrient-dense. If you feel a little better after eating some chocolate, it's not your imagination! Cacao contains the mood-booster anandamide—known as the "bliss molecule"[128]—which gives you a feeling of euphoria. Montezuma, the Aztec emperor who was killed by his own people by stones, spears, and arrows, drank fifty cups of cacao a day from a golden chalice.[129]

While our truffles aren't necessarily as healthy as seaweed or brussels sprouts, they're easy to make, no cooking required, and you get a healthy dose of beneficial herbs!

......................................

125. Butler, "Celebrating Valentine's Day With a Box of Chocolates."

126. "Hershey's Kisses: Fun Facts and Recipes." ABC News.

127. Henderson, "How Chocolate and Valentine's Day Mated for Life."

128. Levy, "What Are Cacao Nibs? Nutrition, Benefits, Uses and Recipes."

129. "Fun Facts about Chocolate." NCA.

## GOJI BERRY GINKGO HAZELNUT CACAO TRUFFLES

Goji berries are believed to protect against eye diseases, but their weird taste (kind of like a tomato and cranberry mixed together) can make them difficult to incorporate into your diet. The cacao and dates in this recipe help camouflage their flavor. Ginkgo improves focus and memory, and stimulates creative thinking.

Goji berries could interact with some drugs. If you take blood thinners, blood pressure medication, or diabetes medication, you may want to avoid goji berries.[130] Avoid ginkgo with anticoagulant drugs. Makes approximately ten truffles.

### INGREDIENTS

½ cup hazelnuts

2 tablespoons raw cacao powder (cocoa powder may be substituted)

6 pitted dates

2 tablespoons goji berries

1 teaspoon ginkgo powder

1 tablespoon coconut oil

2 tablespoons cold water

### INSTRUCTIONS

1. In a food processor, blend hazelnuts, cacao, dates, goji berries, and ginkgo powder until chopped and combined well.

2. Place all ingredients in a mixing bowl. Add coconut oil and cold water.

3. Mix with your hands to combine well. The warmth of your hands is needed to melt the coconut oil (some people prefer to wear gloves since it's kind of a tactile experience).

4. Get ready to roll! Take a small amount of the mixture (about the size of a cherry tomato) and roll it into a ball.

......................................................

130. Flessa, "Goji Berries Trivia: Eighteen Unknown Facts about the Popular Fruit!"

5. Optional: coat the truffles in toppings (like chopped nuts, mini chocolate chips, or shredded coconut). Cover thoroughly by rolling and pressing to cover each ball evenly.

6. Keep refrigerated.

## BENEFITS

- **Ginkgo** (*Ginkgo biloba*): The oldest fossil record of ginkgo is over two hundred million years old, which means it existed when dinosaurs roamed the earth.[131] Ginkgo is considered one of the best herbs for maintaining and improving brain function.

- **Goji berries** (*Lycium barbarum*) are an exceptionally good source of vitamin C and may be nature's most complete eye health food.

# GROUNDED GOODWIFE STORY TIME

### *Give Yourself a Break!* by Ehris

Participants at our workshops continually insist that their memories are failing, and they need help. Today, we're bombarded more than ever before with information—so be kind to yourself. Don't be convinced you're "losing your marbles" if you forget something.

Former Google CEO, Eric Schmidt, explains, "There were five exabytes of information created between the dawn of civilization through 2003, but that much information is now created every two days, and the pace is increasing. ... People aren't ready for the technology revolution that's going to happen to them."[132] Perhaps software creator Mitch Kapor's simile describes it best: "Getting information off the internet is like taking a drink from a fire hydrant."

• • •

131. Cohn, "The Life Story of the Oldest Tree on Earth."

132. Kirkpatrik, "Google CEO Schmidt: 'People Aren't Ready for the Technology Revolution.'"

## TOFFEE CACAo NETTLE TRUFFLES

This is our favorite truffle recipe, primarily because of the crackly, crunchy toffee. Nettle is a nourishing, nutritive tonic herb, rich in a full spectrum of vitamins and minerals, especially calcium and iron. Nettle's antihistamine properties make it an effective remedy for allergies and hay fever. Makes approximately ten truffles.

### INGREDIENTS

½ cup almonds

3 tablespoons raw cacao powder (cocoa powder may be substituted)

6 pitted dates

1 teaspoon nettle powder

5 tablespoons toffee bits (like Heath)

1 tablespoon coconut oil

2 tablespoons cold water

Optional: pinch of cayenne powder

### INSTRUCTIONS

1. In a food processor, blend almonds, cacao, dates, and nettle powder until chopped and combined well.

2. Place all ingredients in a mixing bowl, and add coconut oil, cold water, and optional cayenne powder.

3. Mix with your hands to combine well. The warmth of your hands is needed to melt the coconut oil (some people prefer to wear gloves since it's kind of a tactile experience).

4. Get ready to roll! Take a small amount of the mixture (about the size of a cherry tomato) and roll it into a ball.

5. Optional: coat the truffles in toppings (like chopped nuts, mini chocolate chips, or shredded coconut). Cover thoroughly by rolling and pressing to cover each ball evenly.

6. Keep refrigerated.

## GROUNDED GOODWIFE STORY TIME

### *Nettle* by Ehris

Whenever we mention stinging nettle (*Urtica dioica*) in our green witch workshops, someone always pipes up in horror, "Stinging nettle? I hate stinging nettle!"

If you've ever bumped into a nettle plant, you probably hate the plant, since nettle has little stinging hairs that can leave a rash. But nettle—one of the most nutrient-dense plants that grow on Earth—is my absolute favorite herb. As a green witch, one of my favorite healing tips comes from medical herbalist David Hoffmann, "When in doubt, use nettle."

A few years ago, I was teaching a Healing with Connecticut Weeds class, and we took a field trip to the White Memorial boardwalk in Litchfield, Connecticut. I pointed nettle out to my students, told them about the stinging, and also told them something I'd heard from a fellow herbalist: that if you're nice to nettle, talk to it like it's a person, and say things like, "Hey nettle, I don't want to hurt you, I just want to hang out with you," it won't sting you.

My students rolled their eyes and smirked, "Are you crazy, Ehris? That's ridiculous!"

Convinced they were going to prove me wrong, each of them lovingly snipped off a stalk of nettle. They cradled the nettle in their hands, and as we continued our herb walk, I heard sweet talk such as, "My, you're looking especially green today!" or "I just want to be your friend!" and "You'd never sting me, would you, buddy?" You can probably guess the rest of the story—no rashes, no stings, shocked students.

One of the most unusual (but interesting) uses of nettle is a practice called urtication. Essentially, it's whipping yourself with stalks of nettle on arthritic or swollen joints. It's reported that the nettle rash improves circulation to the area, relieving aches and pains (similar to bee venom therapy, aka apitherapy, for MS and arthritis). Urtication may not be for everyone, but I'd much rather try it over prescription medications!

• • •

## STRAWBERRY CHEESECAKE LAVENDER RuM TRUFFLES

Many people only associate lavender (*Lavandula* spp.) with scented candles, air fresheners, and bath bombs. Don't be fooled by lavender's relaxing and calming effects—it's also an effective antibacterial, antifungal, and antiseptic. Lavender is useful in treating many infections, including staph, strep, colds, and flu. During the Middle Ages, it was used to ward off the plague.[133] People are so used to seeing lavender in its artificially purple, fake-fragrance waxy candle state that they don't realize you can ingest it. At one of our whangs, our guests made a blueberry slump (a colonial fruit dessert similar to a cobber). We sent them off to our herb garden to gather some lavender flowers for a homemade lavender whipped cream. We think they expected it to taste like a Febreze Mediterranean Lavender candle, but it was the hit of the night! Makes approximately twelve truffles.

## INGREDIENTS

1 cup (1 block) cream cheese

4 tablespoons white chocolate chips

⅓ cup freeze-dried strawberries (we've never used fresh strawberries, but frozen strawberries will make this too runny)

2 teaspoons lavender flowers

2 tablespoons rum or cold water

..........................................
133. McIntyre, *The Complete Herbal Tutor*, 141.

## DIRECTIONS

1. Add all ingredients to a food processor and combine well.

2. Place all ingredients in a mixing bowl, and with your hands or a spoon combine well.

3. Get ready to roll! Take a small amount of the mixture (about the size of a cherry tomato) and roll it into a ball.

4. Optional: coat the truffles in toppings (like chopped nuts, mini chocolate chips, or shredded coconut). Cover thoroughly by rolling and pressing to cover each ball evenly.

5. Keep refrigerated.

Maybe you're raising little kids and up to your elbows in poop and snot. Maybe you're busy with work deadlines, and the prospect of emptying the dishwasher one more time, or defrosting yet another package of hamburger meat has pushed you to the brink. It's easy to delay, postpone, or block anything that could bring laughter and joy into our lives when there's dog diarrhea to contend with, traffic to fight, or a mountain of laundry to fold. You spend most of your life in the present, so make sure it's a pleasant place most of the time. Serve a batch of Toffee Cacao Nettle Truffles on the fine china. Binge on Netflix while you're sipping Shatavari Cocoa Cordial from a crystal wine glass. Break out the fancy guest towels. Spritz on that fancy perfume you've been saving. Denying yourself isn't healthy!

## CHAPTER SIX
# GROUNDED GOODWIFE
# PANTRY ESSENTIALS: PART ONE

This chapter details the ingredients, supplies, and equipment needed for part one of this book: Health & Wellness.

Where can you find these ingredients? Your local health food store, online sites, and grocery stores will carry the majority of the items we suggest. We're excluding common ingredients like carrots, onions, apples, and cream cheese, which you probably already have on hand. Links to some of the more unique herbs/items can be found at groundedgoodwife.com.

## SUPPLIES/EQUIPMENT

1-ounce glass spray bottles

2-ounce plastic bottles with flip-top caps

10-milliliter glass roll-on bottles

Blender

Colander

French press

Gallon glass jar

Glass dropper bottles

Half-gallon wide-mouth glass jar

Mason jars (8-ounce, 16-ounce, 24-ounce)

Mini-funnel (to fit in 10-milliliter bottle)

Pressure cooker (8-quart)

Strainer

Tea balls

Tea infusers

## INGREDIENTS

70-proof alcohol: bourbon, rum, vodka, or brandy

Almond butter or peanut butter (natural)

Almonds

Aloe vera gel

Arrowroot starch

Bay leaves

Beets

Blue Lotus Traditional Masala Chai Powder (available online)

Bragg's Liquid Aminos

Cacao

Carrier oils (grapeseed, jojoba)

Cheesecloth or coffee filter

Chicken feet

Coconut oil

Collagen peptides (we recommend pasture-raised, hormone / antibiotic-free)

Dandelion greens

Dates

Essential oils

- Cinnamon
- Clove
- Eucalyptus
- Grapefruit
- Lavender

- Lemon
- Orange
- Peppermint
- Rosemary

Goji berries

Hazelnuts

Honey (if possible, local and raw)

Korean red pepper powder (we use gochugaru)

Leeks

Lemons

Maple syrup (pure)

Milk kefir grains

Pink Himalayan salt

Pumpkin puree

Raw cacao

Raw milk

Raw unpasteurized apple cider vinegar

Real Mushrooms 5 Defenders mushroom powder (available online)

SCOBY for kombucha

Stevia

Toffee bits

Vanilla beans

Watercress

Witch hazel

## HERBS

Alfalfa

Allspice berries

Ashwagandha

Astragalus

Black peppercorns

Catnip

Cayenne (powdered or fresh)

Chamomile

Cinnamon

Elderberries

Elderflower

Eleuthero

Ginger (fresh or powdered)

Ginkgo

Goldenrod

Gotu kola

Green milky oat tops

Hawthorn

Hibiscus

Lavender

Lemon balm

Lemon verbena

Lemongrass

Licorice root

Linden

Maitake mushrooms (dried or fresh)

Motherwort

Mullein leaf

Nettle

Passion flower

Raspberry leaf

Red clover

Rhodiola

Rose hips

Rosemary

Sassafras bark

Shatavari

Shiitake mushrooms (dried or fresh)

Skullcap

Spearmint

Thyme

Turmeric

Vitex (aka chaste tree berry)

# PART TWO
# NATURAL BODY CARE

*Gladden the senses!*

Many people make a point of buying organic cage-free liquid egg whites, wild-caught sockeye salmon fillets, low-fat oat milk, keto pancake and waffle mix, vegan sprouted brown rice cacao crisps, and plant-based bratwurst—but they don't apply the same scrutiny to their beauty products. While we all know that the skin is our largest organ (it weighs eight to nine pounds and covers approximately twenty-two square feet), we tend to forget (or doubt) that what we put on our skin affects our entire body. If you're skeptical, think about nicotine, birth control, and nitroglycerin (for coronary artery disease) patches.

We assume the five-syllable chemicals in cosmetics and personal care items are safe enough to put on our bodies, but the United States cosmetics and personal care industry—everything from makeup to shampoo, lotion, and sunscreen—is largely self-regulated. Since cosmetics and personal care items first came under the control of the United States Food and Drug Administration (FDA) in the 1930s, only nine chemicals have been banned from use. More than twelve thousand chemicals are approved for use today.[134]

Just because a product is labeled "clean," "natural," "nontoxic," or "paraben-free" doesn't necessarily mean that it's safer to use or that its ingredients are superior. In a 2018 article published by Vox, beauty journalist Cheryl Wischhover wrote, "Because the terminology isn't regulated by an agency or governing body like the United States Federal Trade Commission

---

134. Zanolli, "Pretty Hurts: Are Chemicals in Beauty Products Making Us Ill?"

or the FDA, they're all essentially meaningless words when they appear on cosmetics and personal care products. ... So any company can call a product 'natural' or 'clean' and define that term any way it wants. And companies don't hesitate to slap on that label, because shoppers respond to it."[135] A 2018 survey by students in the Fashion Institute of Technology's graduate school of cosmetics and fragrance marketing and management found that "90 percent of consumers believed that natural or naturally-derived beauty ingredients were better for them."[136] Even the FDA agrees that cosmetics made with "organic" ingredients don't necessarily make them better or safer.[137]

Creating your own scrubs, masks, sleep pillows, bath items, shampoos, hair rinses, and perfumes isn't only rewarding—the best part is you'll know exactly what's in the product you've made. The ancient Greeks felt that in order to aid health and beauty, herbal cosmetics should "gladden the senses."[138] Making your own beauty products puts you in control. What could "gladden the senses" more than to know your final products are often so pure, you can eat them?!

## THE 411 ON ESSENTIAL OILS

Many of the recipes in this section include essential oils. Essential oils are extremely trendy, but many people still don't totally get what they are, or know how to use them safely. Technically, an essential oil is an oil extracted from a plant, generally using steam or cold-pressing, that captures the plant's scent, flavor, and essence.

Never use essential oils directly on your skin! They're extremely concentrated and can burn you.

.............................................

135. Wischhover, "The 'Natural' Beauty Industry Is on the Rise Because We're Scared of Chemicals."

136. Bibby, et al., "Transitioning to Transparency."

137. Center for Food Safety and Applied Nutrition. "'Organic' Cosmetics."

138. Askinson, *Perfumes and Cosmetics: Their Preparation and Manufacture*, 253.

# GROUNDED GOODWIFE STORY TIME

## *Essential Oils* by Ehris

For years, I've been telling people to be careful with essential oils—but you know how sometimes, you don't take your own advice? A few Februarys ago, my jasmine plant was in full-bloom, and I became obsessed with everything jasmine. I DIYed jasmine tea, jasmine body scrubs, jasmine flower essence, jasmine perfume, jasmine candles, jasmine lip balm, and jasmine reed diffusers. I got the brilliant idea to make a batch of jasmine shampoo and hair rinse using the fresh flowers and essential oil (as my mom always says in our classes, "Do you see where this story is going?"). I made the hair products and added a bunch of jasmine essential oil, but the jasmine scent wasn't strong enough. I added more drops…and more drops…and more drops…until it finally smelled jasmine-y enough. I washed my hair and used my leave-in hair rinse. The story goes downhill from here! After about thirty seconds, I felt like my head was on fire. When I looked in the bathroom mirror, my stinging scalp was bright red from the insane amount of jasmine essential oil I'd used. My scalp didn't blister or peel, but I learned that "less is more" when it comes to essential oils.

• • •

If essential oils are properly diluted in a carrier oil (our favorites are grapeseed, jojoba, or almond oil), they're safe to use topically. We usually use twenty drops of essential oil in one ounce of carrier oil. There are a few essential oil companies who insist that it's safe to use some of their oils "neat" (directly from the bottle), but we just dilute all of them to be safe.

In all of our workshops and classes, we discuss the controversy of using essential oils internally. Many essential oil companies recommend their oils for both external and internal use. We're not fans of using them internally because we don't think it's necessary. Essential oils are extremely concentrated. For example, it takes six hundred rose petals to make one drop of rose essential oil. If you made a cup of rose petal tea, you'd probably use about fifteen to twenty rose petals. It takes about sixty-three pounds of lemon balm to make one, fifteen-milliliter bottle of lemon balm essential oil. Some people put a few drops of lemon essential oil in their water bottles, but why not just use a real lemon? Why take lavender essential oil for stress reduction when you could just drink a cup of lavender tea made with actual lavender flowers? Taking essential oils internally is too taxing on the body.

We're big believers in "follow the money." Perhaps one reason why these companies advocate internal usage is that you'll go through the bottle more quickly and have to buy more.

## CHAPTER SEVEN

# FACIAL CARE

Many people have no idea what to do with the massive number of skin care products sitting in their bathroom. Skin care has gotten out of hand! While we believe everyone needs a skin care routine, we don't believe in expensive products that promise the face of a cherub. Skin that feels tight after cleansing could be a sign that it was stripped of its natural oils with nothing left to nourish itself. If you cleanse with detergents, over-exfoliate, or use synthetic moisturizers or an alcohol-based toner, you could be disturbing your skin's natural balance. Our skin knows what to do. We just need to learn how to support, rather than suppress, healthy function.

Our simple skincare routine includes cleansers, elixirs, exfoliators, and masks. We believe in a simple wash-and-go approach, and eating your way to beautiful skin. Natural beauty is achieved from the inside out. Your skin is a reflection of your overall health.

## THE CORRECT ORDER OF FACIAL CARE

The skin's job is to keep things *out*, but healthy skin care products have ingredients we want to get *in*. If you don't apply products in the correct order, you won't see the best results from your skin care regime.

- **Cleanser** (daily): You'll need a cleanser to wash off the dirt, makeup, excess oil, dead skin cells, and environmental impurities that end up on your face naturally throughout the day. Washing your face with a gentle cleanser at night is the most important skin care step. Cleansing in the morning is an optional step—some people prefer just to give their face a rinse with cold water.

- **Elixir** (daily): Ultimately, natural hydration has to come from within the body and can't be reversed by applying moisturizer on the skin's surface—but applying an elixir after cleansing will help keep your skin feeling smooth and soft. Elixirs penetrate deep inside the skin to reduce fine lines, deeply hydrate the skin, and provide an excellent base for makeup. Elixirs, the worker bees of skin care, are a combination of various oils and can contain herbal infusions and plant extracts. They're also known as "repair" products because their smaller molecular structure help them penetrate further into the skin. Because the active ingredients are more expensive than water and thickeners, elixirs are also the most expensive products.

### Optional Skincare Steps

- **Exfoliator** (once a week, or every other week after cleansing): Sugar scrubs remove dry, dead skin cells from the surface of the skin, which can help reveal a smoother, brighter complexion.
- **Mask** (twice a month, after exfoliating): Masks are used primarily to deep-clean the skin. Their ingredients will determine whether they will tone and tighten, calm inflammation, hydrate, remove toxins, or soften the skin.

## CLEANSERS

Have you ever experienced a feeling of tightness or dryness after washing your face? That "squeaky clean" feeling is a sign of stripped, imbalanced skin. At the ideal pH level of 5.5, skin is able to maintain a good barrier and function as a true protective defense organ, creating a shield called the "acid mantle."[139]

Think of your acid mantle as your skin's night watchman. Any great deviation in your skin's pH level throws off its "ecosystem." That's why washing away your skin's acid mantle is super damaging.

........................................
139. Oliveira, "Your Skin'S Ph: What Is It And How Do You Restore Its Balance?"

## MINT-CONDITION FACE & BoDY WASH

Peppermint's antiseptic and antibacterial properties help cleanse the skin, while the vanilla oil contains anti-aging properties. If you're feeling sluggish, this invigorating, minty wash can improve mental clarity. It's hard to find an all-natural cleanser that removes mascara, but this one does the trick! Makes one cup.

### INGREDIENTS

4 ounces unscented liquid castile soap

¼ cup peppermint hydrosol

¼ cup water

½ teaspoon jojoba oil

7 drops vanilla oil

### INSTRUCTIONS

1. Add all ingredients to an eight-ounce plastic flip-cap squeeze bottle (we recommend a plastic bottle for this one since you're probably going to be using this in the bathtub or shower and don't want to take a chance with broken glass). Swish gently to blend.
2. To use, shake bottle before each use. Using a washcloth or your fingers, apply about a teaspoon to your face. Rinse well—we recommend using a warm, wet washcloth.

### BENEFITS

- **Castile soap** is made from simple plant oils like coconut, hemp, sunflower seed, jojoba, and olive. It's considered safe for even the most sensitive skin types, and helps clean your skin without drying it out.
- **Peppermint hydrosol:** A hydrosol is an aromatic water containing therapeutic properties (it's the liquid left over from the making of essential oils). Peppermint hydrosol, which smells like freshly crushed peppermint leaves, is energizing, uplifting, and cooling.

- **Jojoba oil** is light, and doesn't leave your skin feeling all greasy. It balances the oil in the skin, rather than adding oil to it. It's considered safe for all skin types, and it won't clog pores or cause acne.[140]
- **Vanilla oil:** There are vanilla extracts, vanilla infusions, vanilla absolutes, and vanilla fragrance oils, but no truly pure vanilla essential oil! Vanilla beans can't tolerate the heat required for steam distillation, and mechanical pressing won't produce any oil. Vanilla beans need a solvent in order to release their aromatic compounds. So, they can't be called essential oils. However, steeping vanilla beans in oil produces an aromatic oil. We use a vanilla bean oil infusion for this recipe.

## IT'S THE BALM! NUTTY VANILLA CLEANSING BALM

A cleansing balm is a solid oil-based cleanser that generally comes in a jar (vs. a tube or bottle), meaning you need to use your finger to dig out the product. When you massage the balm into your skin, it'll warm up and take on a creamy texture. Our Nutty Vanilla Cleansing Balm contains only four ingredients, and we've used it to "melt" even the thickest layers of makeup we've had to wear for TV interviews (including mascara)! The cocoa butter's chocolately-nutty scent, combined with coconut oil's faint undertones, smell delicious! We like to use this cleansing balm in the evening. Makes about four ounces.

### INGREDIENTS

½ cup unrefined cocoa butter

2 tablespoons unrefined coconut oil

5 tablespoons almond oil

5 drops vanilla oil blend (there's no such thing as vanilla essential oil)

### INSTRUCTIONS

1. In a small double boiler, melt the cocoa butter, coconut oil, and almond oil at low heat.

---

140. Rud, "Why Jojoba Oil Is the Only Oil You Should Be Using on Your Face."

2. Add vanilla oil into a mason jar or stainless-steel container.

3. Once the cocoa butter, coconut oil, and almond oil are melted, turn off the heat and pour into the mason jar or stainless-steel container.

4. In the fridge, your balm will solidify in about an hour. Afterward, it can be stored at room temperature, but it may soften in hot weather.

## TO USE

1. Start with a dime-sized amount of the Nutty Vanilla Cleansing Balm on clean, *dry* fingertips. Warm the product between your fingers and apply to a *dry* face (you got the emphasis on *dry*, right?). Massage the balm in circular motions all over your face.

2. Wring out a washcloth in hot water. Place the cloth over your face for about thirty seconds to open up your pores and enjoy the nutty scent as your nutty day dissolves away.

3. Use the washcloth to wipe off any makeup, sweat, or grime. If your makeup's very heavy, you may need to rinse out the washcloth and repeat.

4. Some people then second cleanse with their usual facial cleanser. Some people opt to skip the facial cleanser entirely, using just the balm and a wet washcloth to wash their face. You know your skin better than anyone!

5. Splash with cool water and apply an elixir.

## BENEFITS

- **Almond oil's** emollient properties make it soothing and hydrating to the skin. Almond oil contains vitamin A, which has the ability to stimulate the production of new skin cells and smooth fine lines.

- **Cocoa butter** (theobroma oil) is a natural, meltable oil extracted from the cocoa bean. The fat in cocoa butter forms a protective barrier over skin to hold in moisture. Cocoa butter contains compounds—cocoa mass polyphenols—that have been shown to help diminish signs of aging and soothe sensitive skin.[141]

- **Coconut oil** (virgin or unrefined) is a wonderful face cleanser, moisturizer, and sunscreen, but also it can treat many skin disorders. The fatty acids (caprylic and lauric) in coconut oil may reduce inflammation internally and externally, and moisturize, making coconut oil a great solution for many types of skin conditions.[142]

## FEELS LIKE BUTTAH! WHIPPED COCOA BUTTER CLEANSING CREAM

Having trouble removing makeup? Cold cream, designed to smooth skin and remove makeup, is an emulsion of water and certain fats, usually including beeswax. Variations of cold cream have been used for nearly two thousand years. This thick, oil-based creamy cleanser melts off makeup, but is gentle and beneficial for your skin. The combination of frankincense and lavender essential oils smells clean and calming. Ehris uses this as a makeup remover and also as a nighttime face lotion. Makes about ¾ cup.

### INGREDIENTS

¼ cup + 3 tablespoons apricot kernel oil (almond oil works too)

1 tablespoon coconut oil

1 tablespoon beeswax

1 teaspoon lanolin

½ cup water

¼ teaspoon borax

1 vitamin E capsule

18 drops frankincense essential oil

12 drops lavender essential oil

........................................................

141. Gasser, et al., "Cocoa Polyphenols and Their Influence on Parameters Involved in Ex Vivo Skin Restructuring," 339–45.

142. Lin, Zhong, and Santiago, "Anti-Inflammatory and Skin Barrier Repair Effects of Topical Application of Some Plant Oils," 70.

## INSTRUCTIONS

1. In a small pot over low heat (or you can use a double boiler), warm the apricot kernel oil, coconut oil, beeswax, and lanolin until the beeswax is just melted.

2. In another pot, warm the water and borax over low heat. Stir until borax dissolves.

3. Remove both pots from heat. Pour the oils/beeswax/lanolin mixture into the blender and let cool for about five minutes, until it begins to slightly thicken.

4. Place the lid on the blender. Turn the blender on high and remove the lid's plastic fill cap.

5. Drizzle all of the water/borax mixture through the center of the blender lid. The cream will begin to thicken. Blend for about fifteen to twenty seconds. It should have a smooth consistency. If the blades get clogged up, turn off the blender and free up the blades with a wooden spoon. Put the lid back on and blend for five to ten seconds. Repeat this process if needed until the cream is smooth.

6. With a needle or pin, pierce the Vitamin E capsule, and squeeze the contents into the blender. Add the essential oils. Blend for another five to ten seconds to combine. If you make this recipe in the summer, the cream will be softer than if you make it in the winter.

7. Pour the finished cream into storage containers (we recommend four-ounce glass mason jars). Let the cream cool for about half an hour before putting on the lid. Use within a month (no refrigeration required).

## TO USE

1. Start with a dime-sized amount on clean, dry fingertips. Massage the cream in circular motions all over your face.

2. Wring out a washcloth in hot water. Place the cloth over your face for about thirty seconds to open up your pores.

3. Use the washcloth to wipe off any makeup, sweat, or grime. If your makeup's very heavy, you may need to rinse out the washcloth and repeat.

4. Some people then second cleanse with their usual facial cleanser. Some people opt to skip the facial cleanser entirely, using just the balm and a wet washcloth to wash their face. You know your skin better than anyone! Finally, apply an elixir.

## BENEFITS

- **Apricot kernel oil** (*Prunus armeniaca*) contains softening, rejuvenating, hydrating, and nourishing properties, and closely resembles the natural sebum produced in human skin. Used topically, this moisturizing oil may help lessen blemishes, fine lines, and wrinkles.

- **Coconut oil:** Although coconut water was used to give emergency plasma transfusions to wounded soldiers in the Pacific during World War II,[143] coconut oil is the most nutrient-dense part of the coconut. Coconut oil is 100 percent fat, 80 to 90 percent of which is saturated fat. This gives it a firm texture at cold or room temperatures. Legend has it that sailors aboard one of Vasco de Gama's ships gave the coconut its name. They described the coconut shell as a coco, or "grinning face" of a monkey.[144] When the "coco" came to England, the suffix of "nut" was added.

- **Beeswax** is the substance that forms the structure of a honeycomb. When it's secreted by the bee, beeswax is white, and after contact with honey and pollen it becomes a more intense yellowish color.[145] Unlike petroleum jelly, which is used in a large variety of beauty products, beeswax won't "suffocate" the skin, but it still provides a protective barrier. Interestingly, there is evidence of beeswax being used as filling on a human Neolithic tooth (6,500 years old) in Slovenia![146]

........................................

143. Barclay, "Coconut Water to the Rescue? Parsing the Medical Claims."

144. "The Coconut Story," Coconut Republic.

145. Fratini., et al., "Beeswax: A Minireview of Its Antimicrobial Activity and Its Application in Medicine," 839–43.

146. Bernardini, "Beeswax as Dental Filling on a Neolithic Human Tooth," e44904.

- **Lanolin** is a yellow fat extracted from the sheared wool of sheep. When the wool is washed, the lanolin rises to the top of the water, and is skimmed off. Lanolin forms a nonocclusive barrier (air can penetrate in and out), which means it doesn't smother the skin or feel too gooey or gloppy. Lanolin can hold up to twice its weight in water, which means it's ideal for keeping moisture trapped within the skin. However, lanolin is usually soaked in pesticides to remove any parasites, and it can be very difficult to find organic/pesticide-free lanolin. Be aware that omitting lanolin from this cleansing cream recipe changes its consistency.

- **Cocoa butter** (theobroma oil) is a natural, meltable oil extracted from the cocoa bean. The fat in cocoa butter forms a protective barrier over skin to hold in moisture. Cocoa butter contains compounds—cocoa mass polyphenols—which have been shown to help diminish signs of aging and soothe sensitive skin.[147]

- **Borax** is used (in small amounts) in many skincare recipes. It's used to aid emulsification and to preserve products.

- **Vitamin E** contains moisturizing and healing benefits. Topically, it can be helpful for skin repair, including scars and sun damage.

- **Frankincense** (*Boswellia* spp.) **essential oil** is sometimes called "liquid gold for your face." Its benefits include the ability to strengthen skin, improve its tone and elasticity, and increase defense mechanisms against bacteria or blemishes. Frankincense's earthy, spicy scent is said to lower stress levels, calm anxiety, and promote sleep.[148]

- **Lavender** (*Lavandula* spp.) **essential oil** isn't just a sleep remedy! This essential oil may soothe skin, improve acne, and promote wound healing.[149]

147. Gasser, et al., "Cocoa Polyphenols and their Influence on Parameters Involved in Ex Vivo Skin Restructuring," 339–45.
148. DeFino, "The Skincare Ingredient That Cleopatra Swore by Is Trending Now."
149. Shunatona, "Not Just for Sleep: Here's How Lavender Oil Can Soothe and Heal Your Skin."

# SCRUBS

Exfoliation can be traced back to the ancient Egyptians, who used pumice stones, sand scrubs, and aloe vera plants to rejuvenate the skin.[150] Egyptian women would regularly hang out to relax, bathe, and gossip while they scrubbed their bodies. It's reported that Cleopatra bathed daily in donkey milk (from seven hundred donkeys!) to prevent wrinkles and brighten her skin.[151] Hee haw! The brightening was due to donkey milk's high concentration of vitamin C—four times the amount of vitamin C found in cow's milk.[152] Donkey milk is rich in lactic acid, which is an alpha-hydroxy acid (AHA) and acts as a chemical exfoliant, and is effective in reversing the effects of photoaging and improving wrinkles, skin elasticity, tone, and hydration.[153]

Throughout history, people have exfoliated with wine, corncobs, sand, crushed seashells, and even fire![154]

## Desquamation vs. Exfoliation

Desquamation, the natural shedding of the outer layers of the skin, happens from the inside out. Human skin sheds an average of between two hundred million to one billion cells per day (by the way, the word "desquamation" comes from the Latin, "desquamare," meaning "to scrape the scales off a fish"[155]). Desquamation happens naturally, but if your diet is lacking essential fatty acids (like linoleic acid, found in nuts, seeds, meat, and eggs), it could slow down the process, making your skin dry and scaly.

Exfoliation, on the other hand, works from the outside in. It's an "interfering" process—and you're the interferer. You can speed up the shedding of

......................................

150. Wesley and Talakoub "Winter Exfoliation: A Multicultural Approach."

151. "History of Donkey Milk," Naturare.

152. Li, Liu, and Guo, "The Nutritional Ingredients and Antioxidant Activity of Donkey Milk and Donkey Milk Powder."

153. Kapila, et al., "Donkey Milk: A Very Recent Nutritional 'Pharmafood," 70, 72–77.

154. Loftus, "The History Of Exfoliation."; Wesley and Talakoub, "Winter Exfoliation: A Multicultural Approach." Rosevear, "Exfoliation."

155. Haubrich, *Medical Meanings: a Glossary of Word Origins*, 226.

dead skin cells by using an exfoliant. Exfoliation helps correct the visual signs of a slow natural desquamation—dullness or uneven skin tone.[156]

Every thirty days, our skin gets a new layer of plump, round skin cells that are born at the basal cell layer, the lowest layer of the epidermis (the epidermis is the layer of skin that we see and touch). These plump little guys journey upward through the layers of the epidermis until they reach the surface. Traveling flattens them out (as it does all of us!), and they're eventually sloughed off. This entire journey takes about thirty days in young skin.

At age thirty-five, skin gets an AARP card. Now—gasp!—it's considered "older" skin. The process of cell turnover slows down (picture connecting flights vs. nonstop), and the "trip" can take up to sixty days. The older skin cells remain on the surface far longer, making the skin look tuckered out and gray.

Exfoliation removes the outer layer to reveal the newer skin beneath, and also encourages cell turnover. Exfoliation takes place either through:

- mechanical means—using things like a loofah, Clarisonic, pumice stone, washcloth, or scrub
- chemical means—using fruit enzymes or alpha hydroxyl acids

The easiest, and tastiest, way to mechanically exfoliate is with a sugar scrub. Until we started using sugar scrubs, we didn't really buy into the hype, but they can be incredibly moisturizing and exfoliating to the skin. Those expensive sugar scrubs you see in department stores, health food stores, and spas cost pennies to make! To get your glow on, all you need are ingredients that are probably already in your pantry and fridge.

## Squeeze the Day! Lemon Sugar Scrub Recipe

In all of our workshops, we've yet to meet a person who doesn't love the smell of citrus. It may be the most perfect-in-itself smell that Mother Nature has to offer. Duplicating the sunshine-y fresh-squeezed lemonade essence of the real thing is a challenge, and usually results in some phony version that smells like someone just mopped the floors. This scrub smells just like lemon

........................................
156. "The Difference between Natural Desquamation and Exfoliation: What It Means for Your Skin," Griffin Row.

shortbread cookies—and you'll feel glowing-Greek-goddess amazing after using it. Make sure to open your mouth in the shower while you're rinsing it off—it's that good. Makes one, eight-ounce jar.

## INGREDIENTS

1 ⅓ cup white sugar

Zest and juice from ½ lemon

Up to 30 drops lemon essential oil

⅓ cup grapeseed oil

## INSTRUCTIONS

1. Mix all ingredients in the bowl or cup (for some unknown reason, if you put all the ingredients in the mason jar first, and then try to mix it up, it doesn't fit—but if you mix it up in something else first, it fits perfectly in the eight-ounce mason jar).

2. Spoon into glass jar.

3. To use: Apply a small amount to wet skin. Massage in a circular motion, avoiding the delicate skin around the eyes (you can use this on your whole body too). Rinse.

   – We keep our scrubs in the shower, and they last for over six months. The sugar and oil might separate a little bit after a while, but just mix it up with a spoon or your fingers.

## BENEFITS

- **Lemons,** rich in vitamin C and citric acid, can help brighten, lighten, and even-out your complexion when used over time. According to dermatologist Marina Peredo, MD, "Vitamin C is a great antioxidant for neutralizing free radicals and boosting collagen production."[157]

- **Sugar,** a natural exfoliator, improves overall skin texture by removing dead, dull skin cells.

........................................

157. Women's Health Editors. "Lemon Juice Might Be the Do-It-All Beauty Ingredient You've Been Waiting For."

- **Grapeseed oil,** processed from the tiny seeds of grapes (usually wine grapes), is known for its marvelous skin, hair, and health benefits. It's not a heavy oil—it hydrates the skin but doesn't leave you feeling all greasy. Its mild antimicrobial properties can help prevent accumulation of bacteria that can lead to acne breakouts and clogged pores. It may help heal scars/marks from previous breakouts, improve your skin's appearance, and reduce loss of elasticity and dark spots.[158] Some evidence shows that when topically applied, grapeseed oil can help speed up wound healing.[159]

## GROUNDED GOODWIFE STORY TIME

### *Speaking of Lemons* by Velya

Vastu shastra serves as India's version of feng shui. It aims to harmonize the flow of energy in a house to turn it into a positive home.[160] It's believed that one way to measure the negative or positive vibes in a home or workplace is by keeping a whole lemon in a transparent glass of water. If the lemon floats, it's believed that positive energy exists. If the lemon sinks to the bottom, it's believed that there's negativity. If the water becomes milky, the negativity is being absorbed by the water. If the lemon bursts in the water (yikes!), then the negativity was too much for the lemon to handle. The water should be changed once a week (some people think it's important to do it on a Saturday). If the lemon is rotten or bursts, it should be tossed—probably not the best idea to put it in your compost pile!

• • •

### ESPRESSO YOURSELF! CINNAMON COFFEE SCRUB RECIPE

Sometimes your skin needs some percolating—and this recipe will make you wonder where it's "bean" all your life! If your skin needs a bit of a caffeine

158. Levy, "Have You Tried Grapeseed Oil for Your Skin?"
159. Shivananda, et al., "Wound-Healing Properties of the Oils of *Vitis vinifera* and *Vaccinium macrocarpon*," 1201–8.
160. "Vastu Shastra New Word Suggestion," Collins Dictionary.

jolt and a "latte" love, be sure to make this one. The lightly caramelized, almost nutty, scent will make you feel brew-ti-ful! Words cannot "espresso" how much Ehris loves this scrub. Full disclosure: this one is a bit messy when you rinse it off. FYI, coffee grounds should be used cautiously in showers and sinks—over time, they can coagulate in water and clog drains and pipes. Makes one, eight-ounce jar.

## INGREDIENTS

1 cup brown sugar

3 tablespoons ground coffee (not used coffee grounds)

½ teaspoon cinnamon

20 drops vanilla extract

4 tablespoons + 2 teaspoons olive oil

## INSTRUCTIONS

1. Mix all ingredients in the bowl or cup (for some unknown reason, if you put all the ingredients in the mason jar first, and then try to mix it up, it doesn't fit—but if you mix it up in something else first, it fits perfectly in the eight-ounce mason jar).

2. Spoon into glass jar.

3. To use: Apply a small amount to wet skin. Massage in a circular motion, avoiding the delicate skin around the eyes (you can use this one on your whole body too). Rinse.

   – We keep our scrubs in the shower, and they last for over six months. The sugar and oil might separate a little bit after a while, but just mix it up with a spoon or your fingers.

## BENEFITS

- **Brown sugar** clears away dull, dead skin cells. Your skin will look smoother and glowing!

- **Coffee:** You know how coffee wakes you up in the morning? It does the same thing for your skin. When applied to the skin, its stimulating properties (like caffeine) improve blood flow, making your skin look radiant, bright, awake, and alive. It seems counterintuitive because it's a mild stimulant, but coffee can also calm inflamed and red skin. Not all coffee scrubs are created equal! Some coffee scrub recipes call for used coffee grounds, which means that most of the caffeine has been depleted, so those won't be as effective. Finally, ground coffee gently and effectively buffs your skin, removing dead skin cells.

- **Cinnamon** (*Cinnamomum cassia*): Using cinnamon on your skin can help reduce redness and fade scars, blemishes, and dark spots. Its antibacterial properties make it helpful for acne.
- **Vanilla** (*Vanilla planifolia*) contains anti-inflammatory properties that can help soothe and calm skin. It also smells yummy!
- **Olive oil:** In the ancient world, virgin olive oil was called "liquid gold" by Homer. Hippocrates called olive oil "the great healer."[161] Olive oil has been used for thousands of years in Mediterranean cultures. Ancient Greeks knew of its power to heal wounds, and eventually they used it in oil lamps, cooking, and for beauty.[162] Olive oil penetrates deeply into the skin, and, combined with the exfoliating brown sugar and coffee, these ingredients will remove dead skin cells and leave the skin looking renewed and glowing.

## OH MY GOURD, I LOVE FALL! MAPLE-PUMPKIN SUGAR SCRUB

It's hard to say goodbye to summer, but this scrub makes it easier to transition. If you're a sucker for those warm, comforting scents of the season, maple and pumpkin spice have become the flavors and scents that let us know it's officially fall. Pumpkin contains vitamins A, C, and E, and antioxidants, which help fight sun damage and wrinkles. Its fruit enzymes help naturally exfoliate dead skin cells. Makes about ten ounces.

...........................................

161. Clodoveo, et al., "In the Ancient World, Virgin Olive Oil Was Called 'Liquid Gold' by Homer and 'the Great Healer' by Hippocrates. Why Has This Mythic Image Been Forgotten?" 1062–68.

162. Grufferman, "The Healing Power of Olive Oil."

## INGREDIENTS

1 ¼ cup brown sugar

¼ cup pumpkin puree (not pumpkin pie mix)

⅛ cup maple syrup

⅛ cup oil (olive, grapeseed, jojoba, almond—your choice!)

½ teaspoon pumpkin pie spice, or ¼ teaspoon cinnamon and ¼ teaspoon nutmeg

## INSTRUCTIONS

1. Mix all ingredients in a bowl or cup (for some unknown reason, if you put all the ingredients in the mason jar first, and then try to mix it up, it doesn't fit—but if you mix it up in something else first, it fits perfectly in the mason jar).
2. Spoon into a twelve-ounce glass jar.
3. To use: Apply a small amount to wet skin. Massage in a circular motion, avoiding the delicate skin around the eyes (you can use this one on your whole body too). Rinse.
   - We keep our scrubs in the shower, and they last for over six months. The sugar and oil might separate a little bit after a while, but just mix it up with a spoon or your fingers.

### TOTALLY TOMATO! EXFOLIATING SCRUB RECIPE

Sugar and tomatoes make an ideal combination for use in sugar scrubs, and it's probably the easiest DIY homemade skin care product ever. This scrub came to be when Ehris went a little overboard in her non-GMO vegetable garden. Since Velya's the only one in the house who eats tomatoes, we hosted a Green Goddess Spa day. Our guests PYO'd tomatoes from the garden (that sounds like they did something really bad out there!) and got busy scrubbing. You can use this on a completely dry face (just take your makeup off first) because the tomato will release its juices as you press on it. The memory of twelve women seated at our patio table with tomato seeds all over their faces still makes us smile. Makes one scrub.

## INGREDIENTS

1 tomato

1–3 tablespoons white sugar

## INSTRUCTIONS

1. Cut the tomato in half horizontally (it works best if the tomato has a stem—this will be the "handle" you'll hold onto while you're scrubbing your face).
2. Put the sugar on a small plate or saucer.
3. Dip the cut side of the tomato in the sugar, and twist it around a little to coat the tomato evenly.
4. Get ready to scrub! No need to wet your face first. Gently scrub the tomato in a circular motion around your entire face (not the eyelids or under your eyes since those are sensitive areas).
5. Leave it on for ten to twenty minutes (you might want to eat the other half of the tomato while you're relaxing!). Rinse.

## BENEFITS

- **Tomatoes** (*Solanum lycopersicum*) are extremely rich in the potent antioxidant lycopene. Even more lycopene is released when the pulp is crushed with sugar! Topical application of lycopene can combat age-causing free radicals, and assists in metabolic functions related to growth and repair.[163] You know the gel-like stuff that surrounds tomato seeds? That's the motherlode when it comes to vitamin C—that's where it's most concentrated in a tomato. Don't let it go to waste when cutting tomatoes!

# FACE MASKS

Cleopatra used her sex appeal as a political weapon to win over her enemies. She spoke a dozen languages, rolled herself up in a carpet and had herself delivered to Julius Caesar in his palace, is rumored to have hidden poison in her hair combs, and met Marc Antony on a golden barge with purple sails and

163. Goldfaden and Goldfaden, "How Topical Lycopene Improves Skin Cells."

silver oars dressed as Aphrodite[164] (she also experimented with a goo made of ground horse teeth and deer marrow to help Julius Caesar's baldness).[165] It's rumored that Cleopatra, after her daily milk-of-700-donkeys soak, applied an egg-white face mask to tighten her pores, followed by a crocodile dung face mask for a youthful appearance. If face masks helped Cleopatra be so ambitious and daring, imagine what they could help you accomplish!

Ancient Romans were said to treat age spots with a face mask made from the ashes of snails. Their everyday face masks included a mix of sweat from sheep's wool, placenta, excrement, animal urine, sulfur, ground oyster shells, and bile.[166] Some Victorian women layered raw veal masks over their faces before bed.[167]

In contrast, our mask recipes are incredibly simple and use ingredients commonly found in your kitchen—but you might not associate them with your face.

A face mask can help hydrate skin, remove excess oils, help improve the appearance of pores, and help pull out impurities. Face masks can be applied twice a month, after cleansing and exfoliating. You should let a mask stay on your face for approximately fifteen to thirty minutes. It's easiest to get them off in the shower.

## CACAO-BANANA FACE MASK RECIPE

This edible cacao face mask, featuring simple kitchen ingredients, makes skin healthier—the tasty way! The caffeine in cacao increases circulation, while the antioxidant theobromine has been studied for its ability to protect against sun damage and cancer. Bananas contain a variety of polyphenol and dopamine antioxidants, which help to protect and preserve the integrity of the body's cells. The yogurt's lactic acid gently removes the top layer of the epidermis, revealing smoother and brighter skin. Makes enough for one to two masks.

..................................................

164. Schell, "Cleopatra: A Story of Womanhood."
165. Schwarcz, "Why Did Cleopatra Supposedly Bathe In Sour Donkey Milk?"
166. Laham, *Made Up*, 12.
167. Matthews, "The Beauty Rituals of 19th Century Empress Elisabeth of Austria."

## INGREDIENTS

⅛ banana (the browner, the better)

1 tablespoon raw cacao powder (or cocoa powder, if that's all you have)

1 ½ teaspoons yogurt

½ teaspoon honey

## INSTRUCTIONS

1. Put banana in bowl. With a fork or your fingers, mush up the banana to the consistency of baby food or applesauce. Add cacao, yogurt, and honey, and mix all ingredients well. You want it to look like brownie batter.

2. Generously apply the chocolate mixture to face (and your neck, if you don't mind getting a little messy/gloppy). While you're waiting for it to dry, you might want to eat your leftovers—we recommend adding a little more honey.

3. After twenty to thirty minutes, wash off the face mask. We strongly recommend doing this in the shower because the mask almost dries like a chocolate candy bar on your face.

## BENEFITS

- **Bananas:** Used regularly on your face, bananas may brighten the skin and reduce scars and sunspots.[168] Bananas can also help absorb excess oil on the skin.

- **Cacao** (*Theobroma cacao*), the unprocessed version of cocoa, contains caffeine, which helps increase circulation, decrease redness, and tone the skin.

- **Yogurt** contains lactic acid, which can dissolve dead skin cells—leaving behind soft, evenly-toned skin. The zinc does wonders for lightening sun spots and scars.

- **Honey** is naturally antibacterial, and helps heal skin issues such as acne.

........................................
168. Cherney, "Banana Face Mask Benefits for the Skin and How to Try It."

## GIVE 'EM PUMPKIN TO TALK ABOUT! FACE MASK RECIPE

This mask tastes so good that someone who attended one of our workshops declared, "I'm going to make a batch of this tomorrow morning and put it on my oatmeal!" Nowadays, a real pumpkin isn't even necessary to elicit those nostalgic crisp fall days and old-timey idyllic farm-life feelings. Many pumpkin and pumpkin spice products like beer, cookies, and coffee don't contain any actual pumpkin, but this recipe uses the real thing! This mask is especially helpful for oily or acne-prone skin. Makes enough for one mask.

### INGREDIENTS

1 tablespoon pumpkin puree (not pumpkin pie mix)

¼ teaspoon honey (raw is best)

½ teaspoon lemon juice

2 teaspoons white clay

### INSTRUCTIONS

1. Mix all ingredients together in a small bowl until combined.
2. Use your fingers to spread the face mask in an even layer all over your face (avoiding your eyes).
3. Leave on for fifteen to twenty minutes, then rinse it off.
4. If you have extra, it'll last about a week in the fridge in a sealed container.

### BENEFITS

- **Pumpkin** (*Cucurbita* spp.): Loaded with enzymes, pumpkin naturally exfoliates dead skin cells. Santa Monica-based aesthetician Chanel Jenae praises, "Pumpkin is loaded with natural exfoliating acids and antioxidants, meaning it has amazing resurfacing and retexturing benefits." Chanel uses pumpkin peels to "brighten, calm breakouts, and soften the appearance of fine lines and sun damage."[169]

...........................................

169. Piercy, "What to Do When You're Bored of Thanksgiving Turkey: Make a Fresh Pumpkin Face Mask."

- **Honey** hydrates the skin without making it too oily, which can soften and soothe your complexion.
- **Lemon juice:** Along with the pumpkin in this recipe, lemon juice is also a natural exfoliator, removing dead skin cells that can clog your pores. Lemons contain antibacterial properties, which can help fight break-out-causing bacteria.[170] Lemon juice can also even the skin tone.

## ALOE-CUKE MOISTURIZING MASK RECIPE

This mask is perfect for the summer when your garden is exploding with cucumbers and you've made so many pickles that you're starting to feel pick-led! This cooling, hydrating mask—especially helpful for dry skin—can help refresh a dull complexion. This gentle yet effective recipe is great for sensitive skin, and can be used to soothe a sunburn too! Makes two masks.

### INGREDIENTS

½ cucumber (we leave the peel on since it contains silica, which firms up sagging skin[171])

2 tablespoons aloe vera gel

2 tablespoons green clay

### INSTRUCTIONS

1. In a blender, blend the cucumber and aloe vera gel.
2. Transfer to a bowl and mix in green clay until combined.
3. Gently massage the mixture all over your face, and let sit for fifteen to thirty minutes.
4. Rinse with warm water.

### BENEFITS

- **Cucumbers** (*Cucumis sativus*), a produce-section staple, can also dramatically transform your skin's health and appearance! Cucumber's vitamin

170. Oikeh, et al., "Phytochemical, Antimicrobial, and Antioxidant Activities of Different Citrus Juice Concentrates," 103–9.
171. Oliver, "Three Reasons Why Cucumber Is Your Skin's New Best Friend."

C, caffeic acid, and high water content help to reduce irritated or inflamed skin.[172]

- **Aloe vera gel** is soothing for oily, normal, and normal-to-dry skin. It helps restore the skin's natural pH and relieves irritation from rashes, sunburn, and insect bites.[173]

## COCO-CADo MASK RECIPE

Holy guacamole—this may become your spring and summer go-to! After a day in the sun, this quenching mask soothes parched skin. Then again, it's ideal for cold, dry winters, too! Makes one mask.

### INGREDIENTS

½ avocado

¼ teaspoon honey (preferably raw)

¼ teaspoon coconut milk or heavy cream

### INSTRUCTIONS

1. In a small bowl, mash the avocado to the consistency of baby food or applesauce.
2. Add honey and coconut milk, and mix well.
3. Gently massage the mixture all over your face, and let sit twenty to thirty minutes.
4. Rinse off with warm water.

### BENEFITS

- **Avocado** (*Persea americana*): Avocado's nutritive and conditioning components are especially helpful for dull, dry, or irritated skin. The fats in this

172. Oliver, "Three Reasons Why Cucumber Is Your Skin's New Best Friend."

173. Tourles, *Organic Body Care Recipes: 175 Homemade Herbal Formulas for Glowing Skin & a Vibrant Self*, 58.

creamy fruit nourish your skin's top layer, while creating a protective barrier to prevent moisture evaporation.[174]

- **Coconut milk:** Containing protein, vitamin E, and a high amount of healthy fat—is nourishing and immensely hydrating for the skin.
- **Honey** is a gentle astringent and is extremely moisturizing

## NINJA TURTLE SPIRULINA MASK RECIPE

It's not easy being green! The spirulina (a dark green algae that grows on the surface of lakes) in this nourishing mask is soothing and hydrating. In all honesty, spirulina smells kinda lake-y, but the frankincense essential oil helps camouflage it. Makes two masks.

### INGREDIENTS

1 tablespoon spirulina powder

1 tablespoon + 1 teaspoon aloe vera gel

5 drops frankincense essential oil

### INSTRUCTIONS

1. In a small bowl, mix the spirulina, aloe vera gel, and frankincense essential oil to make a spreadable paste.
2. Apply to your face and let it dry (it'll be dry in about fifteen minutes).
3. Rinse off with warm water.

### BENEFITS

- **Spirulina** (*Arthrospira platensis*): Using the term "algae" when it comes to skin care might conjure up *Creature from the Black Lagoon* images, but spirulina (a type of blue-green algae, not to be confused with a seaweed) can bring about faster cell turnover, so you're naturally shedding those dry skin cells that make your skin appear sallow and dull. Although it tastes like a mouthful of lake water, the chlorophyll in spirulina is exceptionally

174. Tourles, *Organic Body Care Recipes: 175 Homemade Herbal Formulas for Glowing Skin & a Vibrant Self*, 59.

cleansing and creates an environment that's difficult for germs to grow in. Poor spirulina! So beneficial, so green, so misunderstood.

- **Aloe vera gel** is soothing for oily, normal, and normal-to-dry skin. It helps restore the skin's natural pH and relieves irritation from rashes, sunburn, and insect bites.[175]

# ELIXIRS

We've learned firsthand that oil is viewed by many people as the boogeyman of face care. Every time we recommend using grapeseed, argan, or jojoba oil in skin care, our workshop participants eyeball us in horror, as if we've suggested chopping up puppies or burning the American flag! Dendy Engelman, MD, director of dermatologic surgery at Metropolitan Hospital in New York City agrees with us: "Oils will not clog your pores or cause acne. Oil (or sebum) is naturally occurring in the skin—your sebaceous glands are constantly pumping it out. Acne is caused when hair follicles become clogged with oil and dead skin cells. But topical facial oils do not exacerbate this process and can actually help balance and improve acne-prone skin."[176]

Elixirs are lightweight moisturizers that penetrate deep inside the skin to reduce fine lines, deeply hydrate the skin, and provide an excellent base for makeup.

The right time to use an elixir depends on the formula and your skin-care routine. An elixir can be applied in the morning, at night, or both. Common sense is important. If you have chronic skin conditions like rosacea or eczema, elixirs may cause aggravation. Since elixirs are typically very concentrated, a little goes a long way.

Tiny store-bought bottles of face elixirs—fancy little bottles of hope—can come at a hefty cost. The initial price tag of argan, jojoba, rosehip seed, and grapeseed oils for DIY elixirs may seem high, but since they're used in such small amounts, they'll last you for months (if not more than a year). Be prepared for an off-the-charts glow and healthy, plump, happy skin!

......................................

175. Tourles, *Organic Body Care Recipes: 175 Homemade Herbal Formulas for Glowing Skin & a Vibrant Self*, 56.

176. Martin, "Beauty Myth Debunked: Is Oil Bad for Your Face?"

## THE COAST IS CLEAR! BREAKOUT ELIXIR RECIPE

Treating oil with oil seems counterintuitive, but it's usually the best way to help breakouts. This antibacterial elixir will help annihilate subsurface acne bacteria, ridding skin of toxins. Hemp seed oil has a comedogenic rating of zero, meaning it *can't* clog your pores, making it a great acne remedy! Makes about one ounce.

### INGREDIENTS

½ teaspoon witch hazel

2 tablespoons hemp oil

1 teaspoon jojoba oil

4 drops frankincense essential oil

4 drops helichrysum essential oil

2 drops lavender essential oil

2 drops tea tree essential oil

2 drops rose essential oil (optional, but can help with healing scars)

### INSTRUCTIONS

1. Combine all ingredients in a one-ounce glass dropper bottle.
2. Shake bottle well to mix all the ingredients and let sit overnight to allow ingredients to synergize.
3. This elixir can be applied in the morning, at night, or both. Apply three to five drops to skin immediately after cleansing your face and neck.

### BENEFITS

- **Witch Hazel:** If you're looking for cleaner, healthier skin, look no further than witch hazel! Tannins, which are responsible for making witch hazel a natural astringent, remove excess oil from the skin. Applying witch hazel to acne-prone skin can help slow bacteria growth and decrease inflammation, redness, and oiliness.[177]

- **Hemp oil** is hydrating, but once it's been absorbed, it doesn't leave your skin looking greasy. Acne patients have been shown to have low levels of linoleic acid in their skin surface lipids.[178] Since hemp oil is high in linoleic acid, it can help clear up acne.[179]

- **Jojoba oil** absorbs easily and does not clog the pores.

  Sebaceous glands are microscopic glands in our skin that secrete sebum, an oily, waxy matter. Jojoba can balance out too-high levels of sebum—which usually happens during puberty, or when hormone levels are high, and can result in oily skin and acne.

  As an emollient, jojoba oil forms an oily layer on top of the skin that traps water in the skin.[180] Research published in the *International Journal of Molecular Sciences* has proven jojoba oil to have anti-inflammatory effects and potential uses in a variety of skin conditions, including infections, aging, and wound healing. There's also evidence showing jojoba oil to be helpful for acne, seborrheic dermatitis (dry, scaly skin), and eczema.[181]

- **Frankincense essential oil,** sometimes called the "King of Essential Oils," has been used for its anti-aging benefits since antiquity.[182]

  According to Amelia Gartner from Australian plant-based skincare company Cedar and Stone, "Frankincense is great for oily skin and acne [because it's] a natural astringent. It helps regulate sebum and stops your face looking like a hot mess by removing excess oil. Frankincense will soothe and reduce inflammation and can also help prevent acne forming, thanks to the boswellic acids it contains which are capable of killing bacteria associated with acne."[183]

177. Levy, "Witch Hazel Uses, Benefits and Potential Side Effects."
178. Downing, et al., "Essential Fatty Acids and Acne," 221–5.
179. Staky, "DIY Face Serum for Clear & Glowy Skin." The Fox & She.
180. Ruggeri, "Jojoba Oil Benefits for Face, Hair, Body and More."
181. Lin, Zhong, and Santiago, "Anti-Inflammatory and Skin Barrier Repair Effects of Topical Application of Some Plant Oils," 70.
182. "Frankincense Essential Oil," doTERRA.
183. Clark, "The Surprising Beauty Benefits of Frankincense Oil."

Frankincense essential oil promotes the appearance of healthy-looking skin and may help reduce the appearance of uneven skin tones, and improves sun spots and age spots.[184] Frankincense was traditionally burned in temples by the ancient Egyptians, Romans and Greeks, to symbolize prayers rising to the gods. Frankincense resin was discovered in the tomb of a sister of an Egyptian pharaoh of the Twelfth Dynasty (nineteenth century BC).[185]

- **Helichrysum essential oil** is best known for its restorative properties to the skin. Sometimes called the "Immortal Flower," this rejuvenating essential oil promotes a glowing, youthful complexion, and can reduce the appearance of blemishes.[186]

- **Lavender essential oil** is naturally antibacterial, meaning that it kills acne-causing bacteria that might infiltrate your pores. This purple flower is perfect for preventing, calming, and healing painful acne breakouts.[187]

- **Tea tree essential oil** is one of the best essential oils for acne and healing the skin. A 2017 study by the Australasian College of Dermatologists researched the effects of using a tea tree oil gel versus a no-tea-tree face wash. Subjects applied tea tree oil twice a day for three months. The study concluded that tea tree oil can significantly improve mild to moderate acne.[188]

- **Rose essential oil:** Stop and smell the roses! This mood-lifting essential oil can erase scars, moisturize the skin, reduce inflammation, relieve stress, and promote circulation.[189] It has been proven to exhibit extremely high bacteria-killing properties, making it helpful for acne-prone skin.[190]

........................................

184. "Frankincense Essential Oil," Young Living Essential Oils; Axe, "Essential Oils: Eleven Main Benefits and 101 Uses."

185. Simon, "Frankincense and Myrrh."

186. "Helichrysum Essential Oil," doTERRA.

187. "Six Reasons to Use Lavender Oil for Skin," 100% PURE.

188. Malhi, et al., "Tea Tree Oil Gel for Mild to Moderate Acne; a Twelve Week Uncontrolled, Open-Label Phase II Pilot Study," 205–10.

189. Hall, "Why You Need Rose Oil in Your Beauty Regimen."

190. Zu, et al., "Activities of Ten Essential Oils towards Propionibacterium Acnes and PC-3, A-549 and MCF-7 Cancer Cells," 3200–10.

It's among the most expensive of the essential oils, but when you use a drop at a time, it lasts forever!

## DIY HYDRATING FACE OIL RECIPE

We love argan oil because it absorbs so nicely into the skin and doesn't leave an oily residue. It takes approximately sixty-six pounds of argan fruit and about twenty-four hours to produce just one quart![191] The argan tree is endemic to Morocco. For centuries, the harvesting of argan fruits has been performed by Berber, or Amazigh, women who are indigenous to Northern Africa. Their methods and traditional knowledge have been passed down from mothers to daughters.[192] Makes two ounces.

### INGREDIENTS

3 tablespoons jojoba oil

1½ tablespoons argan oil

2 teaspoons rosehip seed oil

¼ teaspoon vitamin E

4 drops carrot seed essential oil

8 drops rose geranium essential oil

### INSTRUCTIONS

1. In a two-ounce dropper bottle, add argan oil, rosehip seed oil, and Vitamin E.
2. Add essential oils.
3. Cap bottle and shake well. Let sit overnight to synergize.
4. This elixir can be applied in the morning, at night, or both. Apply three to five drops to skin immediately after cleansing your face and neck.

...........................................

191. Xingfei, "Value-Added Argan Oil Increasing Women's Independence in Rural Morocco."
192. Argan Project. "How Argan Oil Transforms Lives."

## BENEFITS

- **Jojoba oil** (read about its benefits in our Coast Is Clear elixir recipe).

- **Argan oil,** extracted from a unique tree found only in Morocco, is no stranger to the beauty scene! Packed with nutrients your skin will love—such as antioxidants, vitamin E, and essential fatty acids— research shows that argan oil improves skin elasticity and hydration.[193] A 2015 study indicated that the benefits of using argan oil long-term include its anti-aging effects.[194] Argan oil absorbs quickly and doesn't leave an oily residue. There are no common side effects of using argan oil, but there have been limited reports of allergic reactions in the form of rashes, and in one extreme case, anaphylaxis.

- **Rosehip seed oil** is harvested from the seeds of rose bushes. It's known to hydrate the skin, correct dark spots, reduce scars and fine lines, restore elasticity, and protect against sun and pollution stressors.[195]

- **Vitamin E** has been shown to increase photoprotection, reduce skin inflammation, promote wound healing, and lighten scars.[196]

- **Carrot seed essential oil** comes from the seeds of Queen Anne's Lace, aka wild carrot. Known for its healing and regenerative properties, this essential oil is said to be helpful in reducing fine lines and wrinkles.

- **Rose geranium essential oil** is prized for treating aging and wrinkled or dry skin. It stimulates new cell growth, balances oil production, tightens and tones the skin, and has the power to minimize the look of wrinkles.[197]

193. Bogdan, et al.,"Preliminary Study on the Development of an Antistretch Marks Water-in-Oil Cream: Ultrasound Assessment, Texture Analysis, and Sensory Analysis," 249–55.

194. Boucetta, et al., "The Effect of Dietary and/or Cosmetic Argan Oil on Postmenopausal Skin Elasticity," 339–49.

195. Oliver, "What It Takes To Wake Up Gorgeous Like Miranda Kerr."

196. Michels, "Vitamin E and Skin Health;" Zampieri, et al., "A Prospective Study in Children: Pre- and Post-Surgery Use of Vitamin E in Surgical Incisions."

197. Jacknin, *Smart Medicine for Your Skin: a Comprehensive Guide to Understanding Conventional and Alternative Therapies to Heal Common Skin Problems*, 69; Orchard and van Vuuren, "Commercial Essential Oils as Potential Antimicrobials to Treat Skin Diseases."

## DIY ANTI-AGING ELIXIR RECIPE

It's ironic that the average woman absorbs five pounds of makeup chemicals *per year*, but that doesn't seem as concerning to many of them as the concept of putting oil on their faces![198] Face oils do not make your skin oilier, nor do they make your skin feel greasy. The rose hip seed oil in this anti-aging elixir is high in essential fatty acids and softens and smooths the skin. Put it on at bedtime and your skin will just drink it up! Makes one ounce.

### INGREDIENTS

1 tablespoon jojoba oil

1 tablespoon + 1 teaspoon rose hip seed oil

¼ teaspoon vitamin E

3 drops lavender essential oil

2 drops myrrh essential oil

2 drops frankincense essential oil

2 drops patchouli essential oil

### INSTRUCTIONS

1. In a one-ounce glass dropper bottle, combine jojoba oil, rose hip seed oil, and vitamin E.

2. Add essential oils, cap, and shake well.

3. After washing your face, use ¼–½ dropper full of serum nightly to preserve, smooth, and protect your skin. Can also put on your neck.

### BENEFITS

- **Lavender essential oil's** high antioxidant content may help reduce the appearance of wrinkles and fine lines.[199] It relieves stress and tension,

198. Macrae, "Women Absorb up to Five Pounds of Damaging Chemicals a Year Thanks to Beauty Products."

199. The Hebrew University of Jerusalem, "Antioxidant to Retard Wrinkles Discovered."

and is healing and soothing when applied to acne, burns, and insect bites. Lavender essential oil balances the skin's oil production.[200]

- **Myrrh:** Two thousand years ago, frankincense and myrrh were as valuable as gold, the third gift of the Magi. Myrrh has been used throughout history in medicine and perfume.[201] Myrrh essential oil is popular for its anti-aging, skin rejuvenation, anti-inflammatory, and wound-healing effects. It encourages new cell growth and is used in the prevention and treatment of wrinkles.[202] Myrrh—grounding and soothing on an emotional level—has been shown to improve skin circulation, which improves complexion.[203]

- **Frankincense essential oil** (read about its benefits in our Coast Is Clear elixir recipe).

- **Patchouli essential oil** is grounding and balancing for the emotions, and can also promote and smooth the skin and result in a glowing complexion. Its benefits include reducing the appearance of wrinkles, blemishes, and skin "imperfections."[204]

There are scientists who say that our skin—our body's largest organ—is a barrier between the human body and the external environment, which protects the body against external chemical and physical factors.[205] There are studies that show our skin absorbs whatever we put on it.[206]

Our skin isn't a sponge, but neither is it one of those blue plastic tarps. Although the studies aren't totally conclusive, it's not a risk we're willing to take now that we have the knowledge. We prefer to make our own beauty products.

....................................................

200. Jacknin, *Smart Medicine for Your Skin: a Comprehensive Guide to Understanding Conventional and Alternative Therapies to Heal Common Skin Problems*, 69.

201. Schultz, "There's More to Frankincense and Myrrh Than Meets the Eye."

202. Jacknin, *Smart Medicine for Your Skin: a Comprehensive Guide to Understanding Conventional and Alternative Therapies to Heal Common Skin Problems*, 69-70.

203. "Myrrh Oil Uses and Benefits," doTERRA.

204. "Patchouli Oil Uses and Benefits," doTERRA.

205. Boer, et al., "Structural And Biophysical Characteristics Of Human Skin In Maintaining Proper Epidermal Barrier Function," 1-5.

206. Brown, Bishop, and Rowan, "The Role Of Skin Absorption as a Route of Exposure for Volatile Organic Compounds (VOCs) in Drinking Water," 479-84.

## CHAPTER EIGHT

# HERBAL SHAMPOO
# AND HAIR RINSE

Chances are, if you buy shampoo in a supermarket, the ingredients on the back of the bottle read something like this: Water, Sodium Lauryl Sulfate, Sodium Laureth Sulfate, Cocamidopropyl Betaine, Glycol Distearate, Sodium Citrate, Cocamide Mea, Sodium Xylenesulfonate, Dimethicone, Fragrance, Citric Acid, Sodium Benzoate, Polyquaternium-76, Sodium Chloride, Tetrasodium EDTA, Trisodium Ethylenediamine Disuccinate, Panthenol, Panthenyl Ethyl Ether, Methylchloroisothiazolinone, Methylisothiazolinone.

Rather than analyze all twenty of those ingredients (vs. the handful in our DIY shampoos), let's just look at two of them: sulfates—either sodium lauryl sulfate or sodium laureth sulfate—are detergents. They're responsible for the super-sudsy lather you get out of most shampoos (they also make products like soap and toothpaste foam and lather). Psychologically, the bubbles are supposed to make you feel like cleaning is happening. Actually, that "squeaky clean" feeling we've been taught to achieve is hair that's been stripped of its protective oils. Soaps and shampoos don't have to lather to clean!

In 2016, the FDA banned triclosan (which has been shown to be a hormone disruptor, especially in children[207]) in hand sanitizers, explaining that there was not enough evidence that triclosan was safe. Triclosan is classified as a pesticide by the United State Environmental Protection Agency (EPA),

207. Weatherly and Gosse, "Triclosan Exposure, Transformation, and Human Health Effects,"
447–69.

but, it's still allowed in products like shampoos, deodorants, cosmetics, tooth-pastes, shave gels, and dishwashing liquid.[208]

Don't be tricked! More than ninety-five percent of shampoos, conditioners, and styling products list "fragrance" on their labels, but this catch-all term can actually stand for at least three thousand different ingredients or chemicals.[209] It sounds unbelievable, but the FDA doesn't even currently require fragrance and cosmetic makers to disclose exactly what they're using to scent products since they're considered "trade secrets."[210] So unless you wear a white lab coat and goggles and work in the bowels of a company's lab, no one knows what "fragrance" means, or what effects its ingredients could be having. But you can be sure that if the ingredients were natural, they'd be listing them.

While we're focusing here on shampoos, fake fragrances are also found in lotions, scented candles, dryer sheets, laundry detergents, cleaners, cosmetics, air fresheners, plug-ins, deodorants, soaps, perfumes, colognes, and body sprays.

You don't have to be Sherlock Holmes to know that companies use synthetic scents because they're cheaper than the real thing. High quality, 100 percent pure essential oils aren't cheap, but for good reason. Essential oils are extremely concentrated. One drop of peppermint essential oil contains the equivalent amount of peppermint as twenty eight cups of tea. One drop of chamomile essential oil is equivalent to thirty chamomile tea bags!

The only way to know for sure that there aren't harmful ingredients in your shampoo is to DIY it. Before store-bought shampoo existed, women turned to herb gardens, forests, and meadows for plants that solved their beauty needs. Whether it was thinning, dry, or dull hair, a dandruff cure, or the desire for a new color, there was a plant that could meet their specific demands. We love the idea that every malady has a cousin that heals it.

........................................

208. "Triclosan," United States Environmental Protection Agency.
209. "Why Fragrance Disclosure?" Campaign for Safe Cosmetics.
210. Price, "Dangers of Synthetic Scents Include Cancer, Asthma, and Kidney Damage."

No one cares more about your pocketbook or your hair than you. If you don't like the idea of chemicals disguised beneath layers of suds and phony juicy scents, give some of these recipes a try.

## LOVE IS IN THE HAIR! HERBAL SHAMPOO RECIPE

The beauty of this mild, nondetergent formula is that it can do triple duty as a shampoo, face wash, and body wash. After smelling every fake-fragranced shampoo in our local grocery store, we discovered they all fit into one of these categories: unidentifiable fruit hybrid, sunscreen, salt water taffy, fluffy towels, confused ice cream, vaguely outdoors-y, vaguely tropical drink, Kool-Aid, generic candle, nonoffensive, Christmas dessert, or light jacket weather. This shampoo is naturally scented by herbs and pure essential oils. *Please note*: Don't use castile soap on dyed hair—it's too alkaline and can strip hair color. It's okay on highlighted and hair treated with henna. Makes two and a half cups.

### INGREDIENTS

2 cups water

1 tablespoon nettle leaf

1 tablespoon chamomile flower

1 tablespoon calendula flower

1 tablespoon rosemary leaf

1 tablespoon horsetail herb

½ teaspoon jojoba oil (omit if hair is oily)

½ cup castile soap

15 drops essential oil (see list on page 205)

### INSTRUCTIONS

1. Boil water.
2. Add herbs to a teapot or French press. Pour boiling water over herbs.

3. Steep at least an hour (we sometimes steep overnight)—this will ensure that you're making a very herb-y herbal shampoo! Let cool to room temperature.

4. Strain into a twenty-four–ounce glass bottle or plastic squeeze bottle (an old rinsed-out shampoo bottle works well).

5. Add jojoba oil, castile soap, and essential oils. Gently shake to combine. It'll be more watery than traditional shampoo.

6. Store in the shower/bath, and use as you would a traditional shampoo—just make sure you shake the bottle up a little before using. Use about one tablespoon per application (remember that since it contains castile soap, it won't lather or foam as much as traditional shampoo). Since there are no preservatives in this shampoo, it'll last about a month.

7. Finish with Rapunzel Rosemary Rinse.

## BENEFITS

- **Nettle** (*Urtica dioica*), rich in silica and sulphur, helps increase hair's health and shine. This "weed" can also help in hair regrowth.

- **Chamomile** (*Matricaria chamomilla*) contains cleansing and moisturizing properties. It's excellent for relieving scalp itchiness and dandruff, and improving your hair's sheen.

- **Calendula** (*Calendula officinalis*) flowers are hydrating and moisturizing, and can be used to soothe sensitive scalps and eliminate dandruff. Calendula can strengthen the hair, especially if it's been through a lot of wear-and-tear from styling.

- **Horsetail** (*Equisetum arvense*): When you hear the term horsetail, you probably envision neighing and galloping, but did you know there's an herb of the same name? According to some beauty experts, horsetail is one of the best sources of silica on Earth.[211] This "weed" strengthens weak, brittle, and damaged hair, and may also restore body and luster.

- **Jojoba oil** replenishes moisture and improves the texture of your hair, and removes sticky buildup or excess oil. It treats dry scalp, gets rid of

..................................................
211. Annmarie Skin Care. "11 Ways to Naturally Supercharge Your Hair Growth."

dandruff, adds shine, and naturally eliminates frizz. It's a much better option than using chemical-filled shampoos and conditioners, which only make your hair more dry and limp.[212]

- **Castile soap** is strong enough to cleanse excess sebum and product build-up from the scalp, but gentle enough to not leave your hair stripped and dry. It's non-toxic and biodegradable.

## SOAPWORT "SHAMPOO"

DIY shampoo is the best, no lye! As its name suggests, soapwort (*Saponaria officinalis*) has long been used to make detergent and soap due to the saponins (compounds that make foam when shaken with water) in its roots and leaves that create bubbles. It typically grows in thick patches in waste places like old building sites, along roadsides, railroads, and ditches. Farmers would make soap out of it to bathe sheep before shearing, and it was once used in the wool industry to clean new wool. Colonists brought the plant with them from Europe as a soap substitute.[213] When boiled in water, soapwort produces a slippery substance that has the power to lift grease and dirt. It's believed to be safe for keeping all types of hair healthy and shiny, including color-treated hair. Don't get yourself into a lather if this shampoo doesn't lather as much as you may anticipate. Lather doesn't equal clean. Makes about four cups.

### INGREDIENTS

1 tablespoon chopped soapwort root

1 teaspoon rosemary leaves

4 cups water

15 drops vetiver essential oil

10 drops bergamot essential oil

........................................

212. Ruggeri, "Jojoba Oil Benefits for Face, Hair, Body and More."

213. Jeanroy, "Soapwort Plant Profile."

## INSTRUCTIONS

1. In a saucepan, add soapwort, rosemary, and water. Bring to a boil, then cover and simmer for twenty minutes.

2. Let cool, then strain.

3. Pour into a four-cup flip-cap plastic container (an old, rinsed-out shampoo bottle works well) and add essential oils.

4. Your "shampoo" is ready to use! Store in the fridge (it will last about a week).

5. To use: Depending on the length of your hair, use ½ to 1½ cups on your hair, and massage into your scalp with your fingertips. This recipe won't be as bubbly as store-bought shampoo, but you'll be surprised how clean your hair will feel once it's rinsed. We recommend finishing with our Rapunzel Rosemary Rinse on page 201.

Commercial shampoo strips your hair of its natural oils, causing your scalp to produce more and more oil. This recipe doesn't do this—and that's a good thing!—but it'll take time for your body to adjust its oil production. When you first make the switch to washing with soapwort, your hair might feel a little more greasy or dry than usual. As soon as your body adjusts, your hair will look and feel better than ever, and it'll stay clean longer too. You may find that you only have to wash your hair a few times a week.

# GROUNDED GOODWIFE STORY TIME

### *Washing Your Hair with Baking Soda?* by Ehris

We've opted to include only two shampoo recipes in this book. Love Is in the Hair and Soapwort "Shampoo" are ideal for people who are exploring DIY, sulfate-free hair care options.

I washed my hair with Love Is in the Hair for years, but was always curious about using baking soda and vinegar on my hair. The only thing that held me back was the horror stories I'd heard about how oily my hair would be for a month as I transitioned. As a public speaker, I thought it would ruin my "green witch image" if I showed up at speaking gigs with greasy hair, or wearing a beanie. Three years ago, we had the entire month of December free, and I decided to take the plunge. Possibly because I hadn't used supermarket shampoo for a long time, the switchover really wasn't bad at all. Eliminating shampoo (of any sort) and getting my layers trimmed once a month has left my hair in the best shape it's ever been. I never buy or make shampoo. Instead of shopping in the health and beauty aisle, my haircare product is in the supermarket baking aisle!

Some people report that after a few months of using baking soda, they wind up with dry, frizzy, damaged hair. I think that's because they aren't using it properly. Baking soda has a high pH of nine, but the normal pH of your scalp is between four and five. If your hair's pH level rises above this, its cuticles open and lose moisture, making your hair rough, frizzy, and dry. Once your hair is clean, you have to get your scalp back to its normal four to five pH. A vinegar leave-in rinse will restore pH balance. Also, many recipes instruct making a baking soda/water paste. Instead of the paste formula, I mix a little baking soda with a lot of water (see recipe below), which is just as cleansing, but much more gentle.

• • •

## SIMPLIFY, SIMPLIFY, SIMPLIFY BAKING SODA "SHAMPoO"

Baking soda "shampoo" doesn't contains parabens, sodium laurel sulfate, DEA/diethanolamine, dyes, or fragrance. It's made of one all-natural ingredient: sodium bicarbonate. In case you're curious, the minerals nahcolite and trona are mined (primarily from Wyoming), and refined into soda ash, which then somehow becomes sodium bicarbonate.

Many hair products leave a filmy buildup on the hair, but baking soda clarifies and helps to keep your hair free of dandruff. And the best part? It costs basically nothing, nada. This is the only thing Ehris uses (she washes her hair and uses the Rapunzel Rosemary Rinse about twice a week).

Do not use baking soda on color-treated hair—it can remove coloring on the hair.

## INGREDIENTS

Baking soda

Water

## INSTRUCTIONS

1. In a cup (Ehris uses a sixteen-ounce plastic cup), place a few teaspoons of baking soda. Ehris has thick, curly, shoulder-length hair, so she uses about two teaspoons baking soda and has noticed that if she uses more than that, her hair gets a little too soft. If you have longer or shorter hair, adjust accordingly—you'll figure out exactly how much you need after experimenting a few times.

2. Add about two cups of warm water (if you're using a sixteen-ounce cup, no need to measure the water—just fill the cup to the top), and swish it around a little so the baking soda dissolves.

3. Pour the "shampoo" over wet hair, and gently work it into your scalp. Remember that since it doesn't contain any soap, it won't lather or foam like traditional shampoo.

4. Let it sit on your hair for one to three minutes. Rinse well.

5. Extremely important (in order to close your hair's cuticles and avoid dryness and frizz): finish with the Rapunzel Rosemary Rinse!

## TIPS

- This "shampoo" works best when it's made right before use, so don't make it and then store it for later.

- Commercial shampoo strips your hair of its natural oils, causing your scalp to produce more and more oil. Baking soda doesn't do this—and that's a good thing! But it'll take time for your body to adjust its oil production. When you first make the switch to washing with baking soda, your hair might feel a little more greasy or dry than usual. As soon as your body adjusts, your hair will look and feel better than ever, and it'll stay clean longer too. You may find that you only have to wash your hair a few times a week.

- If you're going to try baking soda shampoo, make sure you finish with a vinegar rinse (like our Rapunzel Rosemary Rinse). Baking soda's high pH opens the hair cuticle. A vinegar rinse will seal the hair cuticle, making the hair shiny and de-frizzed. It'll also balance the pH, helping the scalp stay moisturized and protected.

## GROUNDED GOODWIFE STORY TIME

### *Why Use a Vinegar Hair Rinse?* by Ehris

When I used to use store-bought cream conditioner, it weighed my hair down and made it flat. Switching to a leave-in vinegar hair rinse has made my hair more curly and have more body.

Benefits of vinegar hair rinses:

- removes the buildup left behind by other conditioners and hair products
- seals your hair cuticles, which locks in moisture and leaves your hair looking shiny and smooth
- removes/minimizes tangles (especially helpful for my thick, curly hair)
- balances the pH of your scalp and hair
- is cheaper than any commercial conditioner
- you know exactly what's in it

Many people with color-treated hair report that vinegar rinses actually extend the life of their color job (which makes sense, since vinegar is often used to set clothing and Easter egg dyes).

• ● •

## RAPUNZEL ROSEMARY RINSE

There are two variations to this recipe, Darkening Hair Rinse and Highlighting Hair Rinse, based on your hair color. Don't worry … you won't smell like Italian dressing! Your hair will be scent-free once it dries. You'll also have the option of scenting your vinegar rinse with essential oils. Makes four and a quarter cups.

# GROUNDED GOODWIFE STORY TIME

## *Hair Observations* by Ehris

Not too long ago, we were on our way to one of our speaking gigs, and I was driving. My mom was weirdly peering at my head and said, "Ehris! Your hair looks so dark! It's always been brown, but I've never seen it that dark brown!" I've never colored my hair, so I thought about what she said for a minute.

I said, "You know, I think it's the herbs I've been putting in my hair rinse! Remember, I used to use chamomile and calendula, and you said it looked like I had highlights? I ran out of those herbs like four months ago, so I changed it up to sage, nettle, and rosemary. That's the only thing it could be!"

• • •

## DARKENING HAIR RINSE RECIPE

Used consistently, this recipe can darken your hair, and may even cover gray.

### INGREDIENTS

3 ½ cups water

¼ cup sage leaf (green or clary, not white sage)

¼ cup nettle leaf

¼ cup rosemary leaf

¾ cup vinegar (raw apple cider or plain white vinegar)

15 drops essential oils (see list on page 205)

### INSTRUCTIONS

1. Add sage, nettle, and rosemary to French press or teapot.

2. Pour boiling water over herbs and steep at least an hour (we sometimes steep overnight)—this will ensure that you're making a strong herbal rinse!

3. Strain herbs and pour liquid into glass or plastic bottle.

4. Add vinegar and essential oils, and shake to combine.

## TO USE

- *Ehris:* After washing my hair, I add about ½ cup to a sixteen-ounce plastic cup, fill the rest of the cup with warm water (since I don't like pouring cold stuff on my head), pour it over my hair, and comb it through. Do not rinse!

- *Velya:* I pour about ¼ cup directly on my head and rub it in—do not rinse out! FYI, I have very short, choppy hair and haven't used *any* kind of shampoo, including baking soda, in over three years.

## BENEFITS

- **Sage** (*Salvia officinalis*) leaves are light green, but a strong sage infusion (like the one in this recipe!) will noticeably darken hair over time (this doesn't work like chemical hair dye—don't expect immediate results). Sage also promotes hair growth.

- **Nettle** (*Urtica dioica*) leaf is nutrient-rich, and can help combat hair loss/promote hair growth (drinking nettle tea could help too!). Nettle will balance sebum (the oil that your pores produce), which can make a difference if you suffer from dandruff or dry scalp.

- **Rosemary** (*Salvia rosmarinus*) stimulates and improves circulation to the scalp, encouraging hair growth. It increases shine, and relieves irritated, dry, flaky, dandruff-ridden scalps.

- **Vinegar:** For everything else, we recommend using *only* raw apple cider vinegar, but for this rinse, either raw apple cider vinegar or plain white vinegar work (we've experimented with both of them in the rinse and haven't noticed any difference between the two). Vinegar calms frizzy hair, brings back shine, gets rid of product buildup/residue, decreases dandruff, and removes tangles.

## HIGHLIGHTING HAIR RINSE RECIPE

Use this recipe to bring out golden highlights.

### INGREDIENTS

3 ½ cups water

⅓ cup chamomile flowers

⅓ cup calendula flowers

¼ cup rosemary leaves

¾ cup white vinegar (white vinegar, not ACV, works best with lighter hair)

15 drops essential oils (optional—see choices below)

### INSTRUCTIONS

1. Add chamomile, calendula, and rosemary to French press or teapot.
2. Pour boiling water over herbs and steep at least an hour (longer is better).
3. Strain herbs and pour liquid into glass or plastic bottle.
4. Add vinegar and essential oils, and shake to combine.

### BENEFITS

- **Calendula** (*Calendula officinalis*): Over time, rinsing your hair with calendula can lighten the color and bring out golden tones.
- **Chamomile** (*Matricaria chamomilla*) will nourish and add shine to the hair, while lightening and brightening blonde hair.
- **Rosemary** (*Salvia rosmarinus*) stimulates and improves circulation to the scalp, encouraging hair growth. It increases shine, and can relieve irritated, dry, flaky, dandruff-ridden scalps.

## Essential Oil Options for Shampoo and Hair Rinse

Add up to fifteen drops total.

- "Normal" hair
  - Basil, clary sage, geranium, juniper, lavender, lemon, marjoram, orange, peppermint, rosemary, sage, thyme, ylang ylang

- Dry hair
  - Cedarwood, chamomile, clary sage, geranium, jasmine, lavender, orange, rosemary, sandalwood, ylang ylang

- Oily hair
  - Basil, bergamot, cedarwood, chamomile, clary sage, eucalyptus, geranium, juniper, lavender, lemon, lemongrass, orange, peppermint, rosemary, sage, thyme

While it's important to be concerned about what we eat and drink, it's also important to think about what we're applying to our bodies. Making a change in your shampoo routine can feel a little unsettling, especially if you've used the same product for years. The main difference you'll notice about natural shampoo is that it doesn't lather up the same way your old shampoo did since those foaming agents aren't there. This doesn't mean it's not getting your hair clean, so don't be quick to throw in the towel (you caught the cheesy pun, right?). In the end, your hair could feel cleaner and healthier than it ever has before. If you opt to buy vs. DIY your hair care products, we suggest you search for ones that are free of parabens (synthetic chemicals that are used as preservatives), phthalates (a group of chemicals used to make plastics more flexible and harder to break, often called plasticizers), and sulfates (aggressive detergents made of sulfur-containing mineral salts).

Your body is its own ecosystem. Just as chemicals can throw off ecosystems in nature, they can also disrupt your delicate balance.

# CHAPTER NINE
## UNWINDING

To us, a day of pampering would include a visit to a Korean restaurant, acupuncture, a new stack of library books, clean sheets, and reading on the porch swing. To you, it might mean a mani-pedi, comic books, peanut butter cups, and beach time.

When you treat yourself well, it will trickle down to everything else in life, but that contradicts the prevailing mindset that busier is better. The paradox is that resting your brain can resuscitate it. For most of us, the only parts of the day when our minds are free to wander are our minutes in the shower or when we're trying to fall asleep at night. Seeds can't sprout in an overcrowded pot. Creativity can only take place in a relaxed mind. Think of it like the airplane oxygen masks—we're told to put our own on first before helping someone else. If you're unconscious before you have the chance to help anyone else, you're no help to anyone.

People retain new information best when their minds are given time off to process it—whether it's studying for an algebra exam, or digesting the contents of an important email. A brain-scan experiment on rats demonstrated that when rats are allowed to rest after completing an unfamiliar maze, and are then presented later with the same maze, they find their way through it more quickly.[214] So, even when your (or a rat's) brain is resting, it's working!

Jonathan Schooler, a professor of psychological and brain sciences at the University of California, Santa Barbara, believes that downtime for our brains can aid in creativity and problem-solving. "Our research has found

214. Karlsson and Frank "Awake Replay of Remote Experiences in the Hippocampus," 913–18.

that mind-wandering may foster a particular kind of productivity," and that when our minds have time to roam, we have more *a-ha!* moments.[215] We've all experienced not being able to remember the name of a movie, or a particular word, or name, or song lyric that's right on the tip of your tongue no matter how hard you concentrate. But as soon as you move onto another task, it pops into your head, right?

The magic of basking in a warm bath (can you still remember the ceiling over your childhood bathtub?) or an herbal sleep pillow to induce relaxation and bring on pleasant dreams may be just what your overworked brain needs.

Remember, you are worthy of your own nurturing. *Aha!*

## CALMING WATERS

If you struggle with guilt over taking private time for yourself, remember that you can't pour from an empty glass. We all know that taking a good long soak can cleanse both the body and the mind, but a 2017 study carried out at Loughborough University revealed that slightly raising the body temperature has a positive effect on an individual's metabolic rate, regardless of the activity. Fourteen men took part in the study. They were assigned to either an hour-long soak in a hot bath, or an hour of cycling. The activities were designed to cause a 1.8°F rise in core body temperature over the course of one hour. The calories the men burned in each session were measured. Surprisingly, the calories burned while taking an hour-long bath resulted in about as many calories burned during a half-hour walk (around 140 calories).[216]

Our Calming Waters recipes—which include a sore muscle soak, a milk bath for weather-beaten dry skin, and a luxurious honey bath—will give you the urge to shut the door, turn on some quiet music, and light a candle.

### SORE MUSCLE DETOX SOAK

A landscaper friend of ours, who works outdoors twelve months a year, describes the scent of this soak as "lumberjacky," and uses it weekly. Winters

215. Heid, "Why Your Brain Needs Idle Time."

216. Faulkner, et al., "The Effect of Passive Heating on Heat Shock Protein 70 and Interleukin-6: A Possible Treatment Tool for Metabolic Diseases?" 292–304.

in Connecticut involve a lot of snow shoveling and firewood stacking (we stack/burn eight cords of firewood every winter)! Even healthy Goodwives occasionally have sore muscles. A traditional folk remedy, mustard baths have been used to soothe achy and tired muscles, as well as help with stress, colds, fevers, and congestion. Don't be surprised if this bath makes you sweat! Mustard has been known to open the pores and help the body sweat out toxins. With the addition of the apple cider vinegar and baking soda, this cleansing recipe aids your body's detox process. Makes about two cups.

## INGREDIENTS

¼ cup mustard powder

¼ cup Epsom salts

1 cup baking soda

6 drops peppermint essential oil

6 drops pine essential oil

6 drops eucalyptus essential oil

Raw apple cider vinegar

## INSTRUCTIONS

1. Mix together Epsom salt, baking soda, mustard powder, and essential oils in a sixteen-ounce mason jar. Label the jar.
2. To use, add six tablespoons of mixture and one cup apple cider vinegar to a running bath.
3. Relax and soak!

## BASIC MILK BATH

A milk bath is a bath where you add milk—in liquid or powdered form—to warm water in your bathtub. The proteins and fat in the milk may help soften and soothe the skin. More research is needed, but interestingly, a 2015 study found that topically applying human breast milk was as effective for treating babies with eczema as hydrocortisone ointment.[217] And, as you know from our Cacao Banana Face Mask, lactic acid is a gentle exfoliator. Note: you may want to avoid milk baths if you have sensitive skin, since the lactic acid may be irritating. Makes one bath.

## INGREDIENTS

½ cup milk (We use powdered goat milk, but you can experiment to determine which one you prefer. Full-fat milks will be more nourishing for your skin. Milk options can include: whole, powdered, coconut, raw, rice, almond, soy, buttermilk.)

1 tablespoon oil (we recommend jojoba, grapeseed, almond, or apricot kernel)

5 drops chamomile essential oil

5 drops lavender essential oil

## INSTRUCTIONS

1. Pour whatever form of milk you're using, along with the tablespoon of desired oil, directly under running bath water. Add essential oils just before stepping into the tub. Slosh the water around to mix.

2. Submerge yourself in this moisturizing bath for at least twenty minutes, and relax.

### A HONEY of A SoAK

As Henry David Thoreau said in *Walden*, "Our life is frittered away by detail. ... Simplicity, simplicity, simplicity! I say, let your affairs be as two or three."[218] We like to think that Henry would approve of this simple four-ingredient soak. Honey is rich in antibacterial, antioxidant, and antifungal properties. A natural humectant that promotes moisture retention, it also provides soothing and anti-inflammatory effects. The combo of essentials are calming and uplifting. Makes one bath.

.................................................

217. Kasrae, "Efficacy Of Topical Application Of Human Breast Milk On Atopic Eczema Healing Among Infants: A Randomized Clinical Trial," 966–971.

218. Thoreau, *Walden*, 94.

## INGREDIENTS

5 tablespoons honey

3 drops bergamot essential oil

3 drops orange essential oil

2 drops frankincense essential oil

## INSTRUCTIONS

1. Add all ingredients to a running bath just before you step in the tub.

2. Turn off your brain and relax.

# HERBAL SLEEP PILLOWS

Whenever we offer a DIY Herbal Sleep Pillow workshop, we ask for a show of hands from the audience to the question "Who here has a sleeping issue?" Invariably, most of the participants raise a hand and tell us that they either can't fall asleep, consistently wake up at 2 a.m., have bad dreams, have strange dreams, or can't fall back to sleep after getting up to go to the bathroom (we occasionally hear about a sleepwalker).

If you have sleeping issues, you're not alone. According to a study by the CDC, more than a third of American adults aren't getting enough sleep on a regular basis.[219] It's estimated that fifty to seventy million Americans suffer from a chronic sleep disorder. The cumulative long-term effects of sleep loss and sleep disorders have been associated with a wide range of damaging health consequences, including an increased risk of hypertension, diabetes, obesity, depression, heart attack, and stroke.[220]

A study of 153 healthy men and women (ranging in age from twenty-one to fifty-five years) monitored the development of the common cold after giving all participants nasal drops containing the cold virus (yes, people actually

......................................

219. "1 in 3 Adults Don't Get Enough Sleep," Centers for Disease Control and Prevention.

220. Colten and Altevogt, "Extent And Health Consequences of Chronic Sleep Loss and Sleep Disorders."

agreed to do this!).[221] They found that those who slept less than seven hours were almost three times more likely to develop a cold than those who slept eight hours or more.

Medical interns on a traditional schedule, with extended work hours of more than twenty four hours, made 36 percent more serious medical errors than interns on a schedule that allowed more sleep![222]

Sleep loss affects every major system in the human body.[223] According to Johns Hopkins University, if you've ever felt foggy or groggy after a poor night's sleep, it probably won't surprise you that sleep significantly affects brain function. A healthy amount of sleep is necessary for "brain plasticity," or the brain's ability to adapt to input. If we sleep too little, we become unable to process what we've learned during the day and we have more trouble remembering it in the future. Researchers also believe that sleep may promote the removal of waste products from brain cells—something that seems to occur less efficiently when the brain is awake.[224] And who wants a dirty brain!?

Many people turn to prescription medications to help them sleep because not being able to sleep is a frustrating problem that makes everything seem worse! But, there are many herbs that can help with getting a good night's sleep. Lavender, hops, mugwort, and lemon verbena are examples.

An herbal sleep pillow goes inside your pillowcase to help you (depending on the blend you choose) fall asleep, stay asleep, keep away bad dreams, or interpret your dreams. Ours are no-sewing versions, since neither of us know how to do much more than sew on a button! We suggest making your herbal sleep pillow in a hand-embroidered vintage handkerchief (we collect them at thrift shops for less than a dollar each), and tying them closed with a pretty ribbon (spools of ribbon are also easily found at thrift shops). A thin cloth napkin, a thin sock, or a small piece of fabric also work.

..............................................

221. Cohen, "Sleep Habits and Susceptibility to the Common Cold," 62.

222. Landrigan, et al., "Effect Of Reducing Interns' Work Hours On Serious Medical Errors In Intensive Care Units," 287–89.

223. Perez-Pozuelo, et al., "The Future of Sleep Health: A Data-Driven Revolution in Sleep Science And Medicine."

224. "The Science of Sleep: Understanding What Happens When You Sleep."

# RIP VAN WINKLE

Rip Van Winkle was a (fictitious) Dutch-American villager who falls asleep in the Catskill Mountains and wakes up twenty years later, having missed the American Revolution. While we can't promise that deep of a sleep, the nervine herbs in this blend can help nourish the nervous system, and may aid in relieving stress and anxiety. Makes one sleep pillow.

## INGREDIENTS

4 tablespoons lemon verbena

2 tablespoons lavender

1 tablespoon catnip

1 tablespoon chamomile

1 tablespoon hops

3 drops bergamot essential oil

3 drops chamomile essential oil

## INSTRUCTIONS

1. Spread your fabric out on a flat surface. Place herbs in the center, and add essential oils on top of the herbs.
2. Gather the corners of the fabric, and secure with a ribbon.
3. If you're not going to use it immediately, or if you're giving it as a gift, put it in a baggie so the essential oils don't dissipate into the air.
4. When ready to use, remove from baggie and put it inside your pillowcase. Some people opt to remove the herbal sleep pillow from their pillowcase every morning and put it back in the baggie to prolong the scent. For us, the whole point of the herbal sleep pillow is to make you relax, and adhering to this extra step would give us stress and anxiety.
5. When your herbal sleep pillow starts to lose its fragrance (perhaps after a month), you can untie the ribbon and add some more herbs and essential oils. When it's totally lost its zip, toss it in the bathtub and use as a bath sachet.

## BENEFITS

- **Lemon verbena** (*Aloysia citrodora*): This citrus-scented herb can relieve stress, nervous tension, and anxiety. Including lemon verbena in your sleep pillow can help banish negative thoughts from your mind as you drift off to sleep. Of course, lemon verbena is more fragrant when it's fresh, but putting fresh herbs in a sleep pillow could result in a moldy mess (and then you *really* won't be sleeping!).

- **Lavender** (*Lavandula angustifolia*) is a well-known relaxing herb. It's helpful for nervous exhaustion, anxiety, and stress. Studies have shown that lavender improves anxiety symptoms such as restlessness, disturbed sleep, and somatic complaints, and has a beneficial influence on general well-being and quality of life.[225]

- **Catnip** (*Nepeta cataria*) is calming for humans, but has the totally opposite effect on cats! People always ask us if their cats are going to rip their pillowcases apart in order to get to the catnip inside their blend. We have two cats who sleep on our beds and that's never happened, but if you have concerns, substitute the catnip for another calming herb.

- **Chamomile** (*Matricaria chamomilla*) calms anxiety, lessens tension, and promotes sleep. This aromatic flower is, by far, the most recommended and well-known sleep herb. A 2016 study found that new mothers who drank chamomile tea every day for two weeks slept better and tended to have fewer symptoms of depression than volunteers who didn't drink the tea.[226]

- **Hops** (*Humulus lupulus*) have a long history of being used to treat sleep issues. They're rich in lupulin—a fine, yellow powder—which is a sedative. A randomized, placebo-controlled double-blind study examined the effects of a hops extract on young adults who self-reported with

........................................

225. Kasper, et a.,"Silexan, An Orally Administered Lavandula Oil Preparation, Is Effective In The Treatment Of 'Subsyndromal' Anxiety Disorder: A Randomized, Double-Blind, Placebo Controlled Trial," 277–27; Kasper, et al., "Efficacy and Safety of Silexan, A New, Orally Administered Lavender Oil Preparation, in Subthreshold Anxiety Disorder—Evidence From Clinical Trials," 547–56.

226. Chang and Chen, "Effects of an Intervention with Drinking Chamomile Tea on Sleep Quality and Depression in Sleep Disturbed Postnatal Women: A Randomized Controlled Trial," 306–15.

mild depression, anxiety, and stress levels. The researchers found significant decreases in anxiety, depression, and stress scores with those who had used the hops extract, compared with placebo.[227]

- **Essential oil: Bergamot** (*Citrus bergamia*) is a citrus fruit—but unlike other citrus essential oils that are known to be stimulating, bergamot is calming. It's used to soothe stress and anxiety, and elevate the mood.

- **Essential oil: Chamomile** (*Matricaria chamomilla*) has a sweet, apple-like aroma, calming to mind and body.

## "WHAT HAPPENS TO A DREAM DEFERRED?"

Interpreting your dreams can be a valuable way to better understand yourself. "Dreams are the bridge that allows movement back and forth between what we think we know and what we really know," says Jeffrey Sumber, who studied global dream mythology at Harvard University and Jungian dream interpretation at the Jung Institute in Zurich.[228] The mugwort alone in this sleep pillow blend won't make you a lucid dreamer overnight, but if you include some intention-setting practices before falling asleep, buckle-up—you could be in for a fascinating evening! Makes one sleep pillow.

### INGREDIENTS

4 tablespoons mugwort leaf

2 tablespoons hops strobiles

1 tablespoon spearmint leaf

1 tablespoon rosemary leaf

3 drops spearmint essential oil

3 drops clove essential oil

---

227. Kyrou, "Effects of a Hops (Humulus Lupulus L.) Dry Extract Supplement on Self-Reported Depression, Anxiety and Stress Levels in Apparently Healthy Young Adults: A Randomized, Placebo-Controlled, Double-Blind, Crossover Pilot Study," 171–80.

228. Tartakovsky, "How To Analyze Your Dreams (And Why It's Important)."

## INSTRUCTIONS

1. Spread your fabric out on a flat surface. Place herbs in the center, and add essential oils on top of the herbs.

2. Gather the corners of the fabric and secure with a ribbon.

3. If you're not going to use it immediately, or if you're giving it as a gift, put it in a baggie so the essential oils don't dissipate into the air.

4. When ready to use, remove from baggie and put it inside your pillowcase. Some people opt to remove the herbal sleep pillow from their pillowcase every morning and put it back in the baggie to prolong the scent. For us, the whole point of the herbal sleep pillow is to make you relax, and adhering to this extra step would *give* us stress and anxiety.

5. When your herbal sleep pillow starts to lose its fragrance (perhaps after a month), you can untie the ribbon and add some more herbs and essential oils. When it's totally lost its zip, toss it in the bathtub and use as a bath sachet.

## BENEFITS

• **Mugwort** (*Artemisia vulgaris*): If you dream only in black and white, mugwort may introduce colors. Mugwort-enhanced dreams might engage more of your senses: sound, touch, smell, and taste. If you already have good dream recall, mugwort might help with lucid dreaming (in case you don't know, a lucid dream is one where the dreamer is *aware* that they're dreaming). Edgar Allan Poe once wrote, "All that we see or seem / Is but a dream within a dream." Lucid dreaming can help us explore our own inner worlds. Dr. Denholm Aspy, a researcher at Australia's University of Adelaide who specializes in lucid dreaming, believes that lucid dreaming may actually be therapeutic for people who deal with recurring nightmares that may affect their quality of life.[229]

..................................................

229. Nadorff, "Bad Dream Frequency in Older Adults with Generalized Anxiety Disorder: Prevalence, Correlates, and Effect Of Cognitive Behavioral Treatment for Anxiety," 28–40.

- **Spearmint** (*Mentha spicata*): In our Herbal Sleep Pillow workshops, someone always asks, "Spearmint in a sleep pillow? Doesn't mint wake you up?" Interestingly, spearmint is an *amphoteric* herb, meaning that it knows what your body needs. So, it can be either calming *or* energizing depending on what you require. In this blend, its calming properties help you drift off to sleep, and its energizing properties help make your dreams more vivid.
- **Rosemary** (*Salvia rosmarinus*) can help calm anxiety and lift the spirits, and can have a clarifying effect on dreams.
- **Hops** (*Humulus lupulus*) are rich in lupulin, which is a sedative. Have you ever heard someone described as "loopy?" Interestingly, the term comes from pre-pharmaceutical days. In the days before painkillers, doctors would sedate their patients with compressed lupulin tablets before they amputated limbs, yanked out teeth, or performed surgery. Patients under the influence of lupulin were called "loopy."[230]
- **Essential oil: Clove** (*Syzygium aromaticum*) stimulates the mind, helpful for making you dream more—and can aid in lucid dreaming.
- **Essential oil: Spearmint** (*Mentha spicata*), combined with the other ingredients in this blend, can inspire innovation, artistry, and creativity in your dreams.

## COZY NIGHTS

This blend may help to open a heart which has tightened emotionally and spiritually. In Traditional Chinese Medicine (TCM), the heart is believed to be a physical organ and the seat of consciousness. TCM teaches that rose, one of the main ingredients in this recipe, has a powerful effect on the spiritual state of one's heart.[231] If you'd be happiest in a world of unicorns, rainbows, and skunky-breath puppies, this is the blend for you! Makes one sleep pillow.

..............................................

230. "What The Heck Is Lupulin, And What's It Doin' In My Beer?". 2011. *Great Lakes Hops*.
231. Greene, "The Medicinal Properties Of Roses."

## INGREDIENTS

3 tablespoons rose petals

2 tablespoons lavender

1 tablespoon red clover

1 tablespoon hops

1 teaspoon sweet marjoram

½ teaspoon cinnamon powder

3 drops lavender essential oil

3 drops vanilla oil (there's no such thing as vanilla essential oil)

1 drop vetiver essential oil

## INSTRUCTIONS

1. Spread your fabric out on a flat surface. Place herbs in the center, and add essential oils on top of the herbs.

2. Gather the corners of the fabric and secure with a ribbon.

3. If you're not going to use it immediately, or if you're giving it as a gift, put it in a baggie so the essential oils don't dissipate into the air.

4. When ready to use, remove from baggie and put it inside your pillowcase. Some people opt to remove the herbal sleep pillow from their pillowcase every morning and put it back in the baggie to prolong the scent. For us, the whole point of the herbal sleep pillow is to make you relax, and adhering to this extra step would *give* us stress and anxiety.

5. When your herbal sleep pillow starts to lose its fragrance (perhaps after a month), you can untie the ribbon and add some more herbs and essential oils. When it's totally lost its zip, toss it in the bathtub and use as a bath sachet.

## BENEFITS

- **Rose** (*Rose* spp.) has been valued throughout history for its ability to refresh the spirit. Uplifting and calming, rose petals can be a helpful remedy for insomnia, irritability, anger, grief, heavyheartedness, and physical or mental exhaustion. Simply smelling roses can uplift the heart. According to one study, women with high risk for postpartum depression who regularly smelled rose oil had significant improvements in both anxiety and depression.[232] Curious about exactly how rose oil works, researchers found that it decreased breathing rates, blood oxygen saturation, and systolic blood pressure when applied to the skin.[233] According to Roman mythology, the rose was a favorite flower of Aphrodite, its thorns representing the pain of love. Devastated after the death of Adonis (one of her many lovers), she ran through the woods barefoot and cut herself with the thorns of a white rose, forever turning roses red. Ancient Romans believed that rose pudding was key in rekindling a flame.[234]

- **Lavender** (*Lavandula spp.*) can calm anxiety and stress, as well as ease headaches, migraines, and insomnia. We've found that lavender can help restore energy if we're feeling burned out and exhausted.

- **Red clover** (*Trifolium pratense*), one of nature's best vitamin and mineral supplements, is a calming mild sedative with anti-anxiety effects.

- **Cinnamon** (*Cinnamomum verum*): For most people, the smell of cinnamon is the smell of comfort and warmth. This sweet, spicy, relaxing herb can help lift low spirits. Romantically, it can spice things up in your love life, injecting strong passion into any relationship. If you're looking for a romantic partner, the addition of cinnamon in your sleep pillow may speedup the outcome you're searching for (you might want to get a bigger bed!). Energetically, cinnamon can dispel negativity and help keep your space protected.

- **Sweet marjoram** (*Origanum majorana*) was traditionally used to ease loneliness, bereavement, and heartbreak. It relaxes mental and physical tension, and is an excellent herb for anxiety and insomnia.[235]

232. Conrad, "The Effects Of Clinical Aromatherapy For Anxiety And Depression In The High Risk Postpartum Woman—A Pilot Study," 164–168.

233. Hongratanaworakit, "Relaxing Effect Of Rose Oil On Humans."

234. Gomez-Rejón, "The Ancient Wisdom Of Aphrodisiacs."

235. McIntyre, *The Complete Herbal Tutor*, 147.

- **Hops** (*Humulus lupulus*) have been shown to increase sleep time.[236] Interestingly, hops can help to lower body temperature—falling core body temperature is one important physiological step toward sleep.[237] Hops have also been shown to reinforce the body's daily bio rhythms of rest and activity.[238]

- **Vanilla oil** (*Vanilla planifolia*) calms emotions and uplifts the spirit. Vanilla can have sedative effects on the body. It can reduce restlessness, quiet the nervous system, and lessen anxiety. If the smell of cookies baking in the oven brings you joy, vanilla might be a scent to try for sleep—without having to hit the gym!

- **Essential oil: Vetiver** (*Vetiveria zizanoides*) comes from the roots of the vetiver plant, a tall grass native to tropical Asia. It smells earthy—kind of like moist dirt, which is a good thing—and its grounding properties make it an extremely beneficial oil to use at bedtime. Vetiver is an underated essential oil, and one of Ehris' top three favorites (okay, you may be wondering... the other two are orange and grapefruit).

Sometimes, like little helicopters, new ideas are hovering in a holding pattern in our brain, just awaiting clearance from air traffic control that the heliport is ready to receive them. Relaxation slows our heart rate, reduces blood pressure, relieves tension,[239] and helps us to have a clear mind—all of which makes for an inviting landing pad for all our little helicopters. Neuroscience is finding that our brains are most active when we're idle or relaxing.[240] So (and we're trying hard to take our own advice on this one!), summon the courage to relax.

236. Palmieri, Contaldi, Fogliame, "Evaluation of Effectiveness and Safety of a Herbal Compound in Primary Insomnia Symptoms and Sleep Disturbances Not Related to Medical or Psychiatric Causes," 163–69.

237. "Understanding Valerian and Hop," The Sleep Doctor.

238. Franco, et al., The Sedative Effects of Hop (*Humulus lupulus*), a Component of Beer, on the Activity/Rest Rhythm," 133–39.

239. "Relaxation Techniques: Try These Steps To Reduce Stress," Mayo Clinic.

240. Schulte, *Overwhelmed: Work, Love, and Play When No One Has the Time*, 240.

## CHAPTER TEN
# ADIOS, CoCO CHANEL!
# PERFUMES AND SCENTS

In 1960, Marilyn Monroe was interviewed by Georges Belmont, *Marie Claire* editor-in-chief, for her new film, *Let's Make Love*. The sound clip features her signature breathless voice saying, "You know, they ask me questions. Just an example: 'What do you wear to bed? A pajama top? The bottoms of the pajamas? A nightgown?' So I said, 'Chanel N°5,' because it's the truth ... And yet, I don't want to say 'nude.' But it's the truth!"[241]

Chanel No. 5 was catapulted into fame by a sex symbol. It's composed of jasmine, rose, ylang ylang, iris, amber, and patchouli notes. But historically, some less-than-sexy ingredients have been used as perfume fixatives—including the anal secretions from the Himalayan civet cat and musk deer, castoreum (collected from male and the female beaver castor glands), and ambergris—which originates in the intestines of male sperm whales. Scientists believe that the whales protect themselves from the hard pointy beaks of squids they eat by secreting a fatty substance called ambergris in their intestines to surround the beaks. Eventually, the whales poop out a huge lump of ambergris, up to hundreds of pounds at a time. You'll be happy to hear that American perfume companies no longer mix ambergris into their fragrances.[242]

241. "Marilyn And N°5," Chanel.
242. Gottfried, *Neurobiology of Sensation and Reward*, 375; Graber, "Strange But True: Whale Waste Is Extremely Valuable."

Fortunately for you, we're going to share our DIY herbal perfume recipes that don't require any sort of sketchy secretions and won't cost you an arm and a leg to create!

But first, some perfume history …

# HISTORY of PERFUMES

The Egyptians were huge fans of perfume and used it for both ceremonial and beautification purposes. They thought fragrance was the sweat of the sun god Ra. Their "god of perfume," Nefertum, wore a head dress made of water lilies (one of the most common perfume ingredients at the time).[243]

By AD 100, Romans were using 2,800 tons of frankincense a year. Perfume was used in beauty products, public baths, and even on the soles of feet.[244]

If you were anybody in Europe from the 1200s to about the 1600s, you carried a pomander.[245] Back then, a pomander wasn't a clove-studded-orange that your kid made as a Christmas present for a teacher. It was a waxy, scented blob kept inside an open filigree pendant and worn around the neck to ward off infection and mildly camouflage the stench of open sewers, animal waste, stagnant water, rotting food, garbage, and unwashed bodies.

Until 1370, perfumes were mostly fragrant greasy oils. Hungarian monks figured out that by adding alcohol to these greasy oils, they could be transformed. They created "Hungary Water," the first perfume that resembles the ones we use today. It was originally for Queen Elisabeth of Hungary. There was a belief that in order for it to have the maximum effect, Hungary Water had to be drunk as well as applied to the body![246]

In the 1400 to 1500s, Italy initiated a serious breakthrough in perfume production. The discovery of aqua mirabilis, a clear substance made of 95

243. Thorpe, "The Ancient History Of Perfume."
244. "The Romans: When Fountains Flowed with Rosewater," The Perfume Society.
245. "Ancient Scent-Sations," Kessler Neighbors United.
246. Foley, *Herbs for Use and for Delight: An Anthology from the Herbarist*, 118–19.

percent alcohol, resulted in liquid perfume.[247] For several hundred years, Venice was the center of the world perfume trade.

Perfume (along with high heels, ballet, and eating with a fork) was brought to France and the rest of the world by Catherine de Medici, the Italian bride of King Henry II of France. Catherine had her own signature scent—a scented water with bergamot and orange blossom. Her perfumer also created musk and civet-scented gloves. According to an article written for the Costume Society in the United Kingdom, "Shortly before an arranged marriage in 1572 between Catherine's daughter and the son of Jeanne d'Albret, Queen of Navarre, the groom's mother died. Accusations were made that before her death, Jeanne had been sent a pair of poisoned perfumed gloves by Catherine. There is no evidence to suggest that the allegations were true, and it is far more likely that Jeanne actually died of tuberculosis. Yet the rumors persisted, and the poisoned gloves became the weapon depicted in Alexandre Dumas' novel, *La Reine Margot* (1845), that concerned the events."[248]

Today, there are over thirty thousand designer perfumes on the market. Perfumes are no longer only for the wealthy!

Before we got into making our own herbal perfume, we used to buy it at health food stores. A one-ounce bottle cost around $27, which seemed reasonable to us at the time. When we started making our own perfume, we realized how easy and inexpensive it is to make—and it's a great opportunity to play "mad scientist." In our workshops, we're always impressed by how well the participants combine base, middle, and top notes. Ask any "nose" (a creator of fragrance), and they'll tell you that these notes must be balanced perfectly. The layering of ingredients in a perfume are the essential building blocks of the scent.

## TOP NOTES

Top notes are the lightest of all the notes, and are the first impression of the fragrance. Have you ever smelled a perfume and were instantly in love or

247. "The Strange History of Cologne." Amorq.
248. Scantlebury, "Catherine De' Medici's Scented Gloves."

turned off? That's because you loved—or hated—the top notes. They're the first to fade, but when blended correctly, they lure you in, and smoothly transition to the heart of the fragrance.

## Top Note Essential Oil Examples:

Anise

Basil

Bergamot

Coriander

Eucalyptus

Grapefruit

Jasmine

Lavender

Lemon

Lemon verbena

Lime

Mint (spearmint, peppermint)

Neroli

Orange

Sage

Tangerine

Tea tree

# MIDDLE NoTES

The middle notes—aka the heart notes—are considered the *heart* of the fragrance. They make their appearance once the top notes have faded a bit, and have a strong influence on the base notes.

## Middle Note Essential Oil Examples:

Bay

Black pepper

Chamomile

Cypress

Geranium

Juniper

Lavender

Lemongrass

Marjoram

Nutmeg

Pine

Rosemary

Yarrow

# BASE NOTES

These final fragrance notes create the full body of the fragrance. They provide the lasting impression, and linger on the skin much longer than the top notes. They appear once the top notes are completely evaporated.

**Base Note Essential Oil Examples:**

Cedarwood

Cinnamon

Clove

Frankincense

Ginger

Myrrh

Patchouli

Rose

Rosewood

Sandalwood

Vetiver

Valerian

Vanilla oil (there's no such thing as vanilla essential oil)

Ylang ylang

## DIY HERBAL PERFUME RECIPE

### INGREDIENTS

4–5 drops of base note essential oils (any combination of base note oils that add up to this number)

6–8 drops of middle note essential oils (any combination of middle note oils that add up to this number)

3–4 drops of top note essential oils (any combination of top note oils that add up to this number)

¼ teaspoon vanilla extract

1 ounce spiced rum to preserve and meld scents

### INSTRUCTIONS

1. Mix all essential oils and vanilla extract together in an opaque spray bottle.
2. Let this mixture sit in the bottle for three days to let scents meld.

Then,

1. Add enough spiced rum to fill the spray bottle (leave room for displacement by the spray nozzle), and cap tightly. In our DIY perfume classes, we give each participant a yo-ho-ho (1-ounce shooter) bottle of rum, and tell them, *"Don't* add the rum today! In *three days,* you'll add the rum to your blend." No matter how clearly and dramatically we give the instruction, we always wind up finding at least one empty shooter in the room when the class is over. We're never sure if it went in the perfume bottle, or they chugged it!
2. Your perfume is ready to use! Theoretically, your perfume could include anywhere from three to seventeen different essential oils, so we highly recommend writing down what you put in your blend. It very well could become your signature scent!

# SOME PERFUME BLEND SUGGESTIONS

Some people need a little help getting started in creating a perfume blend (which is understandable, because how in the world is anyone supposed to know what a combination of the essential oils will smell like?). These are some of the "boutique-worthy" blends that have come out of our classes.

# GROUNDED GOODWIFE STORY TIME

## *Bergamot, the Mystery Fruit* by Velya

We call bergamot "the mystery fruit." We've never met anyone who's eaten one, or seen one in real life! In our DIY Herbal Perfume classes, participants always wind up making a "nice" scent, but some people make truly boutique-worthy ones. Those outstanding blends always seem to include bergamot. If a perfume blend just needs a little somethin'-somethin', a drop or two of bergamot can make all the difference!

• • •

## MINT-LAVENDER-VANILLA

### INGREDIENTS

4 drops peppermint or spearmint essential oil

6 drops lavender essential oil

4 drops vanilla oil

¼ teaspoon vanilla extract (see our DIY Vanilla Extract recipe in chapter two)

1 ounce spiced rum to preserve and meld scents

### INSTRUCTIONS

1. Mix all essential oils and vanilla extract together in an opaque one-ounce glass spray bottle.
2. Let this mixture sit in the bottle for three days to let scents meld.

Then,

1. Add enough spiced rum to fill the spray bottle (leave room for displacement by the spray nozzle), and cap tightly.

2. Your perfume is ready to use! We suggest labeling it so you know what you did in case it becomes "your scent."

## ORANGE-NuTMEG-VANILLA

### INGREDIENTS

4 drops orange essential oil

6 drops nutmeg essential oil

4 drops vanilla oil

¼ teaspoon vanilla extract (see our DIY Vanilla Extract recipe in chapter two)

1 ounce spiced rum to preserve and meld scents

### INSTRUCTIONS

1. Mix all essential oils and vanilla extract together in an opaque one-ounce glass spray bottle.

2. Let this mixture sit in the bottle for three days to let scents meld.

Then,

1. Add enough spiced rum to fill the spray bottle (leave room for displacement by the spray nozzle), and cap tightly.

2. Your perfume is ready to use! We suggest labeling it so you know what you did in case it becomes "your scent."

## EARTHy

### INGREDIENTS

2 drops bergamot essential oil

2 drops neroli essential oil

2 drops juniper essential oil

2 drops pine essential oil

2 drops cypress essential oil

2 drops patchouli essential oil

2 drops vetiver essential oil

¼ teaspoon vanilla extract (see our DIY Vanilla Extract recipe in chapter two)

1 ounce spiced rum to preserve and meld scents

## INSTRUCTIONS

1. Mix all essential oils and vanilla extract together in an opaque one-ounce glass spray bottle.
2. Let this mixture sit in the bottle for three days to let scents meld.

Then,

1. Add enough spiced rum to fill the spray bottle (leave room for displacement by the spray nozzle), and cap tightly.
2. Your perfume is ready to use! We suggest labeling it so you know what you did in case it becomes "your scent."

## CITRUSY

### INGREDIENTS

1 drop lemon essential oil

1 drop grapefruit essential oil

1 drop bergamot essential oil

1 drop orange essential oil

6 drops lemongrass essential oil

4 drops vanilla oil

¼ teaspoon vanilla extract (see our DIY Vanilla Extract recipe in chapter two)

1 ounce spiced rum to preserve and meld scents

## INSTRUCTIONS

1. Mix all essential oils and vanilla extract together in an opaque one-ounce glass spray bottle.

2. Let this mixture sit in the bottle for three days to let scents meld.

Then,

1. Add enough spiced rum to fill the spray bottle (leave room for displacement by the spray nozzle), and cap tightly.

2. Your perfume is ready to use! We suggest labeling it so you know what you did in case it becomes "your scent."

## JASMINE-ROSE FLORAL BLEND

### INGREDIENTS

2 drops jasmine essential oil

1 drop neroli essential oil

1 drop bergamot essential oil

2 drops geranium essential oil

4 drops lavender essential oil

2 drops rose essential oil

1 drop sandalwood essential oil

1 drop vanilla oil

¼ teaspoon vanilla extract (see our DIY Vanilla Extract recipe in chapter two)

1 ounce spiced rum to preserve and meld scents

### INSTRUCTIONS

1. Mix all essential oils and vanilla extract together in an opaque one-ounce glass spray bottle.

2. Let this mixture sit in the bottle for three days to let scents meld.

Then,

1. Add enough spiced rum to fill the spray bottle (leave room for displacement by the spray nozzle), and cap tightly.

2. Your perfume is ready to use! We suggest labeling it so you know what you did in case it becomes "your scent."

## HERBAL SOLID PERFUME RECIPES

Instead of a spray, this perfume is solid, like a lip balm. Dab some on pulse points for long-lasting natural scent. The beeswax helps keep the volatile oils in suspension so they won't dissipate in the air as quickly. We make these in one-ounce metal tins with screw-on lids. Makes about five, one-ounce tins.

### INGREDIENTS

For the base:

½ cup grapeseed or jojoba oil

⅛ cup beeswax pellets

### INSTRUCTIONS

1. In a small double boiler (or makeshift double boiler), melt the beeswax.

2. While the beeswax is melting, add the essential oils directly to the one-ounce container (suggestions on the next page). Some recipes suggest combining your essential oils, melted beeswax, and oil right in the double boiler, but we've found that the essential oil smell gets stuck in the double boiler forever.

3. Once your beeswax is melted, add the grapeseed or jojoba oil and stir until everything is warm and liquidy.

4. Remove from heat and carefully pour the beeswax/oil mixture into your container (of course, it will be hot). With a toothpick or chopstick, gently mix to combine with the essential oil.

5. Your perfume will start to set in a few minutes. Once it's completely hardened, it'll be ready for you to enjoy (or give as a gift).

# SCENT SUGGESTIONS

Essential oil proportions are per one-ounce tin (the amount of essential oils has to go in *each* tin).

## Zest

    20 drops lemon essential oil

    15 drops lemongrass essential oil

    8 drops grapefruit essential oil

    3 drops lime essential oil

    3 drops vanilla oil

## Grounded

    13 drops grapefruit essential oil

    12 drops lavender essential oil

    3 drops bergamot essential oil

    4 drops lemon essential oil

    10 drops vetiver essential oil

## Love Swept

    12 drops jasmine essential oil

    12 drops vanilla oil

    8 drops clove essential oil

    5 drops rose essential oil

    4 drops sandalwood essential oil

## Clarity

    15 drops grapefruit essential oil

    13 drops ginger essential oil

    10 drops vetiver essential oil

    5 drops vanilla oil

## Woodsy

10 drops grapefruit essential oil

8 drops tangerine essential oil

8 drop spearmint or peppermint essential oil

4 drops rosemary essential oil

4 drops jasmine essential oil

2 drops vetiver essential oil

2 drops patchouli essential oil

4 drops pine essential oil

## Sunny

12 drops lime essential oil

8 drops tangerine essential oil

8 drops grapefruit essential oil

8 drops vanilla oil

6 drops cedarwood essential oil

Fragrance—just like a necklace, a pair of earrings, or a scarf—can be an accessory to an outfit. Some people wear perfume because it brings them enjoyment or comfort, or it can be evocative of a memory. In much the same way that a musician would study music, or a writer would study literature, being in a swirl of scent and learning the "language" of perfumes can result in a unique finished composition. Perfume can offer little hints about the kind of person you are. The originality of your own unique signature fragrance is a way of sharing a little bit about yourself.

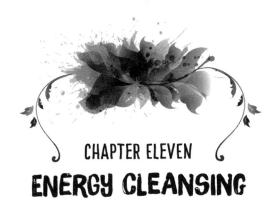

# CHAPTER ELEVEN
# ENERGY CLEANSING

Recently, we hosted a gallery reading at our farmhouse. A gallery reading is a reading by a psychic medium for a group of people together in one room. It's a way to communicate with a spirit, your spirit guides, or to find out if a spirit has a message for you. Spirits decide who they want to connect with, and for how long.

Our 1770 farmhouse already has documented paranormal activity. With twenty people in attendance at the gallery reading inviting in even more "guests," there were a lot of spirits in our house! After everyone had gone home, we both collapsed on the couch, each hoping to enjoy a piece of the gluten-free banana bread we'd served, but we felt dizzy and couldn't focus. The spirits lingering around were guilt-ridden fathers, miscarried babies, heroin addicts, victims of Alzheimer's, and a twin sister. We knew our entire house needed a thorough smoke cleansing!

Feeling stuck, negative, sluggish, or unhappy? It could be due to some stagnant energy in your field that's not allowing positive energy to enter. Smoke cleansing is performed to correct the energy in a home, office, object, or even a person. You do this by burning herbs like white sage, sweetgrass, or mugwort in a focused, intentional way to cleanse negative energy and replenish positive, healing energy. Smoke cleansing creates a blank slate in your environment to ensure that you, your living space, and the things near you are clear of energies that could harm or disturb you. Have you ever gone house-hunting with a realtor? You know that heavy, uncomfortable, blech-y feeling you get in some of the houses? That's a place that needs to be smoke cleansed!

Things aren't just made of physical matter—they also have an invisible energy. Smoke cleansing clears away all the emotional and mental "garbage" that may have gathered over hours, months, or years. You physically dust, clean, and vacuum your house and take showers to clean your body. Smoke cleansing is like an energetic spring-cleaning of your house, or taking a cleansing and purifying shower.

We believe that practices that have been around for a long time—like acupuncture, herbalism, homeopathy, and smoke cleansing—have been around for so long because they work. No one knows for sure when smoke cleansing began, but throughout history, the burning of herbs has been used for cleansing, healing, and spiritual purposes. Smoke cleansing tradition dates back for thousands of years and has been performed in cleansing and blessing rituals by cultures including Native Americans, Aboriginals, Druids, Mayans, Zulus, Chinese, Maoris, and Balinese. Smoke cleansing is used in Buddhism, Hinduism, Islam, Taoism, and Anglican, Roman Catholic, and Orthodox churches.

## COMMON HERBS USED FOR SMOKE CLEANSING

There are many herbs that can be used for smoke cleansing, but each will have its own unique scent and properties. Here are some of our favorites!

### White Sage *(Salvia apiana)*

This is the one item you're sure to find in every single "new age" shop, health food store, and stone shop. People in New England constantly tell us that it thrives in their backyards, but it's most likely that they're describing green sage, since white sage is native to the southwestern United States. We've tried growing white sage in our herb garden, but it withered, dried out, never got bigger, and didn't seem to like Connecticut's icy winters and humid summers. Most people recognize the smell of white sage, and it's probably the most well-known herb used for smoke cleansing. It's ideal for clearing negative energies from people, objects, and spaces. We choose not to use white sage because it was included on the United Plant Savers July 2018 At-Risk/

To Watch list due to irresponsible harvesting and people's disregard for its environment. United Plant Savers writes, "Since every above-ground part of white sage is used for medicinal purposes, it's very easy to be overharvested to the point of death."[249] If you choose to use white sage, look for labels that say "cultivated" (grown on a farm or in a nursery) sources instead of "wild-crafted" (foraged from its wild habitat) ones.

### Sweetgrass (*Hierochloe odorata*)

Smoke cleansing with sweetgrass promotes openheartedness, harmony, and happiness. It helps to invite positive energies into your life as it simultaneously releases what no longer serves you. When walked on, sweetgrass doesn't break—it bends—and because of that, it's believed to symbolize kindness. If you buy a sweetgrass smoke cleansing stick, it'll probably be braided into three strands. Some believe that these three strands can represent love, peace, and harmony or mind, body, and spirit. Sweetgrass smells like vanilla, freshly-cut grass, and fresh bales of hay. It's also known as Mary's grass, vanilla grass, holy grass, bison grass, and the hair of Mother Earth. Sweetgrass naturally grows in wetlands and prairies, but it'll grow in almost any sunny spot. Its natural range is Greenland to Alaska, south to New Jersey, Ohio, Iowa, Arizona, Minnesota, Wisconsin, and Illinois.

Sweetgrass is an aromatic perennial that can grow up to two feet tall. When you pick a planting site, keep in mind that because of its aggressive roots, it might take over an area where it's not wanted. Sweetgrass can be tricky to grow from seed, so we recommend buying a few plants and dividing them after a few years.

### Palo Santo (*Bursera graveolens*)

Palo santo translates to "sacred wood" in Spanish. It's used for deep healing, and clearing energy. We love the smell—like a combo of vanilla and burnt sugar—and we've found firsthand that if you're open to it, palo santo enhances creativity and brings good fortune. Unfortunately, as it becomes more and more popular, the illegal harvesting and cutting of palo santo trees

---

249. "White Sage—*Salvia apiana*," United Plant Savers.

in its native Latin and South America has greatly increased. Consider buying palo santo from reputable indigenous-owned businesses. Read the fine print on packaging, and watch out if you see the word "synthetic"—it means chemicals have been used to produce the signature palo santo scent.

### Mugwort (*Artemisia vulgaris*)

Mugwort brings clarity, deepens intuitive abilities, and removes unwanted energy. Mugwort's Latin name is *Artemisia vulgaris. Artemisia* refers to Artemis, the Greek goddess of the hunt, the wilderness, and wild animals. She's known as the *virgin goddess.* "Virgin" originally meant a woman who was whole unto herself and owned by no one.[250] By AD 1300, the meaning had changed to a "young woman in a state of inviolate chastity."[251] We definitely prefer the original definition! An interesting thought to ponder is how the term "Virgin Mary" fits into all of this etymology ...

## GROUNDED GOODWIFE STORY TIME

### *Mugwort and Dreams* by Velya

Mugwort is known to enhance lucid, prophetic, and vivid dreams— and I always forget this. In midsummer, before it flowers, Ehris and I harvest laundry baskets full of mugwort to use in our DIY Mugwort Smoke Cleansing workshops, as well as for our own smoke cleansing needs. We're careful not to bring any flowering mugwort back to our house because although it has wonderful medicinal benefits, it's invasive, and we don't want it setting up shop in our gardens. We head to our top-secret location in Woodbury, Connecticut, where we know nothing has been sprayed with Roundup.

Armed with gardening shears, we spend hours collecting mugwort stalks. Like sweaty pack mules, we lug the crammed laundry baskets back to our car, our faces buried in the sage-like/chrysanthemum-like odor of the mugwort's tell-tale green above/silver beneath leaves.

---

250. Bennett, *In the Gift of Healing Herbs*, 316.
251. "Virgin (n.)." Etymology Online.

Invariably, the next morning I come downstairs, and with bleary eyes declare to Ehris, "Man, I had the weirdest dream last night..."

That's when I remember that the active compound in some strands of mugwort is thujone, and it's reported to be like a stepping stone to prophetic dreams. According to Gregg Levoy's 2016 *Psychology Today* article titled, "Dreams Don't Come True, They Are True," "Dreams tell you what you really know about something, what you really feel. They point you toward what you need for growth, integration, expression, and the health of your relationships to person, place, and thing. They can help you fine-tune your direction and show you your unfinished business. They're meaning machines. And they never lie."[252] Dreams are an opportunity for the subconscious to go to work on the troubles and questions of the day.

I've recently been weighed down by the baggage of my journey. I've been straddling two different lives: teaching kids and working with adults. For a long time, I've wanted to leave the kid world behind, but it's scary to make a drastic leap like that. Working with kids is something I've always been good at, but it's not what I want to do. As we all know from the book *The Secret*, if you want to attract something into your life, you have to make sure your actions don't contradict your desires. You can't possibly embrace the new life you want while you're still holding on to the baggage of the last one.

My most recent mugwort-induced vivid dream pushed me to make my decision. The dream was so clear and I remember all of it. I was at East Ridge Junior High where I spent the worst two years of my adolescence. I was there as a grown-up, to be interviewed by Kevin O'Leary of *Shark Tank* fame for a teaching position. Kevin, in his trademark black suit and black necktie, danced down the school staircase exactly the way James Cagney did on the White House staircase in *Yankee Doodle Dandy*. When he reached the bottom of the stairwell, he couldn't help but see the diarrhea I'd had all over the hallway—and

252. Levoy, "Dreams Don't Come True, They Are True."

I mean *all* over it. Like a sea of diarrhea. He glared at me and fumed, "Do you think this is funny?!"

"Yeah," I giggled. "I kinda do."

He handed me a push broom and ordered me to clean it up. The hallway lockers had somehow opened up and backpacks, hoodies, tubes of Pringles, clarinets, and spiral bound notebooks spilled onto the diarrhea. I woke up while I was futilely trying to wipe off a Dorito bag and instantly knew what the dream was telling me. That morning, in true *KonMari* style (a Netflix series I expected to snooze through), I purged all of my "teaching stuff" and only kept a few bins of items that "spark joy." I closed my hands-on science company, deleted my website, and today I only work with adults.

•  •  •

## HOW TO MAKE A MUGWORT SMOKE CLEANSING STICK

Mugwort smoke cleansing sticks are available at health food stores or online for around $12 each. You can make your own for a fraction of the price, while doing your part to use invasive plants!

It's important to use mugwort that hasn't been sprayed with pesticides. Inhaling pesticides while you're trying to cleanse your house would be kind of counterproductive! There are two schools of thought on making smoke cleansing sticks. You can either use fresh mugwort and let your stick dry out before using (this could take up to a month), or—the method we prefer— use mugwort that you've already harvested and dried (see chapter four for instructions on drying herbs) and your smoke cleansing stick is ready to use immediately.

While it's possible to make a smoke cleansing stick out of pine or cedar, we don't recommend using them because their volatile oils make them too "sparky" when burned. Palo santo can't be made into a smoke cleansing stick because it's a piece of wood. The best options (besides mugwort) are sweet- grass and white sage, following the same directions below.

## MATERIALS

- Mugwort—approximately 10 stalks, around 12 inches long
- Yarn or string (cotton, hemp … nothing synthetic—the string will burn too, and you don't want to be inhaling polyester fumes!)—approximately 36 inches
- Scissors

## INSTRUCTIONS

1. Gather the mugwort stalks as if you're making a bouquet.
2. Tie a tight double knot about an inch from the base of the stems. Leave a couple of inches of string at the base (you'll need these extra inches of string later).
3. To make a "handle," wrap the string tightly around the base several times.
4. Hold the bundle of mugwort in one hand, and wind the string up the bundle. Once you reach the top, wind the string down the bundle, creating a crisscross design. Wrap as tightly as possible to hold all the leaves in place.
5. Tie another knot at the base, using the string you reserved at the beginning.
6. If you want to make your smoke cleansing stick look neater, trim both ends to tidy it up.

The smoke cleansing sticks you'll see for sale look cute, fat, and perfectly symmetrical. Our first attempts looked *really* sad—puny, uneven, and limp. It's okay if yours don't look professional—they're still going to work just fine. Remember, it's all about your intention!

## HOW To SMOKE CLEANSE A PERSON

A few days ago, someone told us, "I've read that when you smoke cleanse a person, you're supposed to tie your hair back and wear comfortable non-baggy clothing. Is that true?" We were tempted to be sarcastic and tell her, "Actually, we do it in stilettos and pantyhose."

Have the person stand facing you with their feet apart and arms out, as if they're about to do a jumping jack. Light one end of the smoke cleansing stick, let it burn for a few seconds, then blow out the flame to release the smoke. The easiest way to explain this is to picture the person as a gingerbread man, and just trace the outline of their body. We usually start at the person's fingertips, but wherever you want to start is totally fine. Give them a quick smoke cleanse down the center of their body too. Once you're done smoke cleansing the front of their body, have them turn around and trace the outline of the back of their body, and also down the center of their back. Since we absorb everything through the soles of our feet, that's one of the most important places to smoke cleanse. As a reflexologist, Ehris knows that the entire body is mapped out in the feet. Smoke cleansing the soles is grounding and promotes a good connection to Mother Earth.

Some people have concerns about smoke cleansing aggravating allergies or asthma. In our DIY Mugwort Smoke Cleansing workshops, we've smoke cleansed countless people with these health issues, and no one has had a problem. But if you're apprehensive, this might not be the best holistic practice for you.

## HOW To SMOKE CLEANSE A HOUSE

We do two kinds of smoke cleansing: thorough and quickie.

A thorough smoke cleansing involves opening all the cabinets, cupboards, drawers, closets, and doors, and includes your basement and attic. Depending on the size of your house, this can take up to forty-five minutes. This is something we only do when we can "feel" that the house needs it. Since we host so many events at our house and have people constantly coming and going, we probably do this more often than a regular family would need to. We do a thorough smoke cleanse every month, but as a rule of thumb, doing it with every season change is a good idea.

A quickie smoke cleanse is necessary when you have limited time, but you know something's "hanging around" that needs to go. Before we became public speakers, Ehris used to see clients privately in our home for reflexology, herbal and flower essence consultations, and reiki sessions. Using a palo santo stick, she'd do a quickie smoke cleanse in the rooms where a client had been so the next person wouldn't take on their energy.

You'll need a smoke cleansing stick, matches, and something to hold under the stick to catch ashes (like a pie plate or metal pot). First, open at least one window or door on each floor of your house (yes, even in the winter) so any unwanted "stuff" has a way to get out. Light one end of the stick, let it burn for a few seconds, then blow out the flame to release the smoke. After teaching many, many DIY Mugwort Smoke Cleansing workshops, we have a theory that if your stick ignites instantly and flames brilliantly like Katniss Everdeen's *Catching Fire* chariot dress, you and your house majorly need to be cleansed. If you have trouble getting the stick to light, you're probably not carrying around a lot of energetic junk.

Our belief in *all* things holistic is that everything doesn't have to be complicated, serious, and reverential. It's your intention that matters. People ask us:

1. "Where should I start smoke cleansing? I've heard you have to start in the east, then move south, then west, then north." Honestly, we're not quite sure where these cardinal directions even are, so we just start at the front door.

2. "Do I have to ring a bell in each room to awaken the sleeping energy?" No.

3. "Should I get an abalone shell to catch the ashes?" Some people say that using an abalone shell to catch ashes is a bad idea, since you're combining two elements (fire and water). We use metal pots from the thrift shop to catch the ashes.

4. "Should I smoke cleanse at sunrise?" That sounds like a lovely idea, but negative energy doesn't restrict itself to a schedule. Smoke cleansing any time of day or night is fine.

5. "What if I don't have a sacred eagle feather to fan the smoke?" We don't use any kind of feather.

6. "Should I mop the floor with rose tea when I'm done?" Sure, if you want to, but why?

We like to start smoke cleansing at our front door. It's important to trace the outline of the door with the smoldering stick, since the front door is where people come and go. Do the same thing with windows and doorways. Walk slowly around each room, wafting the smoke in all directions. We like to smoke cleanse our furniture, especially if we know someone annoying or unpleasant has been sitting there. Pay attention to corners and fireplaces, since energy can get stuck there. While smoke cleansing, some people recite the Lord's Prayer (either aloud or to themselves). We just say something very basic, like, "Negative energy be gone, only light and love are welcome here." You can say this aloud, or just think it to yourself. Allow the smoke to drift into hidden spaces, like closets and basements. If there are stairs, smoke cleanse them as you make your way to the next floor. Once you feel like you've sufficiently cleansed your home, extinguish the stick by stubbing it against the bottom of the pot, kind of like you're snuffing out a cigar (we guess … we've never smoked cigars).

## HOW To SMOKE CLEANSE AN OBJECT

Along with the actual people coming in and out of our house for events, it's furnished with antiques and thrift shop finds. Thrift shoppers or tag salers often don't stop to think about the history behind the items they choose to bring into their homes. What kind of energy could be attached to that antique English Chippendale armchair? It's important to clear residual energies from secondhand items. Before we even unload purchases from the car, we give them a thorough smoke cleanse. If you're someone who purchases or inherits heirloom jewelry, it's vitally important to cleanse those pieces. It's not that the previous owner had bad energy—it could be that their energy isn't compatible with yours.

To smoke cleanse a small object (like jewelry), have your items ready on a table or countertop, and make sure a door or window is open to let any unwanted energy out. Light your smoke cleansing stick. Pick up the item that needs to be cleansed and hold it over the smoke for a few seconds.

To smoke cleanse a larger object (like a chair), make sure a door or window is open to let any unwanted energy out, then light the stick. Trace the object with the smoldering stick, allowing the smoke to get on all sides of the object.

## GROUNDED GOODWIFE STORY TIME

### *Mugwort Draws a Crowd!* by Velya

Every October in Woodbury, there's a town-wide event called "Meander Down Main Street." Main Street is shut down for the afternoon so that vendors, food trucks, bands, ballerinas from the local dance school, and Cub Scouts can entertain attendees as they mingle with friends and neighbors. Every year at our Grounded Goodwife table, we offer people the opportunity to make a complimentary mugwort smoke cleansing stick, and we lure people to us by burning a pot of dried mugwort. An important thing to note about mugwort is that it smells very much like pot. In the course of this one afternoon, at least three hundred people sidle up to us and wink, "So, what are you girls smokin' down here? It smells like college!"

• • •

## HOW To SMOKE CLEANSE A CAR

One final, often forgotten, place to cleanse is your car, since it can hold unwanted energy you've picked up throughout your day. The process is exactly like smoke cleansing a room. Open all the doors, including the trunk, and make sure the smoke gets in the nooks and crannies of the car (you don't have to cleanse the engine). We like to crack the window for a few hours after we're done smoke cleansing to let out any remaining energetic clutter.

# GROUNDED GOODWIFE STORY TIME

## *Babbling* by Velya

I've never been stopped by a cop or gotten a speeding ticket, but if it ever does happen, it will probably be right after I've given my car a thorough smoke cleanse. I sometimes picture the whole scenario. As I roll down the driver window to hand the cop my license and registration, the overwhelming pot smell hits him in the face. His eyes narrow as he intently observes me, and then I nervously start babbling: "You probably think I was lighting up a joint in here, right? I would never do that... I was just burning mugwort because I was at this antique store, and I was looking at this Victorian settee... and I bought it... see? It's right back there... but the energy in the place felt kind of creepy. You know what smoke cleansing is, right? Like burning herbs to get rid of negative energy?"

• • •

All of us unconsciously process other people's issues and energies throughout the day. With all that our bodies take in from the outside, we're often left feeling overwhelmed, tired, and exhausted as we're confronted with "junk" that doesn't even belong to us! Even though people who are constantly unhappy, uncaring, or ungrateful may suck all the positive energy out of us, we can't always cut these people out of our lives. A good smoke cleansing can be kryptonite to negative energy!

## CHAPTER TWELVE

# GROUNDED GOODWIFE PANTRY ESSENTIALS: PART TWO

This chapter details the ingredients, supplies, and equipment needed for part two of this book: Natural Body Care.

Where can you find these ingredients? Your local health food store, online sites, and grocery stores will carry the majority of the items we suggest. We're excluding common ingredients like twine, white sugar, lemons, and coffee, which you probably already have on hand. Some of the more unique herbs/items are available at groundedgoodwife.com.

## SUPPLIES/EQUIPMENT

1-ounce metal tins with screw-on lids

1-ounce opaque glass spray bottles

2-ounce glass dropper bottles

8-ounce plastic flip-top squeeze bottle

24-ounce plastic flip-top squeeze bottle, or old rinsed-out shampoo bottle

48-ounce plastic flip-top squeeze bottle, or old rinsed-out shampoo bottle

Mason jars (4-ounce, 8-ounce, 12-ounce)

Blender

# INGREDIENTS

Aloe vera gel

Baking soda

Base oils (jojoba, apricot kernel, coconut, grapeseed, olive, hemp, argan, rosehip seed)

Beeswax pellets

Borax

Cinnamon

Cocoa butter

Coconut milk

Epsom salts

Green clay

Honey (raw and local, if possible)

Liquid castile soap (unscented)

Mustard powder

Peppermint hydrosol

Raw, unpasteurized apple cider vinegar

Ribbon

Shea butter

Spiced rum

Vanilla extract

Vanilla oil (vanilla essential oil doesn't exist)

Vintage handkerchief, thin cloth napkin, or small piece of fabric

Vitamin E capsules

White clay

White vinegar

Witch hazel

Yarn or cotton string (nothing synthetic)

Essential oils (see chapter ten for other essential oils you might want to purchase)

- Basil
- Bergamot
- Carrot seed
- Cedarwood
- Chamomile
- Clary sage
- Clove
- Eucalyptus
- Frankincense
- Geranium
- Grapefruit
- Helichrysum
- Jasmine
- Juniper
- Lavender
- Lemon
- Lemongrass
- Marjoram
- Myrrh
- Orange
- Patchouli
- Peppermint
- Pine
- Rose
- Rose geranium
- Rosemary
- Sage
- Sandalwood
- Tea tree

- Thyme
- Vetiver
- Ylang ylang

# HERBS

Calendula

Catnip

Chamomile

Green sage

Hops

Horsetail

Lavender

Lemon verbena

Mugwort

Nettle

Red clover

Rose

Rosemary

Soapwort

Spearmint

Spirulina

Sweet marjoram

# CONCLUSION

Living the green witch life means choosing to live your life and heal your body through natural remedies. What's unique about this way of living is observing everything as a whole. We don't look at sickness and automatically think it's something physical—we observe the entire picture. We believe that those who are in the best health actually heal their body from the inside out. They take care of the inside first, and then the outside follows. Many people focus only on the things they see and try to treat their hair, their skin, and their teeth from the outside. Fuel your body well. If you eat junk, you'll feel like junk.

You may be questioning your world. It's a healthy thing to contemplate and challenge beliefs you've accepted. It's daring to be curious about the unknown and to question the way we live—and both daring and optimum health start from within. Herbs are more courageous than most humans. Many people are content being someone that they're not because it's just easier to go with the flow, but an elderberry bush would rather die than become a horseradish plant. Herbs are true to who they are.

We've created our own paths and encourage you not to follow, but to create your own. By associating with others who are already on this journey, you'll find it much easier to become a green witch. Keep growing! If you truly want to live holistically, you will have to go through a period of changes. There is no growth without change.

# GROUNDED GOODWIFE STORY TIME

### *Question Authority* by Velya

*If you start something, finish it.*
*Always do your best, no matter what you do.*
*Be kind to others.*
*Work hard for everything you get in this life.*

Moms teach us a lot. They give us our voices, and make us who we are. My mother never offered any of those sage words of wisdom, but the most important thing I've learned came from her. She taught me to "question authority." My mother always encouraged me to unapologetically think for myself rather than blindly accept the thinking of parents, teachers, doctors, religion, politicians, the media, and other perceived "authority figures." Because of that, I was never part of the herd, plodding along with all the other people who are plodding along because everyone else is plodding along. I never had to break away from a herd because I never belonged to one, and I didn't have to worry about the things that happen to you when you make the break.

I'm not an allopathic physician or a naturopath, but I do have credentials. When asked, I don't reveal my age because I don't want someone's idea of what thirty, fifty, or seventy is "supposed" to look like to influence their opinion of me. Like Dr. Christiane Northrup, I believe that "age is just a number, and agelessness means not buying into the idea that a number determines everything from your state of health to attractiveness to your value."[253] However, I've been around longer than pocket calculators, smoke detectors, Spandex, lava lamps, weed whackers, barcodes, suitcases with wheels, the internet, and buffalo wings. My "credentials" are my wrinkle-free skin, my full head of hair that needs a haircut every two weeks, my ability to sit criss-cross-applesauce for hours at a time, my perfect vision, my one-filling teeth,

.................................................
253. Northrup, *Goddesses Never Age*, 15.

my energy and enthusiasm, and my ability and fearlessness to jump off a thirty-foot diving platform into a Yucatan cenote.

For a long, long time I kept quiet about my holistic beliefs. People tend to get very squirmy and uncomfortable when they hear nonconformist thinking, and *I* felt bad about making *them* uncomfortable. Dopey, huh? And then something happened that made me realize the importance of not keeping quiet. I was in the faculty room at one of the schools where I used to teach. It was a Friday morning in October, and just about every woman in the room was wearing a pink cancer ribbon because it was Breast Cancer Awareness Month. I had every intention of keeping my mouth shut and just enjoying the spread of pretty-in-pink popcorn, mammo-graham cookies, pink velvet cake pops, and check-your-boobies cupcakes. It was getting close to the start of the school day and the festivities were beginning to wind down when someone handed me a little pink card that instructed: *Get your mammogram. The best five-minute squeeze in your life for early detection of breast cancer.*

Every other time the mammogram talk had come up, I'd just kept quiet. But when you don't speak up, your silence equals approval. So, here's what I said to the room: "I've never had a mammogram, and will *never, ever* get one. Starting at age forty-five, women are told to get regular mammograms. But, studies have shown that routine mammograms can increase a woman's risk of developing radiation-induced breast cancer.[254] Also, only twenty-two pounds of pressure is needed to rupture the encapsulation of a cancerous tumor, which could potentially spread malignant cells into your bloodstream. Today's mammogram equipment applies forty-two pounds of pressure to the breasts! People are convinced that 'early detection saves lives,' but so many of the tumors that mammograms detect are ones that women

............................................

254. Miglioretti, et al., "Radiation-Induced Breast Cancer Incidence and Mortality from Digital Mammography Screening," 205; Epstein, "Dangers and Unreliability of Mammography: Breast Examination Is a Safe, Effective, and Practical Alternative," 605–15.

would die 'with,' not 'from.' They would never become life-threatening if left alone."[255]

As you can imagine, my comments brought the "party" to a screeching halt. But that night, I got an email from a woman who had been in the faculty room. She confided that she was really interested in what I had to say but was afraid to speak up because leaving the pack can be a lonely place. A few years ago, that same woman contacted me again. She said that during a self-exam, she felt a lump in her left breast. She'd been agonizing over what to do and knew that the "right" thing was to get a mammogram, but remembered my antimammogram reasoning. She knew that Ehris was an herbalist and wanted to know if she could help. After a lengthy consultation, Ehris made her a flower essence (since so many dis-eases are caused by emotions), a violet/cleavers tincture to take internally, and a violet/poke roll-on. Lumps are often the result of a "stuck" lymphatic system. Using lymphatic herbs like violet, cleavers, and poke gets lymph fluid flowing—kind of like pulling leaves and debris out of a clogged brook to keep the water running. As Ehris told the woman, "People feel a lump and get so freaked out! They're convinced they have cancer, and that their only 'cure' is chemo. But lumps respond *so* quickly to herbal medicine." Within a week, the woman reported back to Ehris that her lump was gone, and she was so happy she hadn't listened to the "experts" and caved.

While the majority of people in the United States accept that vaccinations, mammograms, and prescriptions are safe and effective, we choose not to have mammograms, not to vaccinate, and not to take prescriptions—but that doesn't mean those are the right choices for you. We're always mindful not to take a "Your feelings are wrong. You should feel the way we do," approach. However, it also means that people who think the way we do shouldn't be insulted, shamed, or persuaded. Personal experiences often motivate us to learn more about our bodies and how we can heal from illness, stress, and trauma.

..............................................
255. Kresser, "The Downside of Mammograms."

As kids, we're trained to follow authority. We were all taught that disobedience is wrong. As a former high school and elementary teacher, I always admired and respected the kids that other teachers found difficult. As long as they were polite, I enjoyed the kids who questioned rules and thought for themselves. Timothy Leary, the American psychologist and writer known for tripping his way through life, was the one who coined the phrase "Question Authority" (or maybe it was Socrates, but it definitely wasn't Ben Franklin.) Thinking for yourself isn't easy. But sometimes your decision to think independently inspires others who secretly yearn to do the same. To think, you must question.

• • •

Throughout history, witches have been depicted as ugly, nasty, wart-nosed women stirring their bubbling toad-filled cauldrons. They were feared and avoided for their "sinister intentions." Really, they were skilled wise-women who knew the power of healing herbs and natural medicine.

Witches are no longer hunted and persecuted to the same degree but we're still misunderstood. If this book has resonated with you and inspired you to harvest the incredible power of nature without harming it, our coven welcomes you. While Velya's dancing naked in the forest, Ehris will be tending the newts. Being a green witch adds a dash of magic to everything you do! When your level of curiosity outweighs your fear of criticism, you'll understand what it means to "dare to be a green witch."

# GLOSSARY

**ADAPTOGEN:** an herb that acts in a nonspecific way to strengthen the body and increase resilience to stress and disease

**ANALGESIC:** pain-relieving

**ANTIBACTERIAL:** active against bacteria

**ANTIBIOTIC:** inhibits the growth of, or destroys, microorganisms

**ANTIMICROBIAL:** destroys microorganisms

**ANTIPARASITIC:** used or intended to kill, repel, or remove parasites

**ANTISEPTIC:** discourages the growth of microorganisms

**ANTIVIRAL:** herbs that may inhibit a virus from attaching to cell walls or inhibit the replication of the virus once it gets into cells, which can then give the immune system the ability to clean up the rest of the infection

**ASTRINGENT:** contract and tighten

**BITTER:** stimulates secretion of digestive juices, encourages appetite

**BITTERS:** stimulate the gallbladder to release bile and the stomach to release hydrochloric acid preparing the body for digestion

**CARRIER OIL:** used to dilute essential oils before they are applied to the skin— they "carry" the essential oil onto the skin. Diluting essential oils is a critical safety practice.

**DECONGESTANT:** used to relieve nasal congestion

**DIAPHORETIC:** an herb that stimulates sweating and may move toxins out of the body

**ESSENTIAL OILS:** a natural oil typically obtained from distillation and having the characteristic fragrance of the plant or other source from which it is extracted

**FLOWER ESSENCES:** extractions prepared from flowering plants used therapeutically for improvement of emotional and mental state

**GARBLE:** the process of separating the leaves, flowers, and stems, and discarding the unwanted parts

**GOITROGENIC:** may inhibit the uptake of iodine by the thyroid gland

**HEPATIC:** liver cleansing

**HYDROSOL:** an aromatic water left over from the making of essential oils, containing therapeutic properties

**NERVINE:** herbs that nourish the nervous system and help relieve stress and anxiety

**TONIC:** nourishing, restoring, and supporting for entire body

**VULNERARY:** soothing and healing

# BIBLIOGRAPHY

"1 in 3 Adults Don't Get Enough Sleep." Centers for Disease Control and Prevention. Last updated February 16, 2016. https://www.cdc.gov /media/releases/2016/p0215-enough-sleep.html.

"11 Ways to Naturally Supercharge Your Hair Growth." Annmarie Skin Care. Last updated January 21, 2021. https://www.annmariegianni.com /natural-hair-growth/.

"About Genetically Engineered Foods." Center For Food Safety. Accessed 2020. https://www.centerforfoodsafety.org/issues/311/ge-foods/about -ge-foods.

Allison, Serene. "Collagen 101: The Merits and the Myths." Trim Healthy Mama. Accessed April 14, 2020. https://trimhealthymama.com/collagen -101-the-merits-and-the-myths/.

Alshatwi, Ali A., Gowhar Shafi, Tarique N. Hasan, Amal A. Al-Hazzani, Mohammed A. Alsaif, Mohammed A. Alfawaz, K. Y. Lei, and Anjana Munshi. 2020. "Apoptosis-Mediated Inhibition Of Human Breast Cancer Cell Proliferation By Lemon Citrus Extract." *Asian Pacific Journal of Cancer Prevention* 12, no. 6 (2011): 1621–25. http://journal.waocp.org /article_25746.html.

"Ancient Scent-Sations." Kessler Neighbors United. Accessed April 23, 2020. https://kesslerneighborsunited.org/ancient-scent-sations/.

Askinson, George William. *Perfumes and Cosmetics: Their Preparation and Manufacture.* London: Crosby Lockwood and Son, 1923. https://archive

.org/stream/in.ernet.dli.2015.162553/2015.162553.Perfumes-And-Cos-metics-Thier-Preparation-And-Manufacture_djvu.txt.

Axe, Josh. "Bone Broth Benefits for Digestion, Arthritis and Cellulite." Dr. Axe. Last updated August 25, 2020. https://draxe.com/nutrition/bone-broth-benefits/.

Axe, Josh. "Essential Oils: Eleven Main Benefits and 101 Uses." Dr. Axe. Last updated April 5, 2019. https://draxe.com/essential-oils/essential-oil-uses-benefits/.

Barclay, Eliza. "Coconut Water to the Rescue? Parsing the Medical Claims." *National Public Radio*, August 15, 2011. https://www.npr.org/sections/health-shots/2011/08/15/139638930/saved-by-the-coconut-water-parsing-coconut-waters-medical-claims.

Bass, Phil. "Bone-In Beef Cuts: A Bone Of Contention." *The National Provisioner*, January 29, 2018. https://www.provisioneronline.com/articles/105755-bone-in-beef-cuts-a-bone-of-contention.

Bell, Keith. "Gut Microbiota and Infant Vaccine Protocol." European Society for Neurogastroenterology. Last updated January 7, 2015. https://www.gutmicrobiotaforhealth.com/gut-microbiota-and-infant-vaccine-proto-col/.

Ben-Noun, Liubov. *Beauty of Humans*. Israel: B.N. Publication House, 2016.

Bennett, Robin Rose. *The Gift of Healing Herbs: Plant Medicines and Home Remedies for Vibrant Healthy Life*. Berkeley, CA: North Atlantic Books, 2014.

Bernardini, Federico, Claudio Tuniz, Alfredo Coppa, Lucia Mancini, Diego Dreossi, Diane Eichert, and Gianluca Turco, et al. "Beeswax as Dental Filling on a Neolithic Human Tooth." *Plos ONE* 7, no. 9 (September 19, 2012): e44904. https://doi.org/10.1371/journal.pone.0044904.

Bibby, Jessica, Bulbul Hooda, Marlene Lam, Jeanne Loftus, Tanuj Puri, Elizabeth Rentschler, Alexandra Repetto, Lindsay Powell Schwartz, Gina Surphlis, and Jasmine Yoon. "Transitioning to Transparency," The Fashion Institute of Technology's Master of Professional Studies Program, 2018. http://docplayer.net/148778359-Transitioning-to-transparency.html.

Boer, Magdalena, Ewa Duchnik, Romuald Maleszka, and Mariola Marchle-wicz. "Structural and Biophysical Characteristics Of Human Skin In Maintaining Proper Epidermal Barrier Function." *Advances In Dermatology and Allergology* 33 (2016): 1–5. https://doi.org/10.5114/pdia.2015.48037.

Bogdan, Cătălina, Mirela L Moldovan, Ioana Manuela Man, and Maria Crişan. "Preliminary Study on the Development of an Antistretch Marks Water-in-Oil Cream: Ultrasound Assessment, Texture Analysis, and Sensory Analysis." *Clinical, Cosmetic and Investigational Dermatology* 9 (September 6, 2016): 249–55. https://doi.org/10.2147/CCID.S107298.

Bomgardner, Melody. "The Problem with Vanilla." *Scientific American*, September 14, 2016. https://www.scientificamerican.com/article/the-problem-with-vanilla/.

Boucetta, Kenza Qiraouani, Zoubida Charrouf, Hassan Aguenaou, Abdelfat-tah Derouiche, and Yahya Bensouda. "The Effect of Dietary and/or Cosmetic Argan Oil on Postmenopausal Skin Elasticity." *Clinical Interventions in Aging* 10 (January 30, 2015) 339–49. https://doi.org/ 10.2147 /CIA.S71684.

Brown, H. S., D. R. Bishop, and C. A. Rowan. "The Role of Skin Absorption as a Route of Exposure For Volatile Organic Compounds (VOCs) in Drinking Water." *American Journal of Public Health* 74, no. 5 (1984): 479–84. https://doi.org/10.2105/ajph.74.5.479.

Buscemi, Silvio, Davide Corleo, Francesco Di Pace, Maria Letizia Petroni, Angela Satriano, and Giulio Marchesini. "The Effect of Lutein on Eye and Extra-Eye Health." *Nutrients* 10, no.9 (September 18, 2018): 1321. http://doi.org/10.3390/nu10091321.

Butler, Stephanie. "Celebrating Valentine's Day with a Box of Chocolates." History. Last updated February 8, 2013. https://www.history.com/news /celebrating-valentines-day-with-a-box-of-chocolates.

Bystritsky, Alexander, Lauren Kerwin, and Jamie D. Feusner. "A Pilot Study of Rhodiola Rosea (Rhodax) for Generalized Anxiety Disorder (GAD)." *Journal of Alternative and Complementary Medicine* 14, no. 2 (March 2008): 175–80. https://doi.org/10.1089/acm.2007.7117.

Campbell-McBride, Natasha. *Gut and Psychology Syndrome: Natural Treatment for Autism, Dyspraxia, A.D.D., Dyslexia, A.D.H.D., Depression, Schizophrenia.* Cambridge, UK: Medinform Publishing, 2017.

"Can Gut Bacteria Improve Your Health?" Harvard Health Publishing. Last updated October 2016. https://www.health.harvard.edu/staying-healthy/can-gut-bacteria-improve-your-health.

Captain Hale. "Beetroots." Accessed November 13, 2019. https://captainhale.com/recipes/beetroots/.

Center for Food Safety and Applied Nutrition. "'Organic' Cosmetics." U.S. Food and Drug Administration. Accessed April 22, 2020. https://www.fda.gov/cosmetics/cosmetics-labeling-claims/organic-cosmetics.

Chang, Shao-Min, and Chung-Hey Chen. 2015. "Effects of an Intervention with Drinking Chamomile Tea on Sleep Quality and Depression in Sleep Disturbed Postnatal Women: A Randomized Controlled Trial." *Journal of Advanced Nursing* 72, no. 2 (2015): 306–315. https://doi.org/10.1111/jan.12836.

Charles, Dan. "Why Greek Yogurt Makers Want Whey To Go Away." *National Public Radio*, November 21, 2012. https://www.npr.org/sections/thesalt/2012/11/21/165478127/why-greek-yogurt-makers-want-whey-to-go-away.

Cherney, Kristeen. "Banana Face Mask Benefits for the Skin and How to Try It." *Healthline*, December 6, 2019. https://www.healthline.com/health/banana-face-mask.

Childress, Cerena. "Tomato Varieties! Humble to Humongous & More!" Green Bean Connection. Last updated February 4, 2018. https://greenbeanconnection.wordpress.com/2018/02/04/tomato-varieties-humble-to-humongous-more/.

Chonpathompikunlert, Pennapa, Jintanaporn Wattanathorn, and Supaporn Muchimapura. "Piperine, the Main Alkaloid of Thai Black Pepper, Protects against Neurodegeneration and Cognitive Impairment in Animal Model of Cognitive Deficit like Condition of Alzheimer's Disease." *Food and Chemical Toxicology : An International Journal Published for the British*

*Industrial Biological Research Association* 48, no.3 (March 2010): 798–802. https://doi.org/10.1016/j.fct.2009.12.009.

Christensen, R., E.M. Bartels, R.D. Altman, A. Astrup, and H. Bliddal. "Does the Hip Power of *Rosa canina* (Rosehip) Reduce Pain in Osteoarthritis Patients?: A Meta-Analysis of Randomized Controlled Triasl." *Osteoarthritis and Cartilage* 16, no. 4 (September 2008): S220. https://doi .org/10.1016/s1063-4584(08)60552-x.

Clark, Lucie. "The Surprising Beauty Benefits of Frankincense Oil." *Vogue Australia*, August 30, 2018. https://www.vogue.com.au/beauty/skin /the-surprising-beauty-benefits-of-frankincense-oil/news-story /2dd732d9e485802248d53002bf2c9831.

Clodoveo, Maria Lisa, Salvatore Camposeo, Bernardo De Gennaro, Simone Pascuzzi, and Luigi Roselli. "In the Ancient World, Virgin Olive Oil Was Called 'Liquid Gold' by Homer and 'the Great Healer' by Hippocrates. Why Has This Mythic Image Been Forgotten?" *Food Research International* 62 (2014): 1062–68. https://doi.org/10.1016/j.foodres.2014.05.034.

"The Coconut Story." Coconut Republic. Accessed July 30, 2020. http:// www.coconutrepublic.org/coconut_story.php.

Cohen, S.G. and R. Evans 3rd. "Asthma, Allergy, and Immunotherapy; A Historical Review: Part II." *Allergy and Asthma Proceedings* 13, no.1 (January/ February 1992): 47–58. https://doi.org/10.2500/ 108854192778878999.

Cohen, Marc. "Rosehip - An Evidence Based Herbal Medicine For Inflammation And Arthritis." *Australian Family Physician* 41, no. 7 (July 2012): 495–8. https://pubmed.ncbi.nlm.nih.gov/22762068/.

Cohen, Sheldon, William J. Doyle, Cuneyt M. Alper, Denise Janicki-Deverts, and Ronald B. Turner. "Sleep Habits and Susceptibility to the Common Cold." *Archives of Internal Medicine* 169, no. 1 (2009) : 62. https://doi .org/10.1001/archinternmed.2008.505.

Cohn, Roger. "The Life Story of the Oldest Tree on Earth." *YaleEnvironment360*, May 1, 2013. https://e360.yale.edu/features/peter_crane _history_of_ginkgo_earths_oldest_tree.

Colletti, Michelle. "Gut and Psychology Syndrome: GAPS: Part III." Elite Learning. Last updated August 26. 2020. https://www.elitecme.com /resource-center/behavioral-health/gut-and-psychology-syndrome-gaps -part-iii.

Colten, Harvey R., and Bruce M. Altevogt. 2006. "Extent And Health Consequences of Chronic Sleep Loss and Sleep Disorders." *Institute of Medicine Committee On Sleep Medicine And Research* (2006). htttps://doi .org/10.17226/11617.

Conrad, Pam, and Cindy Adams. "The Effects of Clinical Aromatherapy for Anxiety and Depression in the High Risk Postpartum Woman: A Pilot Study." Complementary Therapies in Clinical Practice 18, no. 3 (2012): 164–68. https://doi.org/10.1016/j.ctcp.2012.05.002.

Crowell, Pamela L., Michael N. Gould. "Chemoprevention and Therapy of Cancer by d-Limonene." *Critical Reviews in Oncogenesis* 5, no. 1 (February 20, 1994): 1–22.https://doi.org/10.1615/critrevoncog.v5.i1.10.

Crum, Hannah. "Best Tea for Kombucha - How to Choose a Tea Blend Recipe." Kombucha Kamp. Last updated August 7, 2019. https://www .kombuchakamp.com/tea-and-kombucha-what-to-use-and-what-to-avoid.

Crum, Hannah. "Top Ten Questions about Sugar and Kombucha." Kombucha Kamp. Last updated August 14, 2019. https://www.kombuchakamp .com/sugar-and-kombucha-faq-top-10.

Culpeper, Nicholas. *Culpeper's Complete Herbal*. Edited by Stephen Foster. New York: Sterling, 2019.

D'Adamo, Peter, and Catherine Whitney. *Eat Right for Your Type (Revised and Updated): The Individualized Blood Type Diet Solution*. Berkley: New American Library, 2016.

DeFino, Jessica. "The Skincare Ingredient that Cleopatra Swore by Is Trending Now." The Zoe Report. Last updated June 7, 2019. https://www. thezoereport.com/p/frankincense-oil-is-like-liquid-gold-for-your -face-17939541.

Dhar, Michael. "What Is Jell-O?" LiveScience. Last updated December 19, 2013. https://www.livescience.com/42088-what-is-jello-jell-o.html.

Dickson, EJ. "Don't Panic, You Don't Need Hand Sanitizer to Fight Corona-virus." *Rolling Stone*, March 5, 2020. https://www.rollingstone.com /culture/culture-news/hand-sanitizer-effective-coronavrus-covid -19-962027/.

"The Difference between Natural Desquamation and Exfoliation: What It Means for Your Skin." Griffin Row. Accessed April 22, 2020. https://www .griffinandrow.com/education/skin-biology/skin-physiology /difference-natural-desquamation-exfoliation-means-skin/

Dotinga, Randy. 2020. "Hip Replacements Skyrocket In U.S." Health Beat Spectrum Health. Last updated March 5, 2015. https://healthbeat .spectrumhealth.org/hip-replacements-skyrocket-in-u-s/.

Downing, D. T., M. E. Stewart, P. W. Wertz, and J. S. Strauss. "Essential Fatty Acids and Acne." *Journal of the American Academy of Dermatology* 14, no. 2 (February 1986): 221–5. https://doi.org/10.1016/s0190-9622(86)70025-x.

Epstein, Samuel S., Rosalie Bertell, and Barbara Seaman. "Dangers and Unre-liability of Mammography: Breast Examination Is a Safe, Effective, and Practical Alternative." *International Journal of Health Services* 31, no. 3 (July 2001): 605–15. http://doi.org/10.2190/2rhd-05t6-bry0-1cex.

Etkin, Caryn D. and Bryan D. Springer. "The American Joint Replacement Registry—The First Five Years." *Arthroplasty Today* 3, no. 2 (June 2017): 67–69. https://doi.org/10.1016/j.artd.2017.02.002.

Farnworth, Edward R., ed. *Handbook of Fermented Functional Foods*. 2nd ed. Boca Raton, FL: CRC Press, 2008.

Fattorusso, Antonella, Lorenza Di Genova, Giovanni Battista Dell'Isola, Elisabetta Mencaroni, and Susanna Esposito. "Autism Spectrum Disorders and the Gut Microbiota." *Nutrients* 11, no. 3 (February 28, 2019): 521. https://doi.org/10.3390/nu11030521.

Faulkner, S. H., S. Jackson, G. Fatania, and C. A. Leicht. 2017. "The Effect Of Passive Heating on Heat Shock Protein 70 and Interleukin-6: A Possible Treatment Tool For Metabolic Diseases?" *Temperature* 4, no. 3 (2017): 292–304. https://doi.org/10.1080/23328940.2017.1288688.

Fenster, Michael S. *Eating Well, Living Better: The Grassroots Gourmet Guide to Good Health and Great Food*. Lanham, MD: Rowman & Littlefield Publishers, 2012.

Ferry MP, M. Gessain, R. Geeain. "Vegetative Propagation of Shea, Kola and Pentadesma." Cocoa Research Institute, Ghana Annual Report (1987/88): 98–100.

Flessa, Maria-Elpida. "Goji Berries Trivia: Eighteen Unknown Facts about the Popular Fruit!" Useless Daily. Last updated September 19, 2016. https://www.uselessdaily.com/uncategorized/goji-berries-trivia-18 -unknown-facts-about-the-popular-fruit/#ixzz6CvJP4NJK.

Foley, Daniel J. *Herbs for Use and for Delight: An Anthology from the Herbarist*. New York: Dover Publications, 1974.

Foxcroft, Louise. *Hot Flushes, Cold Science: A History of the Modern Menopause*. London: Granta, 2010.

Franco, L., C. Sánchez, R. Bravo, A. Rodriguez, C. Barriga, and Javier Juánez. 2012. "The Sedative Effects of Hops (*Humulus lupulus*), a Component of Beer, on the Activity/Rest Rhythm." *Acta Physiologica Hungarica* 99, no. 2 (June 2012): 133–139. https://doi.org/10.1556/aphysiol.99.2012.2.6.

"Frankincense Essential Oil." doTERRA. Accessed April 21, 2020. https://www.doterra.com/US/en/education/pe/frankincense-oil.

"Frankincense Essential Oil." Young Living Essential Oils. Accessed April 23, 2020. https://www.youngliving.com/en_US/products/frankincense -essential-oil.

Fratini, Filippo, Giovanni Cilia, Barbara Turchi, and Antonio Felicioli. 2016. "Beeswax: A Minireview of Its Antimicrobial Activity and Its Application in Medicine." *Asian Pacific Journal of Tropical Medicine* 9, no. 9 (September 2016): 839–43. https://doi.org10.1016/j.apjtm.2016.07.003.

"Fun Facts about Chocolate." National Confectioners Association. Accessed February 1, 2020. https://www.candyusa.com/story-of-chocolate/fun -facts-about-chocolate/.

Gasser, P., E. Lati, L. Peno-Mazzarino, D. Bouzoud, L. Allegaert, and H. Bernaert. "Cocoa Polyphenols and their Influence on Parameters Involved in Ex Vivo Skin Restructuring." *International Journal of Cosmetic Science* 30, no. 5 (September 8, 2008: *339–45*. https://doi.org/10.1111/j.1468 -2494.2008.00457.x.

Geuenich, Silvia, Christine Goffinet, Stephanie Venzke, Silke Nolkemper, Ingo Baumann, Peter Plinkert, Jürgen Reichling, and Oliver T Keppler. "Aqueous Extracts from Peppermint, Sage and Lemon Balm Leaves Display Potent Anti-HIV-1 Activity by Increasing the Virion Density." *Retrovirology 5*, no. 27 (March 20, 2008). https://doi.org/10.1186/1742-4690-5-27.

Gladstar, Rosemary. *Rosemary Gladstar's Medicinal Herbs: A Beginner's Guide.* North Adams, MA: Storey Publishing, 2012.

Gladstar, Rosemary. *Rosemary Gladstar's Herbal Recipes for Vibrant Health: 175 Teas, Tonics, Oils, Salves, Tinctures, and Other Natural Remedies for the Entire Family.* North Adams, MA: Storey Pub., 2008.

Goldfaden, Gary, and Robert Goldfaden. "How Topical Lycopene Improves Skin Cells." *Life Extension*, September 2012. https://www.lifeextension .com/magazine/2012/9/topical-lycopene-improves-skin-cellular-function.

Gomez-Rejón, Maite. "The Ancient Wisdom of Aphrodisiacs." The Getty Iris. Last updated February 13, 2014. https://blogs.getty.edu/iris/the -ancient-wisdom-of-aphrodisiacs/.

Goreja, W.G. 2004. *Shea Butter: The Nourishing Properties Of Africa's Best-Kept Natural Beauty Secret.* Amazing Herbs Press.

Gottfried, Jay A., ed. *Neurobiology of Sensation and Reward.* Boca Raton, FL: CRC Press, 2019.

"Gotu Kola." Penn State Hershey Health Information Library. Accessed April 14, 2020. http://pennstatehershey.adam.com /content.aspx?productid=107&pid=33&gid=000253.

Götz, Jürgen and Alan Woodruff. "What Is the Blood-Brain Barrier?" The Conversation. Last updated April 5, 2017. https://theconversation .com/explainer-what-is-the-blood-brain-barrier-and-how-can-we -overcome-it-75454.

Graber, Cynthia. "Strange But True: Whale Waste is Extremely Valuable." *Scientific American*, April 26, 2007. https://www.scientificamerican.com/article/strange-but-true-whale-waste-is-valuable/.

Green, Matthew. "How the Decadence and Depravity of 18th-Century London Was Fueled by Hot Chocolate." *The Telegraph*, January 25, 2018. https://www.telegraph.co.uk/travel/destinations/europe/united-kingdom/england/london/articles/surprising-history-of-london-chocolate-houses/.

Greene, Patrice. 2015. "The Medicinal Properties Of Roses". Herbstalk. Last updated March 16, 2015. http://www.herbstalk.org/blog/the-medicinal-properties-of-roses.

Gross, Paul M., Xiaoping Zhang, and Richard Zhang. *Wolfberry: Nature's Bounty of Nutrition and Health*. Booksurge Publishing, 2006.

Grossmann, Kayla. "Homemade Whey vs. Protein Powder: Rediscovering Nutrient Dense Foods." The Radiant Life Blog. Accessed July 22, 2020. https://blog.radiantlifecatalog.com/bid/62826/Homemade-Whey-vs-Protein-Powder-Rediscovering-nutrient-dense-foods.

Grufferman, Barbara Hannah. "The Healing Power of Olive Oil." *HuffPost*, November 10, 2011. https://www.huffpost.com/entry/olive-oil-health-benefits_b_945506.

"Gut Microbiome Can Suppress Food Allergies: Just Add "Good" Bacteria," *Genetic Engineering and Biotechnology News*, June 26, 2019. https://www.genengnews.com/news/gut-microbiome-can-suppress-food-allergies-just-add-good-bacteria/.

Haan, M.N. 2001. "Women's Health." *International Encyclopedia of the Social & Behavioral Sciences* (2001): 16528–32. https://doi.org/10.1016/B0-08-043076-7/03866-3.

Hajeski, Nancy J. *National Geographic Complete Guide to Herbs and Spices*. Washington, DC: National Geographic Society, 2016.

Hall, Chloe. "Why You Need Rose Oil in Your Beauty Regimen." *ELLE*, February 15, 2019. https://www.elle.com/beauty/makeup-skin-care/news/a26761/why-you-need-rose-oil-in-your-beauty-regimen/.

Hall, Jenny. "Do Hand Sanitizers Really Work?". University Of Toronto News. Last updated January 10, 2012. https://www.utoronto.ca/news/do-hand-sanitizers-really-work.

Haubrich, William S. *Medical Meanings: a Glossary of Word Origins*. Philadelphia: American College of Physicians, 2003.

The Hebrew University of Jerusalem. "Antioxidant to Retard Wrinkles Discovered." *ScienceDaily*, September 1, 2007. https://www.sciencedaily.com/releases/2007/08/070830102601.htm.

Heid, Markham. "Why Your Brain Needs Idle Time." Elemental. Last updated February 14, 2019. https://elemental.medium.com/why-your-brain-needs-idle-time-e5d90b0ef1df.

Heid, Markham. "Science Can't Explain Why Everyone Is Drinking Bone Broth." *Time*, January 6, 2016. https://time.com/4159156/bone-broth-health-benefits/.

"Helichrysum Essential Oil." doTERRA. Accessed April 13, 2020. https://www.doterra.com/US/en/p/helichrysum-oil.

Henderson, Amy. "How Chocolate and Valentine's Day Mated for Life." *Smithsonian Magazine*, February 12, 2015. https://www.smithsonianmag.com/smithsonian-institution/how-chocolate-and-valentines-day-mated-life-180954228/.

Hensley, Tim. "A Curious Tale: The Apple in North America." Brooklyn Botanic Garden. Last updated June 2, 2005. https://www.bbg.org/gardening/article/the_apple_in_north_america.

"Hershey's Kisses: Fun Facts and Recipes." *ABC News*, September 18, 2012. https://abcnews.go.com/blogs/lifestyle/2012/09/hersheys-kisses-fun-facts-and-recipes.

Hirose, Ryohei, Takaaki Nakaya, Yuji Naito, Tomo Daidoji, Risa Bandou, Ken Inoue, Osamu Dohi, Naohisa Yoshida, Hideyuki Konishi, and Yoshito Itoh. "Situations Leading to Reduced Effectiveness of Current

Hand Hygiene against Infectious Mucus from Influenza Virus-Infected Patients." American Society For Microbiology 4, no.5 (September 2019): 1–16. https://doi.org/10.1128/mSphere.00474-19.

"History of Donkey Milk through the Ages." Naturane. Accessed 2020. https://www.naturanecosmetics.com/en/content/26-faits-historiques.

Hongratanaworakit, Tapanee. "Relaxing Effect of Rose Oil on Humans." *Natural Product Communications* 4, no. 2 (February 2009): 291–6.https://doi.org/10.1177/1934578x0900400226.

Hopkins, Alan. "Chicken Soup Cure May Not Be a Myth." The Nurse Practioner 28, no. 6 (June 2003): 16. https://10.1097/00006205-200306000-00005.

Horeja Ndow, Sirra. "'Women's Gold'—Shea Butter From Burkina Faso." Case Study In Women's Empowerment. Accessed July 30, 2020. https://wideplus.org/wp-content/uploads/2012/10/sixthstoryofwomen.pdf.

"How Argan Oil Transforms Lives." Argan Project. Accessed April 23, 2020. https://arganproject.com/blogs/news/how-argan-oil-transforms-lives.

"Hyaluronic Acid: The Fountain of Youth." DÉCAAR. Last updated August 27, 2019. https://decaar.com/news/hyaluronic-acid-the-fountain-of-youth/.

"Interview Michael Pollan." Frontline: Modern Meat. Public Broadcasting Service, WGBH Educational Foundation, 2014. https://www.pbs.org/wgbh/pages/frontline/shows/meat/interviews/pollan.html.

"Inventing the Modern Total Knee Replacement." Hospital for Special Surgery. Last updated May 1, 2013. https://www.hss.edu/conditions_inventing-the-modern-total-knee-replacement.asp.

"Is Plastic a Threat to Your Health?" Harvard Health. December 2019. https://www.health.harvard.edu/healthy-eating/microwaving-food-in-plastic-dangerous-or-not.

Jacknin, Jeanette. *Smart Medicine for Your Skin: a Comprehensive Guide to Understanding Conventional and Alternative Therapies to Heal Common Skin Problems*. Garden City Park, NY: Avery, 2001.

Jamieson, Amanda M. "Influence of the Microbiome on Response to Vaccination." *Human Vaccines & Immunotherapeutics* 11. no. 9 (2015): 2329–2331. https://doi.org/10.1080/21645515.2015.1022699.

Jeanroy, Amy. "Soapwort Plant Profile." The Spruce. Last updated September 15, 2020. https://www.thespruce.com/herb-soapwort-4107277.

Johnson, Jon. "Superbugs: Everything You Need to Know." *Medical News Today*, November 21, 2019. https://www.medicalnewstoday.com/articles/327093.

Johnson, Rebecca L., Steven Foster, and Andrew Weil. *National Geographic Guide to Medicinal Herbs: The World's Most Effective Healing Plants*. Washington, DC: National Geographic, 2014.

Kapila, Suman, Kamal Gandhi, Sumit Arora, Seema Rana, and Savita Devi. "Donkey Milk: A Very Recent Nutritional 'Pharmafood.'" *Indian Dairyman* 70 (July 2018): 72–77.

Karlsson, Mattias P., and Loren M. Frank. "Awake Replay of Remote Experiences in the Hippocampus." Nature Neuroscience 12, no. 7 (June 14, 2009): 913–18. https://doi.org/10.1038/nn.2344.

Kasper, Siegfried, Markus Gastpar, Walter E. Müller, Hans-Peter Volz, Hans-Jürgen Möller, Angelika Dienel, and Sandra Schläfke. "Efficacy and Safety of Silexan: A New, Orally Administered Lavender Oil Preparation, in Subthreshold Anxiety Disorder—Evidence from Clinical Trials." *Wiener Medizinische Wochenschrift* 160 (2021-2022): 547–556. https://doi.org/10.1007/s10354-010-0845-7.

Kasper, Siegfried, Markus Gastpar, Walter E. Müller, Hans-Peter Volz, Hans-Jürgen Möller, Angelika Dienel, and Sandra Schläfke. "Silexan, An Orally Administered Lavandula Oil Preparation, Is Effective In The Treatment Of 'Subsyndromal' Anxiety Disorder: A Randomized, Double-Blind, Placebo Controlled Trial". *International Clinical Psychopharmacology* 25, no. 5 (2010): 277–87. https://doi.org/10.1097/yic.0b013e32833b3242.

Kasrae, Hengameh, Leila Amiri Farahani, and Parsa Yousefi. "Efficacy of Topical Application of Human Breast Milk on Atopic Eczema Healing

Among Infants: A Randomized Clinical Trial." *International Journal of Dermatology* 54, no. 8 (February 2015): 966–71. https://doi.org/10.1111/ijd.12764.

"Kefir's History." La Coprologie sur le Web. Accessed April 5, 2020. http://coproweb.free.fr/kefiranglais.htm.

Kirkpatrik, Marshall. "Google CEO Schmidt: 'People Aren't Ready for the Technology Revolution,'" *Read Write*, August 4 2010. http://readwrite.com/2010/08/04/google_ceo_schmidt_people_arent_ready_for_the_tech#awesm=~or9ZvGJTDdkf01.

Klatell, Penny. "How Much Caffeine Is in That Piece Of Chocolate?" Eat Out Eat Well. Last updated February 8, 2019. https://eatouteatwell.com/tag/valentines-day-candy/.

Koutsos, Athanasios, Samantha Riccadonna, Maria M. Ulaszewska, Pietro Franceschi, Kajetan Trošt, Amanda Galvin, Tanya Braune, et al. "Two Apples a Day Lower Serum Cholesterol and Improve Cardiometabolic Biomarkers in Mildly Hypercholesterolemic Adults: a Randomized, Controlled, Crossover Trial." *The American Journal of Clinical Nutrition* 11, no.2 (February 2020): 307–318. https://doi.org/10.1093/ajcn/nqz282.

Kresser, Chris. "The Downside of Mammograms." Kresser Institute. Last updated April 6, 2017. https://kresserinstitute.com/the-downside-of-mammograms/.

Kyrou, Ioannis, Aimilia Christou, Demosthenes Panagiotakos, Charikleia Stefanaki, Katerina Skenderi, Konstantina Katsana, and Constantine Tsigos. "Effects Of A Hops (Humulus Lupulus L.) Dry Extract Supplement On Self-Reported Depression, Anxiety And Stress Levels In Apparently Healthy Young Adults: A Randomized, Placebo-Controlled, Double-Blind, Crossover Pilot Study." *Hormones* 16, no. 2 (2017): 171–80. https://doi.org/10.14310/horm.2002.1738.

Laham, Martha. *Made Up: How the Beauty Industry Manipulates Consumers, Preys on Women's Insecurities, and Promotes Unattainable Beauty Standards.* Lanham, MD: Rowman & Littlefield, 2020.

Landrigan, Christopher P., Jeffrey M. Rothschild, John W. Cronin, Rainu Kaishal, Elisabeth Burdick, Joel T. Katz, and Craig M. Lilly, et al. "Effect of Reducing Interns' Work Hours on Serious Medical Errors in Intensive Care Units." *Yearbook of Critical Care Medicine* (2006): 287–89. https://doi .org/10.1016/s0734-3299(08)70200-4.

Lee, Choong Jae, Leslie Wilson, Mary Ann Jordan, Vy Nguyen, Jessica Tang, Gregory Smiyun. "Hesperidin Suppressed Proliferations of Both Human Breast Cancer and Androgen-Dependent Prostate Cancer Cells." Phyto-therapy Research 24, no. 1 (January 2010): S15–S19. https://doi .org/10.1002/ptr.2856.

Levoy, Gregg. "Dreams Don't Come True, They Are True." *Psychology Today,* April 16, 2016. https://www.psychologytoday.com/us/blog /passion/201604/dreams-dont-come-true-they-are-true.

Levy, Jillian. "Have You Tried Grapeseed Oil for Your Skin?" Dr. Axe. Last updated November 12, 2019. https://draxe.com/beauty/grapeseed-oil-for-skin/.

Levy, Jillian. "What Are Cacao Nibs? Nutrition, Benefits, Uses and Recipes." Dr. Axe. Last updated December 2, 2019. https://draxe.com/nutrition /cacao-nibs/.

Levy, Jillian. "Witch Hazel Uses, Benefits and Potential Side Effects." Dr. Axe. Last updated July 16, 2019. https://draxe.com/nutrition/witch-hazel/.

Li, Ling, Xinfeng Liu, and Hong Guo. "The Nutritional Ingredients and Anti-oxidant Activity of Donkey Milk and Donkey Milk Powder." *Food Science and Biotechnology* 27, no.2 (April 2018): 393–400. https://doi.org/10.1007 /s10068-017-0264-2.

Li, Qinrui, Ying Han, Angel Belle C. Dy, and Randi J. Hagerman. "The Gut Microbiota And Autism Spectrum Disorders." Frontiers in Cellular Neu-roscience (April 28, 2017). https://doi.org/10.3389/fncel.2017.00120.

Lin, Tzu-Kai, Lily Zhong, and Juan Santiago. "Anti-Inflammatory and Skin Barrier Repair Effects of Topical Application of Some Plant Oils". *Inter-national Journal of Molecular Sciences* 19, no. 1 (December 27, 2017): 70. https://doi.org/10.3390/ijms19010070.

Link, Rachael. "Kefir Benefits, Nutrition Facts, Types and How to Make." Dr. Axe. Last updated April 11, 2019. https://draxe.com/nutrition/kefir-benefits/.

Link, Rachael. "This 'Immortal Health Elixir' Protects Your Gut and Fights Food Poisoning Pathogens (and More!)." Dr. Axe. Last updated August 13, 2019. https://draxe.com/nutrition/7-reasons-drink-kombucha-everyday/.

Loftus, Catherine. "The History of Exfoliation." Cinta Aveda Institute. Last updated November 27, 2014. https://blog.cintaaveda.edu/2014/11/the-history-of-exfoliation/.

Mackeen, Dawn. "Are There Benefits to Drinking Kombucha?" *The New York Times*, October 16, 2019. https://www.nytimes.com/2019/10/16/style/self-care/kombucha-benefits.html.

Macrae, Fiona. "Women Absorb up to Five Pounds of Damaging Chemicals a Year Thanks to Beauty Products." *Daily Mail Online*, June 19, 2007. https://www.dailymail.co.uk/health/article-462997/Women-absorb-5lbs-damaging-chemicals-year-thanks-beauty-products.html.

Malhi, Harsimran Kaur, Jenny Tu, Thomas V. Riley, Sujith Prasad Kumarasinghe, and Katherine A. Hammer. "Tea Tree Oil Gel for Mild to Moderate Acne; a Twelve Week Uncontrolled, Open-Label Phase II Pilot Study." The Australasian Journal of Dermatology 58, no. 3 (August 2017) 205–10. https://doi.org/ 10.1111/ajd.12465.

"Marilyn and N°5." Chanel. Last updated November 16, 2012. YouTube, 2:32. https://www.youtube.com/watch?v=Wo8UtWiYiZI.

Martin, Crystal G. "Beauty Myth Debunked: Is Oil Bad for Your Face?" *Essence*, October 12, 2013. https://www.essence.com/beauty/skin/beauty-myth-debunked-oil-bad-your-face/.

Matthews, Mimi. "The Beauty Rituals of 19th Century Empress Elisabeth of Austria - Including Brandy Shampoo and Raw Veal Face Masks." Bust. Accessed April 1, 2021. https://bust.com/style/16369-the-beauty-rituals-of-19th-century-empress-elisabeth-of-austria-featuring-brandy-shampoo-and-raw-veal-face-masks.html.

McIntyre, Anne. *The Complete Herbal Tutor: The Ideal Companion for Study and Practice*. London: Gaia, 2010.

Michels, Alexander J. "Vitamin E and Skin Health." Linus Pauling Institute, Oregon State University. Accessed January 2, 2020. https://lpi.orego nstate.edu/mic/health-disease/skin-health/vitamin-E.

Miglioretti, Diana L., Jane Lange, Jeroen J. van den Broek, Christoph I. Lee, Nicolien T. van Ravesteyn, Dominique Ritley, and Karla Kerlikowske et al. "Radiation-Induced Breast Cancer Incidence And Mortality From Digital Mammography Screening." *Annals of Internal Medicine* 164, no. 4 (February 2016): 205. https://doi.org/10.7326/m15-1241.

Mills, Deborah. *Daily Doses of Deborah Volume 5*. Lulu, 2018.

Milner, Conan. "Why Whey?" *The Epoch Times*, June 26, 2015, last updated July 1, 2015. https://www.theepochtimes.com/why-whey_1407605.html.

Ming Lee, Nellie. 2016. "Steeped in History: A Cordial, Liqueur or Schnapps Is a Tonic Whatever You Call It." *South China Morning Post*, October 4, 2016. https://www.scmp.com/lifestyle/food-drink/article/2024975 /steeped-history-cordial-liqueur-or-schnapps-tonic-whatever-you.

Mitts, Gigi. "How to Make Kefir (the Only Guide You Need)." My Fermented Foods. Last updated July 30, 2019. https://myfermentedfoods .com/how-make-kefir/.

"Mountain Rose Herbs: Gotu Kola." Mountain Rose Herbs. Accessed March 14, 2020. https://www.mountainroseherbs.com/products/gotu-kola /profile.

"MSG: A Neurotoxic Flavor Enhancer." Truth in Labeling. Accessed 2020. https://truthinlabeling.org/.

Mumcuoglu, Madeleine, Daniel Safirman, and Mina Ferne. "Elderberry." In *Encyclopedia of Dietary Supplements, Second Edition*, edited by Paul M. Coates 235–40. Boca Raton, FL: CRC Press, 2010.

"Myrrh Oil Uses and Benefits." doTERRA. Accessed April 16, 2020. https:// www.doterra.com/US/en/blog/spotlight-myrrh-oil.

Nadorff, Michael R., Ben Porter, Howard M. Rhoades, Anthony J. Greisinger, Mark E. Kunik, and Melinda A. Stanley. "Bad Dream Frequency in Older Adults with Generalized Anxiety Disorder: Prevalence, Correlates, and Effect of Cognitive Behavioral Treatment for Anxiety." *Behavioral Sleep Medicine* 12, no.1 (2013): 28–40. https://doi.org/10.1080/15402002.2012.755125.

"Native American Sweetgrass: Its Meaning and Use." Traditional Native Healing. Last updated May 30, 2015. https://traditionalnativehealing.com/native-american-sweetgrass-its-meaning-and-use.

Neufeld, K. M., N. Kang, J. Bienenstock, and J. A. Foster. "Reduced Anxiety-like Behavior and Central Neurochemical Change in Germ-Free Mice." Neurogastroenterology and Motility 23, no. 3 (November 5, 2010): 255–65. https://doi.org/10.1111/j.1365-2982.2010.01620.x.

Niaz, Kamal, Elizabeta Zaplatic, and Jonathan Spoor. "Extensive Use of Monosodium Glutamate: A Threat to Public Health?" *EXCLI Journal* 17 (2018): 273–78. https://doi.org/10.17179/excli2018-1092.

Northrup, Christiane. *Goddesses Never Age.* Carlsbad: Hay House, Inc., 2015.

Ody, Penelope. *The Complete Medicinal Herbal.* Toronto: Dorling Kindersley, 1993.

Ohry, Abraham, and Jenni Tsafrir. "Is Chicken Soup an Essential Drug?" *Canadian Medical Association Journal* 161, no. 12 (December 14, 1999): 1532–33. https://www.cmaj.ca/content/161/12/1532.

Oikeh, Ehigbai I., Ehimwenma S. Omoregie, Faith E. Oviasogie, and Kelly Oriakhi. "Phytochemical, Antimicrobial, and Antioxidant Activities of Different Citrus Juice Concentrates." *Food Science & Nutrition* 4, no. 1 (July 30, 2015): 103–9. https://doi.org/ 10.1002/fsn3.268.

Oliveira, Marilyn. "Your Skin'S Ph: What Is It and How Do You Restore Its Balance?" Dermstore blog. Last updated May 29, 2019. https://www.dermstore.com/blog/how-to-balance-your-skins-ph-level.

Oliver, Dana. "Three Reasons Why Cucumber Is Your Skin's New Best Friend." *HuffPost*, December 7, 2017. https://www.huffpost.com/entry/cucumber-skin-benefits_n_7645976.

Oliver, Dana. "What It Takes To Wake Up Gorgeous Like Miranda Kerr." *HuffPost*, June 7, 2013. https://www.huffpost.com/entry/rosehip-seed-oil-benefits_n_3375871.

Orchard, Ané, and Sandy van Vuuren. "Commercial Essential Oils as Potential Antimicrobials to Treat Skin Diseases." Evidence-Based Complementary and Alternative Medicine (2017). https://doi.org/10.1155/2017/4517971.

Palmieri, Giancarlo, Paola Contaldi, and Giuseppe Fogliame. "Evaluation of Effectiveness and Safety of a Herbal Compound in Primary Insomnia Symptoms and Sleep Disturbances Not Related to Medical or Psychiatric Causes." *Nature And Science of Sleep* 9 (2017): 163–69. https://doi.org/10.2147/nss.s117770.

Paramithiotis, Spiros. *Lactic Acid Fermentation Of Fruits And Vegetables*. Boca Raton, FL: CRC Press, 2017.

"Patchouli Oil Uses and Benefits" doTERRA. Accessed April 20, 2020. https://www.doterra.com/US/en/blog/spotlight-patchouli-oil.

Patra, Jayanta Kumar, Gitishree Das, Spiros Paramithiotis, and Han-Seung Shin. "Kimchi and Other Widely Consumed Traditional Fermented Foods of Korea: A Review." *Frontiers in Microbiology* (September 28, 2016). https://doi.org/10.3389/fmicb.2016.01493.

Pärtty, Anna, Marko Kalliomäki, Pirjo Wacklin, Seppo Salminen, and Erika Isolauri. "A Possible Link Between Early Probiotic Intervention and the Risk of Neuropsychiatric Disorders Later in Childhood: A Randomized Trial." *Pediatric Research* 77, no. 6 (March 11, 2015): 823–828. https://doi.org/10.1038/pr.2015.51.

Perez-Pozuelo, Ignacio, Bing Zhai, Joao Palotti, Raghvendra Mall, Michaël Aupetit, Juan M. Garcia-Gomez, Shahrad Taheri, Yu Guan, and Luis Fernandez-Luque. "The Future of Sleep Health: A Data-Driven Revolution in Sleep Science and Medicine." *npj Digital Medicine* 3, no. 1 (2020). https://doi.org/10.1038/s41746-020-0244-4.

Perlmutter, David. "Autism Spectrum Disorder and Gut Bacteria: Hope Moving Forward." David Perlmutter M.D. Last updated June 15, 2017. https://www.drperlmutter.com/autism-and-gut-bacteria-hope-moving-forward/.

Perry, Susan. "Study: Washing Your Hands—Even without Soap—Is More Effective than Hand Sanitizers for Flu Prevention." *Minnpost*, September 20, 2019. https://www.minnpost.com/second-opinion/2019/09/study -washing-your-hands-even-without-soap-is-more-effective-than-hand -sanitizers-for-flu-prevention/.

Piercy, Catherine. "What to Do When You're Bored of Thanksgiving Turkey: Make a Fresh Pumpkin Face Mask." *Vogue*, February 1, 2017. https://www.vogue.com/article/what-to-do-when-youre-bored-of-thanksgiving -turkey-make-a-fresh-pumpkin-face-mask.

"Planned Knee and Hip Replacement Surgeries Are on the Rise in the U.S." BlueCross and BlueShield, January 23, 2019. https://www.bcbs.com /the-health-of-america/reports/planned-knee-and-hip-replacement -surgeries-are-the-rise-the-us.

Pollan, Michael. *Cooked: a Natural History of Transformation*. New York: The Penguin Press, 2014.

Pothuraju, Ramesh, Vengala Rao Yenuganti, Shaik Abdul Hussain, and Minaxi Sharma. "Fermented Milk in Protection Against Inflammatory Mechanisms in Obesity." *Emerging Roles of Nutraceuticals and Functional Foods in Immune Support* (2018) 389–401. https://doi.org/10.1016/B978 -0-12-805417-8.00029-9.

Prado, Maria R., Lina Marcela Blandón, Luciana P. S. Vandenberghe, Cristine Rodrigues, Guillermo R Castro, Vanete Thomaz-Soccol, and Carlos R. Soccol. "Milk Kefir: Composition, Microbial Cultures, Biological Activities, and Related Products." *Frontiers in Microbiology* 6 (October 30, 2015): 1177. https://doi.org/10.3389/fmicb.2015.01177.

Price, Annie. "Dangers of Synthetic Scents Include Cancer, Asthma, and Kidney Damage/" Dr. Axe. Last updated November 17, 2016. https://draxe .com/health/dangers-synthetic-scents/.

Raimondo, Stefania, Flores Naselli, Simona Fontana, Francesca Monteleone, Alessia Lo Dico, Laura Saieva, Giovanni Zito, et al. "Citrus Limon-Derived Nanovesicles Inhibit Cancer Cell Proliferation and Suppress CML Xenograft Growth By Inducing TRAIL-Mediated Cell Death." *Oncotarget* 6, no. 23 (August 14, 2015): 19514–27. https://doi.org/10.18632/oncotarget.4004.

"Relaxation Techniques: Try These Steps to Reduce Stress." Mayo Clinic. Accessed 2020. https://www.mayoclinic.org/healthy-lifestyle/stress-management/in-depth/relaxation-technique/art-20045368.

Rivas, Magali Noval, Timothy R. Crother, and Moshe Arditi. "The Microbiome In Asthma". Current Opinions In Pediatrics 28, no. 6 (December 2016): 764–71. https://doi.org/10.1097/MOP.0000000000000419.

Robertson, Ruairi C., Amee R. Manges, B. Brett Finlay, and Andrew J. Prendergast. "The Human Microbiome and Child Growth—First 1000 Days and Beyond." *Trends In Microbiology* 27, no. 2 (February 2019): 131–147. https://doi.org/10.1016/j.tim.2018.09.008.

"The Romans: When Fountains Flowed with Rosewater." The Perfume Society. Accessed April 23, 2020. https://perfumesociety.org/history/the-romans-when-rosewater-flowed-through-fountains/.

Rosevear, Christina. "Exfoliation." Healthy Beginnings. Last updated March 31, 2008. https://hbmag.com/exfoliation/.

Rosner, Fred. *The Medical Legacy Of Moses Maimonides.* Hoboken, NJ: KTAV Publishing House, 1998.

Rovner, Sandy. "Health Talk: The Myths of Menopause." *The Washington Post,* May 2, 1980. https://www.washingtonpost.com/archive/lifestyle/1980/05/02/healthtalk-the-myths-of-menopause/5c7a427b-3ebc-48d4-90be-30ce13eae73f/.

Rud, Melanie. "Why Jojoba Oil Is the Only Oil You Should Be Using on Your Face." Shape. Last updated on April 20, 2019. https://www.shape.com/lifestyle/beauty-style/jojoba-oil-skin-care-benefits.

Ruggeri, Christine. "Jojoba Oil Benefits for Face, Hair, Body and More." Dr. Axe. Last updated August 12, 2019. https://draxe.com/beauty /jojoba-oil/.

Sasannejad, P., M. Saeedi, A. Shoeibi, A. Gorji, M. Abbasi, and M. Forough-ipour. "Lavender Essential Oil in the Treatment of Migraine Headache: A Placebo-Controlled Clinical Trial." *European Neurology* 67 (2012): 288–91. https://doi.org/10.1159/000335249.

Scantlebury, Francesca. "Catherine de' Medici's Scented Gloves." The Costume Society. Accessed October 21, 2018. http://costumesociety.org.uk /blog/post/catherine-de-medicis-scented-gloves.

Schapira, Joel, David Schapira, Meri Shardin, and Karl Schapira. *The Book of Coffee & Tea: a Guide to the Appreciation of Fine Coffees, Teas, and Herbal Beverages*. New York: St. Martins Griffin, 1996.

Schell, Regan Elizabeth. "Cleopatra: A Story of Womanhood." *The Annotation*, January 14, 2017. https://theannotation.com/cleopatra-a -story-of-womanhood-19e5713cf6df.

Schoffro Cook, Michelle. "Here's Why You Shouldn't Eat Foods with MSG." *EcoWatch*, January 8, 2017. https://www.ecowatch.com/msg-health -effects-2182662411.html.

Schulte, Brigid. *Overwhelmed: Work, Love, And Play When No One Has The Time*. New York: Picador, 2014.

Schultz, Colin. "There's More to Frankincense and Myrrh Than Meets the Eye." *Smithsonian Magazine*, December 24, 2014. https://www .smithsonianmag.com/smart-news/chemically-theres-lot-more -frankincense-and-myrrh-meets-eye-180953727/.

Schwarcz, Joe. "Why Did Cleopatra Supposedly Bathe in Sour Donkey Milk?" McGill Office For Science And Society. Last updated March 20, 2017. https://www.mcgill.ca/oss/article/science-science -everywhere-you-asked/why-did-cleopatra-supposedly-bathe-sour -donkey-milk.

"The Science of Sleep: Understanding What Happens When You Sleep." Johns Hopkins Medicine. Accessed 2020. https://www.hopkinsmedicine

.org/health/wellness-and-prevention/the-science-of-sleep-understanding
-what-happens-when-you-sleep.

Scutti, Susan. "More Men, Younger Americans Having Joint Replacement
Surgery." *CNN Health*, March 6, 2018. https://www.cnn
.com/2018/03/06/health/hip-knee-replacement-surgeries-earlier-study
/index.html.

"'Second Brain' Neurons Keep Colon Moving." *ScienceDaily*, May 29, 2018.
https://www.sciencedaily.com/releases/2018/05/180529132122.htm.

Seifi, Philip. "Magical Kefir." Russian Life. Accessed April 21, 2020. https://
russianlife.com/stories/online/magical-kefir/.

Shavit, Elinoar. "Renewed Interest in Kefir, the Ancient Elixir of Longevity."
*Fungi* 1, no. 2 (2008): 14–18.

Shaw, Sarah, Katrina Wyatt, John Campbell, Edzard Ernst, and Joanna
Thompson-Coon. "Vitex Agnus Castus for Premenstrual Syndrome." *The
Cochrane Database of Systematic Reviews* (March 2, 2018). https://doi
.org/10.1002/14651858.CD004632.pub2.

Shivananda, B. Nayak, D. Dan Ramdath, Julien R. Marshall, Godwin Isitor,
Sophia Xue, and John Shi. "Wound-Healing Properties of the Oils of *Vitis
vinifera* and *Vaccinium macrocarpon*." Phytotherapy Research 25, no. 8 (February 9, 2011): 1201–8. August 2011. https://doi.org/10.1002/ptr.3363.

Shunatona, Brooke. "Not Just for Sleep: Here's How Lavender Oil Can
Soothe and Heal Your Skin." Byrdie. Last updated June 16, 2020. https://
www.byrdie.com/lavender-oil-for-skin-4801192.

Simo, Cotton. "Frankincense and Myrrh." Chemistry World. Last updated
December 24, 2014. https://www.chemistryworld.com/podcasts
/frankincense-and-myrrh/8106.article.

"Six Reasons to Use Lavender Oil for Skin." 100% PURE. Last updated
November 22, 2019. https://www.100percentpure.com/blogs/feed
/6-reasons-to-use-lavender-oil-for-skin.

Smith, Matt. "There's a Downside to All That Greek Yogurt You're Eating."
*Vice News*, March 13, 2015. https://www.vice.com/en_us/article
/kz5mkm/theres-a-downside-to-all-that-greek-yogurt-youre-eating.

Spiegel, Alison. "What's the World's Most Used Spice?" *Huffington Post*, May 8, 2014. https://www.huffpost.com/entry/peppercorns_n_5274212.

Staky, Blair. "DIY Face Serum for Clear & Glowy Skin." The Fox & She. Last updated February 1, 2021. https://thefoxandshe.com/diy-face-serum -essential-oils/.

"The Strange History of Cologne." Amorq. Accessed August 26, 2019. http://amorq.com/article/3958/the-strange-history-of-cologne.

Sukley, Bernadette. *Pennsylvania Made: Homegrown Products by Local Craftsmen, Artisans, and Purveyors*. Guilford, CT: Globe Pequot Press, 2016.

"Supplement and Herb Guide for Arthritis Symptoms." Arthritis Foundation. Accessed 2020. https://www.arthritis.org/health-wellness /treatment/complementary-therapies/supplements-and-vitamins /supplement-and-herb-guide-for-arthritis-symptoms.

Sussman, Lisa. *Cold Press Juice Bible: 300 Delicious, Nutritious, All-Natural Recipes for Your Masticating Juicer*. Berkeley, CA: Ulysses Press, 2014.

Tanaka, Masaru, and Jiro Nakayama. "Development of the Gut Microbiota in Infancy and Its Impact on Health in Later Life." *Allergology International* 66, no.4 (October 2017): 515–522. https://doi.org/10.1016/j .alit.2017.07.010.

Tartakovsky, Margarita. "How to Analyze Your Dreams (And Why It's Important)." Psych Central. Last updated May 17, 2016. https:// psychcentral.com/lib/how-to-analyze-your-dreams-and-why-its -important/.

Thoreau, Henry David. *Walden: Life in the Woods*. Layton, UT: Gibbs Smith, 2017.

Thorpe, JR. "The Ancient History of Perfume." *Bustle*, July 31, 2015. https://www.bustle.com/articles/101182-the-strange-history-of-perfume -from-ancient-roman-foot-fragrance-to-napoleons-cologne.

"Top 10 Benefits of Eating Watercress." Watercress. Last updated October 17, 2019. https://www.watercress.co.uk/blog/2019/3/28/what-are-the -benefits-of-eating-watercress.

Tourles, Stephanie L. *Organic Body Care Recipes: 175 Homemade Herbal Formulas for Glowing Skin & a Vibrant Self*. Pownal, VT: Storey Communications, 2007.

"Triclosan." United States Environmental Protection Agency. Accessed 2020. https://www.epa.gov/ingredients-used-pesticide-products/triclosan.

Troitino, Christina. "Kombucha 101: Demystifying the Past, Present, and Future of the Fermented Tea Drink." *Forbes*, February 17, 2017. https://www.forbes.com/sites/christinatroitino/2017/02/01/kombucha-101-demystifying-the-past-present-and-future-of-the-fermented-tea-drink/#32690d184ae2.

"Understanding Valerian and Hops." The Sleep Doctor. Last updated June 19, 2017. https://thesleepdoctor.com/2017/06/19/understanding-valerian-hops-how-valerian-and-hops-can-help-you-de-stress-relax-and-sleep-better/.

"Vastu Shastra New Word Suggestion." Collins Dictionary. Accessed 2020. https://www.collinsdictionary.com/us/submission/6714/Vastu+Shastra.

Ventola, C. Lee. "The Antibiotic Resistance Crisis, Part 1: Causes And Threats." *Pharmacy and Therapeutics* 40, no. 4 (April 2015): 277–83. https://www.ncbi.nlm.nih.gov/pmc/articles/PMC4378521/.

"Virgin (n.)." Etymology Online. Accessed February 3, 2020. https://www.etymonline.com/word/virgin.

Wallace, Susan. "Commonly Used Medicinal Plants." Mostly Medieval. Accessed April 1, 2020. https://www.mostly-medieval.com/explore/plants2.htm.

Wang, Hao, Chuan-Xian Wei, Lu Min, and Ling-Yun Zhu. "Good or Bad: Gut Bacteria in Human Health and Diseases." *Biotechnology and Biotechnological Equipment* 32, no. 5 (June 2018): 1075–80. https://doi.org/10.1080/13102818.2018.1481350.

Weatherly, Lisa M., and Julie A. Gosse. "Triclosan Exposure, Transformation, and Human Health Effects." *Journal of Toxicology and Environmental Health Part B* 20 no. 8 (2017): 447–69. https://doi.org/10.1080/10937404.2017.1399306.

Wells, Katie. "What Is Collagen Powder (and How to Use It)." Wellness Mama. Last updated January 3, 2020. https://wellnessmama.com/3058/collagen-hydrolysate/.

Wells, Patricia. "Sauerkraut: It All Began in China." *The New York Times*, November 14, 1979.

Wesley, Naissan, and Lily Talakoub. "Winter Exfoliation: A Multicultural Approach." MD Edge Dermatology, January 28, 2019. https://www.mdedge.com/dermatology/article/192994/aesthetic-dermatology/winter-exfoliation-multicultural-approach.

"What the Heck Is Lupulin, and What's It Doin' in My Beer?" Great Lakes Hops. Last updated September 25, 2011. https://www.greatlakeshops.com/hops-blog/what-the-heck-is-lupulin-and-whats-it-doin-in-my-beer.

"White Sage—*Salvia apiana*." United Plant Savers. Accessed February 3, 2020. https://unitedplantsavers.org/white-sage-salvia-apiana/.

Whitney, Alyse. "The 5 Best Bone Broths You Can Buy Off the Shelf." Bon Appétit. Last updated January 5, 2021. https://www.bonappetit.com/gallery/5-best-bone-broths.

"Why Fragrance Disclosure?" Campaign for Safe Cosmetics. Accessed April 23, 2020. http://www.safecosmetics.org/fragrance-/learn-more/.

"Winter Exfoliation: A Multicultural Approach." MDedge Dermatology. Frontline Medical Communications, Inc., February 7, 2019.

Wischhover, Cheryl. "The 'Natural' Beauty Industry Is on the Rise Because We're Scared of Chemicals." *Vox*, September 18, 2018. https://www.vox.com/the-goods/2018/9/18/17866150/natural-clean-beauty-products-feinstein-cosmetics-bill-fda.

Women's Health Editors. "Lemon Juice Might Be the Do-It-All Beauty Ingredient You've Been Waiting For." *Women's Health*, May 6, 2019. https://www.womenshealthmag.com/beauty/a19934865/uses-for-lemons/.

Woolf, Aaron, dir. *Independent Lens: King Corn*. Public Broadcasting Service, April 1, 2008. https://www.pbs.org/independentlens/kingcorn/cows.html.

Xingfei, Zhong. "Value-Added Argan Oil Increasing Women's Independence in Rural Morocco." UNIDO. Accessed April 20, 2020. https://www.unido.org/news/value-added-argan-oil-increasing-womens-independence-rural-morocco.

Young, Gary, Ronald Lawrence, Marc Schreuder. *Discovery of the Ultimate Superfood: How the Ningxia Wolfberry and Four Other Foods Help Combat Heart Disease, Cancer, Chronic Fatigue, Depression, Diabetes and More.* Life Sciences Publishing, 2005.

Zakay-Rones, Z., E. Thom, J. Wadstein, and T. Wollan. "Randomized Study of the Efficacy and Safety of Oral Elderberry Extract in the Treatment of Influenza A And B Virus Infections," *Journal Of International Medical Research* 32, no.2 (April 1, 2004): 132–40. https://doi.org/10.1177/147323000403200205.

Zakay-Rones, Zichria, Noemi Varsano, Moshe Zlotnik, Orly Manor, Liora Regev, Miriam Schlesinger, and Madeleine Mumcuoglu. "Inhibition of Several Strains of Influenza Virus In Vitro and Reduction of Symptoms by an Elderberry Extract (Sambucus Nigra L.) During an Outbreak of Influenza B Panama." *The Journal Of Alternative And Complementary Medicine* 1, no. 4 (August 27, 2007): 361–69. https://doi.org/10.1089/acm.1995.1.361.

Zampieri, Nicola, Veronica Zuin, Roberto Burro, Alberto Ottolenghi, and Francesco Saverio Camoglio. "A Prospective Study in Children: Pre- and Post-Surgery Use of Vitamin E in Surgical Incisions." *Journal of Plastic, Reconstructive & Aesthetic Surgery* 63, no. 9 (September 2010):1474–78. https://doi.org/10.1016/j.bjps.2009.08.018.

Zanolli, Lauren. "Pretty Hurts: Are Chemicals in Beauty Products Making Us Ill?" *The Guardian*, May 23, 2019. https://www.theguardian.com/us-news/2019/may/23/are-chemicals-in-beauty-products-making-us-ill.

Zhang, Yu-Jie, Sha Li, Ren-You Gan, Tong Zhou, Dong-Ping Xu, and Hua-Bin Li. "Impacts of Gut Bacteria on Human Health and Diseases." *International Journal Of Molecular Sciences* 16, no. 4 (April 2, 2015): 7493–7519. https://doi.org/10.3390/ijms16047493.

Zu, Yuangang, Huimin Yu, Lu Liang, Yujie Fu, Thomas Efferth, Xia Liu, and Nan Wu. "Activities of Ten Essential Oils towards Propionibacterium Acnes and PC-3, A-549 and MCF-7 Cancer Cells." *Molecules* 15, no. 5 (April 30, 2010): 3200–10. https://doi.org/10.3390/molecules15053200.

# INDEX